DATE DUE

DEMCO 38-296

THE ROAD TO LOVE CANAL

THE ROAD TO LOVE CANAL

Managing Industrial Waste before EPA

CRAIG E. COLTEN
and
PETER N. SKINNER

 UNIVERSITY OF TEXAS PRESS, AUSTIN

American Geographical Society for permis-
l Perspective on Industrial Wastes and
al Review 81 (1991): 215–228, and to
Environmental History Review for permission to reprint material from "Creating a
Toxic Landscape: Chemical Waste Disposal Policy and Practice, 1900–60," Environmental History Review 18 (1994): 85–116.

COPYRIGHT © 1996 BY THE UNIVERSITY OF TEXAS PRESS

Printed in the United States of America

First edition, 1996

Requests for permission to reproduce material from this work should be sent to
Permissions, University of Texas Press, Box 7819, Austin, TX 78713-7819.

∞ The paper used in this publication meets the minimum requirements of American
National Standard for Information Sciences—Permanence of Paper for Printed
Library Materials, ANSI Z39.48-1984.

LIBRARY OF CONGRESS CATALOGING-IN-PUBLICATION DATA

Colten, Craig E.
    The road to Love Canal : managing industrial waste before EPA / by Craig E.
Colten and Peter N. Skinner. — 1st ed.
        p.   cm.
    ISBN 0-292-71182-4 (hardcover : alk. paper). — ISBN 0-292-71183-2
(paperback : alk. paper)
    1. Chemical industry—Waste disposal—United States—History—20th century.
2. Hazardous wastes—United States—Management—History—20th century.
3. Hazardous wastes—Law and legislation—United States—History—20th
century. I. Skinner, Peter N.   II. Title.
TD899.C5C65   1996
363.72'875'0973—dc20   95-15399

TO CLARENCE KLASSEN AND OTHERS OF HIS CALIBER WHO SERVED AS
ENVIRONMENTAL STEWARDS IN THE YEARS BEFORE SUPERFUND

Contents

FIGURES

TABLE

Foreword

Craig Colten and Peter Skinner have written a significant book. In a thorough and readable presentation, they have reconstructed the mind set surrounding our waste disposal choices that led to disasters like Love Canal. By reassembling expert opinion and the scientific literature prior to the creation of the U.S. EPA in 1970, they provide us with a definitive account of a damaging decision process. In addition Chapter 6, on the social and political "sensitizers" to important decisions, is well worth a second read.

This book's penetrating mixture of legal and technical details constitutes environmental history at its best. Without distracting the reader with intent or ideology, the authors show how the dominant informing institutions of science and law became inexpert amid inadequate environmental policy. While many historians have done the same for the making of a president, few have paused so deliberately on these topics of massive economic and social consequence.

This is a book to be read by the policy development community, those interested in the linkages between science and the law, as well as corporate decision makers. Moreover, because of its bold clarity and insistent pursuit of historical perspective, it provides a useful read to anyone concerned with the origins of our environmental predicament. I found its thoroughness insightful.

Colten and Skinner's work forewarns us to beware of a return of the cultural pattern they discuss. Without mentioning ozone depletion or global warming, this book explains how long and how comprehensive the cultural path to environmental problem solving remains.

Be readied. In this book you will find a historical lesson of great consequence and intrigue.

BRUCE PIASECKI
Rensselaer Polytechnic Institute

Preface

William Faulkner once observed that "the past is not dead, it is not even past." Certainly, Faulkner's characters, tortured by phantoms of their past, and his region, burdened with an immense history of its own, bore the outward scars of previous generations that would not disappear with the passage of time. Although Faulkner never had to concern himself with the issue of hazardous wastes, his observation aptly applies to this topic. For seldom has society had to grapple with a more enduring problem than long-lived deposits of industrial residue.

After the public discovery of the country's most notorious waste dump, Love Canal, but in the short interim before the passage of the Superfund legislation (1980), Congressman Eckhardt of Texas chaired a committee that surveyed chemical waste disposal methods. His committee obtained amazingly frank responses from 1,605 chemical plants, which reported discarding approximately 762 million tons of waste since 1950. By far the most common methods of disposal were landfills, pits, ponds, or lagoons. It is precisely these techniques that have produced the persistent dilemmas associated with hazardous wastes.

We have asked ourselves why these particular methods, of the many available, were selected. This book attempts to trace the long history of this question and, in so doing, probes an issue that is rooted in early twentieth-century industrial practices, yet one that continually intrudes in our lives today.

Acknowledgments

This project came about somewhat by happenstance when the authors met while researching historical hazardous waste questions. Each saw in the other a similar viewpoint and valuable resources, but also a unique opportunity to collaborate. After exchanging information and working together briefly on the Love Canal case, they decided to merge their extensive files and interests. Thus this project was launched.

Along the way, many others aided the authors. In Illinois, the staffs of the Illinois State Museum, the Hazardous Waste Research and Information Center, and the Illinois State Library provided essential support. In addition, the Illinois Environmental Protection Agency, the State Water Survey, and the State Geological Survey opened historical files for our examination. Short research forays to the Beckman Center for the History of Chemistry and the Hagley Museum and Library, underwritten by those institutions, permitted the review of extremely important documents. Historical resources at the Michigan State Archives and Rocky Mountain Arsenal also significantly influenced our understanding of past events. Diane Mulville-Friel, Dan Haag, and Gerard Breen served as researchers at the Illinois State Museum and in that capacity provided extremely valuable assistance. And not to be forgotten is Julie Snider, who expertly crafted the illustrations.

Funding for this project came, in part, from the Hazardous Waste Research and Information Center, a division of the Illinois Department of Energy and Natural Resources. The opinions expressed by the authors are their own and do not necessarily reflect the views of their present or past employers or other organizations with which they are affiliated.

In New York we obtained assistance from a crew of student interns including valuable contributions from Jeannette Meade, Paul Kelly, and Michael Montysko. Special thanks to Michael Bryce for his ongoing contributions to our research. Staffs at the New York State Library and from the Department of Law Library deserve recognition for supplying critical documents. The National Archives and the New York Public Library also offered access to vital historical records. To all these individuals and institutions we are deeply indebted, along with numerous others we failed to mention.

We also would like to acknowledge the valuable contribution of several reviewers. Martin Melosi and an anonymous reviewer provided critical comments that allowed us to sharpen many passages of the manuscript and thereby improve its focus and clarity. Ongoing discussions with Clarence Klassen, Joel Tarr, Bruce Piasecki, Shelley Bookspan, and numerous other colleagues also helped refine the final product. Our students offered a forum for expounding our ideas and posed critical questions. In addition, the editors and reviewers for the *Geographical Review* and the *Environmental History Review* offered valuable guidance on portions of this text that originally appeared in the pages of those journals; we greatly appreciate receiving permission to reprint them here. Our editors at the University of Texas Press contributed in many ways to help us draw out important points and express them more effectively. To all, we offer our gratitude. We, of course, accept responsibility for any shortcomings.

Finally, we must also commend our families, who endured our absences, both mental and physical, and our frantic scrambles to meet deadlines as we pressed this project toward its completion. As much as our professional peers, they too deserve our thanks and recognition.

Introduction

ONE

Love Canal, a once comfortable suburban neighborhood in the industrial community of Niagara Falls, New York, has been seared into the collective memory of the country, although particular segments of society view its significance differently. For the former residents of the now largely evacuated district, it denotes an example of corporate irresponsibility.[1] Free-market environmentalists portray it as governmental failure on an unprecedented scale.[2] For environmental activists, it symbolizes a tragedy that finally compelled assertive government action to correct decades of land waste disposal abuses. In the environmental consulting field, it is a watershed event that has led to prosperity for countless environmental firms.[3] Chemical manufacturers might perceive it as both a transgression by one of the fold and a media phantom that continues to haunt industry long after its discovery. A federal judge concluded that the creation of Love Canal reflected "many specific instances of Hooker's negligence," but did not meet the legal test of "the reckless disregard for the safety of others."[4] From a historical perspective, Love Canal is but one of thousands of industrial waste sites that illustrates a pattern of corporate and government behavior during the past three-quarters of a century.[5]

Legal proceedings and treatises on hazardous waste issues present a similarly perplexing view of industrial, particularly chemical, waste management for the period before 1970. On one extreme, expert witnesses for industrial waste disposers contend that indiscriminate disposal of toxic substances in pits, ponds, or lagoons was the best available treatment during the

1940s, 1950s, and 1960s. Such opinions bolster the position that what constitutes mismanagement now was acceptable and even recommended industry practice before 1970. Defenders of waste producers make the case that the consequences of their actions were not foreseeable and therefore not irresponsible. Other experts in fields such as toxicology, hydrology, public health, and industrial history have offered contrasting views. Casual waste management practices were common, some argue, and did not conform with practices recommended by industry itself.[6] We will explore the technical literature that documents contemporary scientific knowledge that called for the adoption of alternatives to commonly used practices.

This book will examine the historical context of chemical waste management from viewpoints of waste disposers and the contemporary experts on hazardous substance use and public health during the first two-thirds of this century. We will focus our review on the technical and popular literature published prior to the formation of a national environmental protection agency, the testimony of expert witnesses in environmental litigation, municipal and state regulatory materials, and some internal corporate communications.

Before 1970 and the passage of the National Environmental Protection Act, there was no uniform regulation of chemical waste disposal.[7] This does not imply an atomistic, locally based process of waste management decision making. To the contrary, there were numerous national organizations, in the fields of both manufacturing and public safety, that provided guidance on waste treatment technologies and served as networks for disseminating vital information. In fact, the staffs of many large manufacturers were by far the best informed and most capable of making critical decisions about proper waste disposal methods. There were government organizations and independent standards-setting associations that also provided mechanisms for introducing individuals and smaller companies to existing knowledge. These groups guided the formulation of local legislation and regulations regarding sewage and solid waste. Common law also acted to impose, albeit weakly, a degree of liability on waste disposers. Furthermore, professional journals, government reports, the popular press, symposia, and numerous other organs served effectively to disseminate information. The complex nexus of trade organizations, technical capabilities, economic constraints, and legal expectations contributed to the shaping of waste management practices.

The goal of this work is to analyze the historical context within which chemical manufacturers made decisions about the methods that they chose for discarding unwanted by-products. This framework consisted of several key elements and numerous smaller contributing factors. Of primary importance was the composition and volume of waste products. The increasing volume of chemical wastes during the twentieth century created increasing pressure on waste generators to find inoffensive and secure means of disposal. Likewise, the development of ever more toxic and persistent by-products called for a higher degree of control. Waste treatment technologies evolved in response to, although somewhat behind, the demands of both industry and society. Treatment options involved isolation, chemical alteration, destruction, and recovery and were selected on the basis of a multitude of variables: local environmental conditions, scientific understanding of both chemical and environmental processes, and managements' consideration of these factors. A cohesive analysis of these factors, and additional influences on management decisions such as economics, internal policy, and social responsibility, will dispel much of the confusion surrounding the fragmented presentation of past waste management capabilities and practices. It will lend insight into the modus operandi of chemical waste producers and provide a clearer understanding of the sequence of events and choices made that produced thousands of Superfund sites across the country.

The analysis will demonstrate that—within the contemporary framework of technical knowledge, technological capability, and legal liability—there were lapses in appropriate waste management choices. Conversely, there were numerous success stories as well—examples of manufacturers that selected adequate means to ensure long-term control over hazardous wastes.

THE HISTORICAL IMPERATIVE

When Congress passed the Superfund legislation (Comprehensive Environmental Response, Compensation, and Liability Act) in 1980, it chose to include stringent liability provisions. Enforcement of this act holds any and all former owners or operators of severely contaminated sites both jointly and severally responsible for cleanup costs and damages. And there is no statute of limitations. In general, when the U.S. Environmental Protection Agency seeks to initiate cleanup or to recoup expenditures for mitigation of environmental damage, it identifies the major contributors to a site's contamination and forces them to bear the costs. This requires an unusual amount of historical research—to identify former owner/occupants, to document contemporary production of hazardous substances, and to determine their contribution to the site's contamination. In claims against former insurers, past waste management practices also have become critical issues. This has inspired an unprecedented interest in industrial history and placed historical inquiry as a key component in current environmental litigation.

There are two main thrusts to the research agenda into Superfund litigation. The first involves government agency efforts to identify "potentially responsible parties" or PRPs and to determine their role in contamination and waste disposal incidents. An initial list of PRPs inevitably instigates a second round of inquiries—to identify contributors omitted by the government inventories and to show that they played a substantial role. The parties often call upon eyewitnesses and retired practitioners who are generally familiar with former activities. They are requested to provide the second element: an assessment of past standards of waste management practices. Beyond a consulting opportunity for many retired hydrologists, sanitary engineers, and public health officials, it has produced a wealth of historical testimony and research materials that relate to former waste management practices.

These historical materials frequently have been confined to court cases about specific sites, and consequently there has been no overarching review of the testimony or technical literature of the day. The fragmented delivery of countless witnesses and the volumes of reports and articles collected create a unique opportunity to consider the broad landscape of toxic waste management from a historian's perspective. Individual witnesses, tied to a somewhat particular body of experience, do not always provide a professionally detached, comprehensive perspective. Furthermore, their testimony, offered in a highly adversarial situation with millions of dollars at stake and further limited by evidentiary rules and case strategies, does not offer a holistic and more objective view of the general nature of pre-1970 waste management. Nevertheless, the fundamental issues deliberated call for a reasonable historical account. We hope to create a balanced and more complete account by assembling the contemporary observations and merging them with recent expert testimony. More than evidence assembled to support the agenda for particular cases, this panoramic view will provide a context for historical investigations into other environmental, social, and political issues associated with hazardous waste management.

We also intend to contribute to the ongoing historical inquiry into environmental and engineering topics. The historian Joel Tarr has offered an interpretation of toxic waste management that suggests past practices were in accord with existing levels of knowledge and analytical capabilities. He argues that public health authorities, principally sanitary engineers, were concerned with biological wastes and the potentially harmful bacteria they nurtured, not with the toxic effects of industrial by-products. Samuel Hays contends that public concern with toxics was largely a post-1945 issue. Nonetheless, Christopher Sellers has pointed out that expertise in toxicology resided in the community of industrial hygienists, many of whom worked closely with or for industry before 1950. Indeed, manufacturers often turned to their own toxicological experts when formulating policy involving hazardous substances. Despite the public's belated concern with this subject, industry vigorously sought to maintain exclusive dominion over toxics and waste management expertise.[8] We will show that qualified individuals in the appropriate positions had access to sufficient tools to recommend, and some did recommend, more complete and technologically available waste control measures than were commonly implemented.

Martin Melosi and Christine Rosen have reviewed developments in the emergence of legal liability for hazardous substances. Melosi concluded that the judicial and legislative tools drew a narrow definition of environmental liability before 1940. Nonetheless, he found that decisions and legislative actions of the early twentieth century provided a legal context for grappling with hazardous waste problems today.[9] Rosen demonstrated that during the early twentieth century justices in several northeastern states attached greater value to the social benefits of abating pollution than to the economic costs faced by polluters.[10] These observations illustrate that there was a legal means to contest pollution and impose costs on polluters. We will consider actions and developments both before and after 1940 in an attempt to establish a more complete historical context that includes the critical decades of the 1940s and 1950s.

A ROAD MAP FOR SELECTING WASTE DISPOSAL METHODS

As long as there has been industry, there have been manufacturing wastes to get rid of. Except for plating, smelting, and certain refinery wastes, however, most persistent and toxic industrial wastes were manageable, at least until the 1930s—largely because the volumes produced were relatively small. During the 1930s and 1940s, the organic chemicals industry flourished and created a new spectrum of wastes whose quantities, toxicity, and persistence took quantum leaps. These industries created wastes which half a century later continue to tax society's cleanup capabilities.

Research chemists formulated specific synthetic organic chemicals for the purpose of destroying certain undesirable organisms. By the 1940s, organic

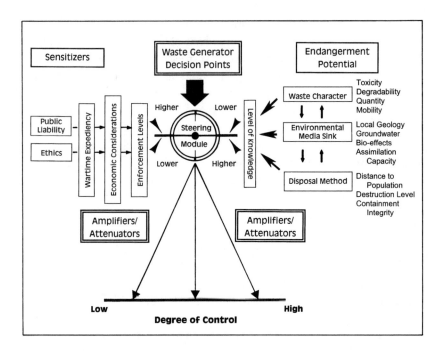

FIGURE 1.1. Industrial waste management decision-making process. In making decisions about disposal options, waste producers balanced knowledge of the potential hazards posed by wastes and their presence in the environment against sensitizing concerns such as liability and ethics. The emphasis given to one element or the other steered their choice of waste management toward a higher or lower degree of control.

chemical pesticides and fungicides were replacing the more traditional lead- and cadmium-based predecessors. Thionyl chloride-based chemical warfare agents replaced the more traditional mustard gas. Manufacturing these chemicals created toxic by-products, often in copious quantities, that were not useful for reclamation and thereby required disposal. Other organic chemical synthesis processes created toxic wastes even though the products were not particularly hazardous.

The degree to which toxic and persistent wastes impinge on current activities generally depends on how much environmental control was chosen at the time of disposal. To illustrate, a high-control example would be incineration coupled with scrubbers—a method which destroyed the wastes and limited dispersal of combustion products into the community. Another example is deposition of wastes in lined pits with groundwater monitoring systems following some waste neutralization or immobilization coupled with appropriate trusteeship arrangements.

Examples of low-level control are off-site waste deposition and release on land used for public purposes. In either case, transfer of control had both environmental and institutional aspects. By placing hazardous wastes on land not controlled by the generator, the disposal site owner implicitly became the custodian of a substance that could move through the environment and inadvertently impact the owner and/or neighbors. Although land disposal in some cases sufficed to maintain control of waste migration, the failure to preclude exposure of unsuspecting visitors to the wastes was a different but just as dangerous loss of control.

The methods for disposal of chemical wastes varied from incineration to burial in lined and monitored landfills, open dumping, and deposition in waterways and quarries. Our study of waste management choices is based in part on historical cases and reveals a decision-making process that encompassed many considerations. Although responsibility for choosing a disposal method fell to a wide range of management and plant personnel, all too often, short-term considerations dictated the method selected.

Graphically, we can depict an arrangement of considerations which guided decision makers in selecting their methods of disposal (Fig. 1.1). The center rotatable circle depicts the position of the decision maker(s). A decision about the appropriate disposal method would be affected by many factors that would amplify or attenuate the degree of control chosen. This decision inevitably determined how well the public was protected from exposure to toxic materials through subsequent years. Viewed another way, these factors can be seen to have steered the choice of disposal method to the high end or the low end of the continuum.

The decision maker's thinking can be pushed one way or the other by various factors and can be sensitized by still others. Knowledge of a waste's endangerment potential is the foremost consideration in choosing an appropriate waste disposal method. If the decision makers believed the waste innocuous, they would give little thought to protecting the public from exposure to it. The waste managers had to consider a number of waste characteristics:

- toxicity, reactivity, or explosivity
- degradability
- quantity
- mobility

If land or watercourse disposal were options, the disposers considered the following:

- geological integrity
- local groundwater hydrology
- proximity of downstream/down-gradient biological receptors
- assimilation capability of local water courses

The decision makers also had to reflect on other waste-specific considerations, such as

- proximity to human populations
- destructive capabilities of treatment technology
- containment integrity
- by-product recovery potential

As one example, if the industrial waste needing disposal is very toxic and refractory (i.e. nondegradable), the disposal choice should feature a higher level of environmental control. Similarly, a higher level of control is warranted for land disposal options if the proposed dump site is close to residences or if the groundwater flows toward water supply sources. Finally, if a waste can be effectively burned, incineration options are good choices for toxic materials. Similarly, if the waste is easily recoverable, this option should rise to the top of the pile.

The degree to which these considerations were important to decision makers' choices depended inextricably on the level of knowledge that they had about any of these matters. If they were unaware of a waste's endangerment potential or understood the waste to be fairly innocuous or readily immobilized in the ground, they would feel less pressure to choose a high-control disposal method. If they knew nothing about the characteristics of the chosen disposal site, they were likely to assume the site was safe and require a relatively low level of environmental control. Knowledge of chemistry, geological sciences, and local land use played important roles in decision making as well.

On the left side of the diagram (Fig. 1.1) it can be seen that exogenous factors such as public liability and ethical considerations played roles in defining the social expectations for decision makers. In other words, when faced with choices about how to manage wastes, the decision makers considered or were guided by the public and corporate mores of the time, by statutory or common-law requirements, and by their own private value systems. These sensitizers helped define the "should do's" in their value systems.

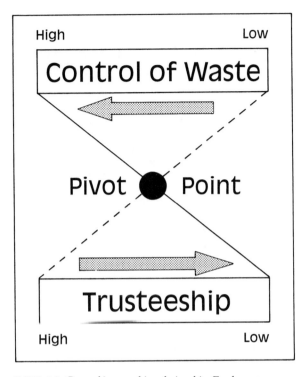

FIGURE 1.2. Control/trusteeship relationship. For long-term care, a higher degree of control allowed waste disposers to implement a lesser degree of trusteeship. Conversely, low control called for more extensive trustee arrangements.

The "should do's" were modified or dictated by other pressures, however. Other elements such as wartime imperatives, competition or economic cycles, level of enforcement, and availability of funds to capitalize more expensive, safer methods all played a role. These sensitizers amplified or attenuated any pressure the decision makers felt to choose better disposal methods owing to considerations described on the right-hand side of the diagram. In other words, if a particular waste was thought to be very toxic or hazardous, attentive decision makers[11] would generally first consider high-control options. Their final choices, however, would probably reflect practical realities communicated to them about the cost or difficulty of the option, the likelihood of being caught for a violation of laws or ethical expectations, or by the countervailing pressures of war.

The foundation of environmental control was and is today the engineering options available to the decision makers. Some offered high degrees of physical control (i.e., waste destruction, recovery, or physical/chemical isolation in high-integrity encapsulation), while others offered low levels of control, such as open dumping. There were and are today many methods for increasing control or maintaining isolation, however. By maintaining ownership, posting warning signs, and erecting fences, waste managers can reduce inadvertent exposures to unsuspecting visitors. By installing covers and drainage systems, hazardous leachates and runoff can be collected and treated. By purchase of buffer lands around a dumping area, the risk of public exposure can be limited. In short, decision makers could in the past and can today engineer a blend of disposal technologies, institutional arrangements, and site enhancements to reduce long-term public exposure and thereby achieve a chosen level of waste control. All of these control/enhancement mechanisms reflect a degree of trusteeship.

We have added a second conceptual diagram to describe a corollary thought process for decision makers. For situations in which long-term care is appropriate, society has devised a number of trusteeship arrangements to provide appropriate levels of control.[12] Figure 1.2, which depicts the decision maker's thought process, features a nomograph with two parallel bars illustrating the level of isolation needed against the level of trusteeship required. For wastes and/or dump sites needing a high level of long-term isolation, a decision maker could establish a rigorous and well-funded trusteeship arrangement. For a less hazardous site, a less rigorous arrangement would be satisfactory. The line connecting the two parallel bars pivots about a center point and reflects how these considerations change the level of trusteeship among the range of possibilities.

If waste disposal methods that guaranteed high control had been inexpensive and widely available, most attentive decision makers would have chosen them (as they would do today as well) without agonizing over the many decision criteria depicted in Figure 1.1. Although technologically available and understood, incineration and lined landfills (which increase control of wastes) were considered more expensive, at least as an initial cost, and were not widely used during the 1940s and 1950s for waste management. Consequently, low control often characterized land disposal practices of the period. One result was the Love Canal-type problems of the 1970s.

Some decision makers were unaware of the toxic and persistent nature of the wastes that they were expected to dispose of. The yard foreman who sometimes chose the dump sites was probably not a toxicologist. The third-party landowner who offered to take waste often knew very little about the site or the wastes. Without that knowledge, there would be little motivation to choose high-level control. Others may have been morally blank or simply unaware of public protection expectations. Nonetheless, industry guidelines called for educating personnel at all levels and retaining control over hazardous substances. Still, even better-informed decision makers may have been too easily swayed by higher costs, wartime imperatives, economic cycles, or minimal enforcement. Whatever the reason, many hazardous waste sites dot the U.S. landscape and have caused substantial degradation of natural resources and exposure to the public.

The upcoming chapters will examine the various components of the waste disposal choice process in turn. We will first focus on endangerment potential, tracing the recognition of chemical hazards among specialists and public officials. Next, we will look at the methods used to accommodate hazards or reduce the endangerment potential. Taking steps to develop and implement treatment technologies and to distinguish between garbage and sewage and other harmful wastes was an obvious expression of the recognition of endangerment. A following section explores the legal context and enforcement pressures that impinged upon waste disposers. Level of knowledge about endangerment potential and disposal options within industry and among corporate managers serves as the core of the next chapter. A section on sensitizers considers such ever changing forces as economic cycles, wartime exigencies, and corporate ethics. Finally, we review outcomes of the process (e.g., actual waste sites) or the actual waste management procedures that were put into place.

Recognizing Dangers

TWO

INTRODUCTION

Before society undertakes steps to protect itself from a harmful substance, it must recognize the inherent dangers or become alert to the endangerment potential of the suspect material. When medical authorities in cholera-plagued London established a relationship between the consumption of water from certain public water wells and contraction of this dreaded disease, they halted use of the wells.[1] In a like manner, before authorities undertook steps to control hazardous substances emanating from U.S. industry, they had to be aware of both the risk they posed and the pathways to unsuspecting individuals. To recognize the sometimes indirect routes of exposure and the often latent effects of harmful chemicals, experts in diverse specialties had to share information vital to establishing linkages among their respective fields of academic and applied knowledge. During the first half of the twentieth century, there did exist both the fundamental understanding of industrial waste hazards and the networks among the various branches of science that were necessary to alert specialists to risks posed by toxic by-products; however, the barriers of specialization impeded the free flow of information.[2] In terms of hazardous substances, not only were there institutional barriers separating certain interested professions, but frequently there was neither a prompt nor precautionary response to the recognition of a hazard.

Society has dealt with many hazardous conditions and substances over the past two centuries and has worked out many sensible safeguards. One of the fundamental protective tools has been to isolate things with endangerment potential. From the quarantine policies of nineteenth-century medicine to the practice of "out of sight, out of mind" for municipal garbage, society has relied on isolation, and it handled industrial wastes in a similar manner during the early years of this century. George Price, writing in 1914, itemized several ways to prevent industrial by-products from causing a nuisance. Among them were two that reflect the control techniques of his day: "removal of all noxious matter by either destroying or utilizing same . . . [and] storage of all offensive materials in closed and tight vessels."[3] Price's solutions for minimizing exposure to offensive wastes included recovery, isolation (which could take the form of dilution in waterways or the atmosphere or segregation at remote or nonpublic locations), and containment. For many wastes, disposers simply discarded unwanted by-products in a generally isolated location—a geographic and expedient solution. The second method involved technical means: When there was inadequate space to seclude or quarantine wastes, engineered solutions, such as fences, vaults, or liners, provided extra security. From the turn of the century deliberations over physical isolation and engineered security proceeded to debates over nuclear waste management practices.[4] This chapter will examine the developing recognition of hazardous properties inherent in industrial products and by-products and explore the ramifications of the geographic and technical means that are used to manage them. The fundamental question we seek to answer is, Did sufficient recognition exist to allow persons in positions of authority to prepare for emerging environmental problems?

RECOGNITION OF HARMFUL PROPERTIES

In the Workplace

Previous discussions of workplace hazards have focused on the evolution of safety and industrial hygiene practices and the impacts of worker's compensation policies.[5] While some of this literature seeks to explain labor-related issues, we will review developments in the specialized medical field of industrial hygiene, which provided the means for the medical community and industry to anticipate and prepare for many of the emerging environmental problems caused by hazardous wastes of the post-1940 period. Research by the historian Christopher Sellers clearly demonstrates that industrial hygienists had a substantial understanding of health hazards posed by hazardous substances. He concludes that this information was not generally shared by pollution scientists.[6] Nonetheless, we found that health and engineering specialists in industry were aware of, shared, and consulted industrial hygiene and pollution engineering studies.

Specialists progressed through several stages to a recognition of the links between internal (workplace) and external (environmental) problems caused by hazardous substances. The first phase simply inventoried hazards within factory settings and the associated worker maladies and encouraged separating employees from potential harm—or isolating the hazard. A second phase followed and overlapped with the first. It offered engineered solutions to exposure, through the development of devices that would physically remove hazards, place a barrier in their way, or substitute nonhazardous materials. Third, in response to workers compensation policies that covered certain workplace illnesses, toxicologists tried to determine the precise exposures required to produce a human ailment or death and inaugurated operational modifications to reach safe limits. Finally, as industrial hygienists more completely understood conditions within the workplace, their attention shifted to environmental releases of hazardous substances and the processes by which people encountered these releases.

In 1902 Thomas Oliver proclaimed that "there is not necessarily any danger to the workman in manufacturing the most poisonous substances, *if reasonable precautions are taken*" (emphasis ours).[7] This statement of principle illustrates that contemporary experts were aware of hazards posed by raw materials and finished products in the manufacturing environment. It also underscores the perception that adequate preventive measures could minimize exposure—whether through isolation or by engineering operational modifications.

The initial workplace studies cataloged substances that posed hazards to workers and contained a startling number of nineteenth-century toxic materials. By the outset of the twentieth century, private industry and government institutions compiled lists of hazardous substances, where they were used, and the symptoms they produced. Compilers initially had to determine which symptoms were related to specific materials among the many workers encountered. Although arsenic (used in coloring wallpaper and carpets), for example, had acute health effects on workers,[8] many of the workplace hazards caused less obvious reactions. The effects of lead, one of the early plagues of occupational health, often acted in a progressive or chronic manner—the longer the exposure to small doses the worse the health condition that resulted.[9] Lead received the greatest attention, because of its widespread use and its clearly recognized symptoms: wrist drop and lip discoloration.[10] Other occupational illnesses were not so easily diagnosed. Silicosis was less immediate in its impacts and presented greater difficulty in diagnosis.[11]

Government agencies and medical professionals in Germany and England inventoried various industrial maladies and their associated causes. By 1910, the U.S. Department of Commerce and Labor had published a list, based in part on European research, of hazardous trades and occupational sicknesses. The preliminary inventory focused on gases or dusts that entered the body via respiration. It recognized lead and chromium as problems caused by oral ingestion, not inhalation.[12] Although the early inventories were limited, they pointed out an emerging concern with metals, organic chemicals, acids, and other industrial materials. They did not indicate specific tolerance levels but warned against prolonged exposure to even small doses. Most importantly, they pointed out the widespread use of hazardous chemicals in industry. To improve and expand their inventories, hygienists called for employers to compile detailed worker exposure statistics that would illuminate linkages between substance and response. As results from this tracking came in, the inventories grew progressively, and the U.S. Bureau of Labor issued updates in 1922 and 1933.[13]

Academic institutions began training physicians to deal with the expanding range of workplace health and safety problems. As the number of practitioners grew, professionals in the field convened the first national conference on occupational diseases in Chicago in 1910.[14] Within a decade there were numerous industrial hygiene programs at some of the leading universities, including MIT, Harvard, Johns Hopkins, Ohio State, and Pennsylvania University. The U.S. Public Health Service lent further credibility to the subject when it established a Division of Industrial Hygiene and Sanitation in 1915.[15] Stymied initially by a lack of appropriations, this division ultimately served as a clearinghouse and coordinator for state industrial hygiene programs.[16] Through training institutions and government bodies, the medical community became alert to the problems of worker exposure and participated in cataloging causes and symptoms.

Early in this century hygienists offered two extremely important and fundamental observations regarding worker exposure. The first considered the means of ingestion of hazardous substances and the second centered on long-term exposure. The U.S. Bureau of Labor reported in 1910 that "industrial poisons may enter the body . . . (1) through the mouth and digestive system; (2) through the respiratory system; [and] (3) through the skin."[17] Initial investigations focused primarily on airborne dusts and vapors that affected workers via the respiratory system. A survey of ailments acquired by chemical plant employees found that there were especially high rates of respiratory passage diseases.[18] During the 1920s, concern with dermal absorption of organic chemicals also emerged. Although industrial hygienists did not focus on the direct consumption of toxic substances, they certainly recognized the hazard and included it in all inventories.

The second aspect of worker exposure involved the distinction between acute and chronic responses. By the 1920s, Alice Hamilton, one of the foremost experts on lead toxicology, repeatedly warned that industrial illnesses were not solely a function of acute reactions. Rather, she advised that most industrial poisoning was due to chronic exposures to relatively small doses.[19] Hygienists also noted that heart aliments were associated with extended exposure among chemical workers, thereby supporting Hamilton's warnings.[20] As occupational health statistics accumulated and measurement techniques improved, researchers eventually turned their attention to determining maximum allowable concentrations (MACs) for toxic substances encountered in the workplace.[21]

In addition to the recognized chronic hazards, occupational health authorities considered substances such as chlorine and ammonia to be accident hazards—that is, they were more likely to harm people in the event of sudden, unexpected releases.[22] Nonetheless, chronic ingestion of minute quantities remained a principal concern in much of the early industrial hazards research.

To remedy the dual problems of long-term exposure and low-level doses, industry sought to divert hazardous substances away from its workers. To control fumes and dust, engineers developed air circulation systems. The complexity of these systems ranged from rudimentary practices, such as open windows and fans, to sophisticated duct work that removed the hazardous substance and vented it to the outside atmosphere.[23] By mechanically removing hazardous fumes and dusts and by closely monitoring workers' health, industrial physicians felt that they would have time to detect early reactions and respond to them, generally by transferring affected workers out of high-exposure jobs.[24]

Protective clothing was another means of reducing exposure. Nineteenth-century manufacturers discovered that they could reduce the deadly effects of chlorine by having bleach packers wrap their heads in wet flannel and don leather goggles.[25] For workers handling many hazardous liquids, hygiene experts recommended wearing gloves, goggles, and special footwear. Although specific standards were lacking, a leading national organization advised that protective gear should fit the work situation and "reduce the hazards to the lowest feasible minimum in each case."[26] A Saint Louis chemicals producer outfitted certain employees with special color-coded jumpsuits to indicate that they handled toxic chemicals.[27] If a worker in one of the special outfits became incapacitated, medical staff would know immediately to suspect a toxic reaction.

Early twentieth-century concern focused on direct exposure but took indirect contacts into account as well. For example, manufacturers and hygienists knew that a worker could transfer lead from his clothes to his hands, and from there it could enter his digestive system on food he handled. Likewise, hygienists realized that ingestion of drinking water left exposed to airborne contaminants could poison a worker.[28] Dermal absorption from stained clothes was another possible means of entry. Solutions to these problems included the provision of hand-washing facilities for workers and the separation of eating and working quarters. Manufacturers also assumed responsibility for washing clothes that collected hazardous substances.[29] This ensured that workers would not wear garments saturated with toxic substances for extended periods of time, and it also protected their families from inadvertent exposure. Such actions illustrate that manufacturers were aware that individuals outside the workplace could suffer from inadvertent exposure to relatively small dosages.

Industry participated in identifying toxic substances and harmful doses and exhibited particular concern with threshold levels for chronic responses before 1950. Perhaps the best-known work was that of DuPont's Haskell Laboratory. Following the death of several workers exposed to tetraethyl lead and a rash of bladder cancer among employees at its dyeworks, DuPont established a laboratory to investigate the toxic effects of chemicals in 1935. The laboratory staff analyzed the causes of bladder tumors but was unable to determine the threshold level for benzene, which caused the cancerous growth. Nonetheless, the researchers recommended solutions segregating hazardous and nonhazardous operations and improving ventilation.[30] They also undertook experiments to determine the toxic doses for such chemicals as carbon disulfide, chlorprene, duprene, and dioxan. In each research project they attempted not only to determine how much exposure workers could endure, but they generally recommended preventive techniques such as protective clothing, regular physical exams, and removal from exposure when toxic symptoms emerged.[31]

Other companies also participated in internal toxicity investigations.

Beyond establishing MACs, another objective behind internal hazardous substance research was to reduce the cost of training replacement employees and to minimize insurance costs associated with workers' compensation policies.[42] The chemical industry in particular had a wealth of toxicological information and used it as the basis for minimizing lost-time conditions and compensatory claims.[43] This prompted a fundamental policy of investigating new products as they were developed. In the early 1930s, experts urged chemical plants to develop plant safety protocols suited to each new manufacturing process.[44] At about the same time, a major work on industrial hygiene argued essentially the same point: "It is the duty of every engineer, whether he be chemical, mechanical, structural, electrical, or architectural, to determine for new products and new processes whether or not there exists therein dangers to workers who may be engaged in the manufacture or to the public who may utilize or consume these products."[45] Such procedures were evident in the work of the Haskell Laboratory of DuPont, and industry spokesmen advocated such a policy. In fact, by the 1940s the general attitude was that workers and the public should be protected from items about which little was known. The New York Department of Labor suggested that "where new materials are in use, or where a material whose toxicity is unknown is being used, the proper procedure is to protect workers against these materials."[46]

In conjunction with controlling exposures within the factory, a common view was that manufacturers had a responsibility to prevent the escape of hazardous substances to areas surrounding their facilities. For decades prior to 1900, chlorine had been recognized as an acutely toxic substance. In the late nineteenth century, the English Parliament appointed inspectors to monitor escaping chlorine gas in the vicinity of production plants.[47] In this country, Price noted, in 1914, that smoke from certain industries damaged vegetation and he encouraged steps to isolate such processes.[48] Manufacturers were warned, in order to prevent explosions or fires off site, not to release volatile liquids into public sewers.[49] Standard advice to chemical engineers and administrators was to guard against contamination of public water supplies.[50]

Industrial hygienists were called upon to solve problems associated with workers' health both on and off the property of their employer. Frank Patty, a noted toxicologist and hygienist, recounted a case from the early 1940s in which over a hundred workers developed rashes while refurbishing a freighter. An investigation to determine the cause initially focused on the ship, but broadened to other possible causes when workers who had not been on the ship reported the condition. Eventually, investigators discovered that the dermatitis resulted from exposure to a cashew-shell liquid encountered on a vacant lot where workers took their lunch breaks. A contractor had dumped the contents of damaged drums on the ground, and the workers had unwittingly relaxed on the contaminated soil. After the nut oil spills had been covered and neutralized, the symptoms quickly abated.[51] This example illustrates the awareness among hygienists of the possibility that air, land, or water could serve as temporary repositories for hazardous substances that could eventually affect human health. Careless disposal of industrial wastes was one route recognized by hygienists that could create such conditions.

Explicit concern with toxic contamination of public waters had emerged by 1941 when the public health authority L. T. Fairhall noted the linkage between manufacturing activity and surface waters. He contrasted natural and artifactual (industrial) contaminants and acknowledged that toxics often were highly diluted in larger water bodies. Nonetheless, he argued that they still demanded strict surveillance and that sanitary engineers must be prepared to deal with industrial contamination of water supplies.[52] English hygienists identified several incidents in which industrial spills and waste disposal had contaminated private wells. They reported that "it is evident that contamination by compounds of this nature [trichloroethylene] is likely to be very persistent and there is some evidence of toxicity at very low concentrations [only 18 ppm]."[53] Furthermore, industrialists and hygienists were the target audience for National Safety Council advisories that urged them to avoid endangering neighboring properties with oil wastes.[54]

During World War II, the U.S. Public Health Service advised that dumping toxic wastes in public waters could have fatal consequences and analyzed the effluent of munitions plants for toxic characteristics.[55] After the war, the National Safety Council released disposal guidelines for chemical wastes. This document warned that "disposal practices should be examined for possible sources of personal injury (either in the plant or outside), property damage, or nuisance."[56] Thus, before 1950 those charged with responsibility for industrial health and safety recognized that air or water could transport industrial wastes to neighboring populations.[57]

Product testing during the early 1950s shifted to establishing minimum lethal doses for toxics discharged to public waters.[58] At the outset, analysis focused on marine life, but in 1954 hygienists proclaimed that the critical issue should be determining the effects of toxic wastes on human populations and they thus brought together concerns of hygiene and sanitary science.[59] The Kettering Laboratory in Cincinnati, funded in part by chemical and steel manufacturers, conducted extensive laboratory animal testing to determine the toxic dosage of organic chemicals and metals. Their investigations sought to establish safe levels of industrial toxic waste discharges.[60] While the notion that industries would continue to release toxic substances was implicit in their work, they wanted to know how much they could discharge without causing injuries. Also, researchers recognized that human ingestion of toxic chemicals could result from indirect exposures. In 1955, the principal investigator of the Kettering team reported that "water-borne chemicals that accumulate in the tissues of animals used for food also are an indirect source of human exposure to chemicals."[61]

Clearly by the mid-1950s investigators were seeking to detect direct workplace exposures as well as off-site human exposure to toxic wastes released by factories. The 1950s pronouncements of industrial hygienists reflect decades of experience in tracing the pathways of workers' exposure to hazardous substances. The fact that industrial raw materials, finished products, and by-products could contribute to health problems was acknowledged both implicitly and explicitly. By hiring industrial hygienists, manufacturers took steps to understand the effects of hazardous substances, and engineers designed safety systems to minimize worker exposure. When they contributed to disability insurance funds, industrial concerns sought to provide protection for at-risk employees and also secure protection from litigation that could follow work-related illnesses. Engineering manuals and textbooks advised plant officials to take steps to minimize the escape of hazardous substances from the factory grounds and to beware of the potential harm that toxic substances could cause to public waters. Appropriate specialists understood the relationship between the workplace and the greater community and also the risks posed by dangerous substances to these groups.

In the Environment

A wide range of scientific specialists and public policy participants had come to recognize the potential for hazardous chemical transmission to human and animal populations throughout much of this century. Although hydrological, biological, sanitary, and toxicological investigations repeatedly acknowledged the risks posed by toxic releases, seldom did waste disposal methods reflect this level of knowledge.

Before 1900, biologists and legislative bodies both recognized that industrial by-products could damage the environment. The formation of commissions to encourage the development of commercial fisheries in several states reflects this knowledge. Endowed with a mission to protect and foster the propagation of fish populations, they restricted industrial pollution that might harm aquatic life. Initially, they concentrated on what were viewed as hazardous discharges at the time, that is, sediment contaminants and biological wastes. To prevent their introduction into waterways, states defined certain wastes as nuisances: Examples included gashouse wastes, distillery slop, slaughterhouse refuse, and textile and paper mill effluent.[62] Legislation focused on the oxygen-depleting qualities of biological wastes, and by prohibiting their release, state governments acknowledged current understanding of biological processes.

By the 1920s, public agencies devoted greater attention to chemical wastes as evidenced by the U.S. Bureau of Fisheries' testimony before Congress that oil pollution caused fish to acquire an offensive taste and could have a toxic effect as well.[63] Authorities identified several effects of oily wastes on wildlife: (a) direct toxic effect, (b) smothering of their young, (c) killing of aquatic vegetation and other benthic food sources, and (d) destruction of spawning grounds.[64] The testimony of biologists indicated that science was aware of both the direct toxic qualities of oil and its indirect impacts on habitat. These arguments bolstered the position of proponents of a federal bill to outlaw oil discharges, which eventually won passage in 1924. While the bill applied only to maritime waters, its significance lies in the fact that it regulated a vast expanse of water with a diluting capacity infinitely greater than inland waters and one that was not used for drinking water.

Although there was a recognition that industrial effluent could kill aquatic life, state fish commissions could accomplish only so much within the existing legal framework. The Illinois Board of State Fish Commissioners voiced a typical frustration:

> We are frequently in receipt of complaints of fish being killed by
> the introduction of refuse from different manufacturing or other
> establishments, which is being turned into the rivers and
> streams. . . . We have found also that no matter how flagrant the
> case appeared, we as fish commissioners, having no authority
> further than that of any citizen, could only point out the sole means
> of relief, a suit for damage by nuisance.[65]

Illinois allowed the interests of riparian manufacturers to override those of the commercial fishermen.[66] In addition, state laws could not block effluent released by manufacturers in neighboring states. Despite policies that could not stop discharges of factory effluents, authorities recognized a linkage between industrial wastes and wildlife at the outset of this century and certainly understood by the 1920s that toxic wastes, even when highly diluted, could be fatal to wildlife.

In terms of water supplies and human consumption, concern with industrial wastes spread slowly. This stemmed in part from turn-of-the-century beliefs that toxic wastes acted as effective bactericides and from the choice of water, rather than sewage, treatment techniques by sanitary engineers.[67] Nevertheless, by the early 1920s the American Water Works Association (AWWA) proclaimed that "most industrial wastes are detrimental to water supplies." The aesthetically unpleasant appearance and the offensive tastes and odors that industrial wastes imparted to public water supplies became the central issues, not toxicity. From a practical standpoint, turbidity added to the cost of treating municipal water supplies, and the interaction of phenols with chlorine produced unpalatable water. Beyond the merely troublesome effects, however, the AWWA noted that toxic wastes such as cyanide poisoned water supplies. An internal committee reported that industrial wastes had tainted 248 public water supplies. As remedies, they called for the treatment of polluted water and the elimination of industrial wastes from public water supplies. In addition, they encouraged passage of legislation to deal particularly with interstate problems caused by industrial effluent.[68] The attention given to industrial waste problems clearly indicates that those charged with providing domestic water supplies recognized the hazardous nature of industrial discharges to waterways and suggests that they increasingly saw dilution as an unsatisfactory waste management method. Nonetheless, decision makers customarily chose inexpensive water treatment systems over the more costly waste treatment facilities, which delayed implementation of the option that would lead to cleaner streams.[69]

Public health and wildlife officials continued to monitor the impacts of liquid wastes released from municipalities and manufacturers during the 1930s.[70] Gradually, as society discovered more and more diverse applications for industrial chemicals, efforts to assess the indirect consequences on the environment got under way. Most significantly, concern with the impacts caused by land application of industrial products and wastes appeared in the pages of various trade and technical publications. In 1934, for example, West Virginia authorities summarized the effects of road oils on public water supplies. The increasing use of oil to control dust on rural roads led to its inevitable transport by surface runoff to reservoirs. The chief complaint was that phenols in road oils produced foul tastes and odors in drinking water. West Virginia researchers concluded that asphalt roads did not pose a significant contamination danger, but advised using low-phenol oils to minimize water-supply contamination following road oiling.[71] Such investigations reflect the efforts to trace indirect contamination.

Public health officials discovered another indirect means of contamination when a municipal garbage dump tainted groundwater near Indianapolis in the early 1930s. Authorities presumed that impounding high-BOD (biochemical oxygen demand) waste liquor produced by a garbage reduction plant would not affect nearby domestic wells. They assumed that the solids in the garbage liquor would seal the base of the impoundment and that the local groundwater movement would transport any contaminants away from the wells. Apparently, pore-space clogging did not occur and the recharge effect beneath the dump caused a groundwater mound that directed leachate outward from the impoundment. Within nine months, contaminants had reached two wells over 500 feet from the disposal site. This finding clearly alerted authorities to the potential for migration of leachate from land disposal sites, and they reported it in a national publication aimed at public water-supply officials.[72]

Authorities in southern California began monitoring groundwater supplies in the 1930s for saline and industrial contaminants. Chemical works, paper mills, railroad yards, and refineries discharged effluent into the intermittent Los Angeles River, where effluent could percolate into aquifers serving as public water supplies. By 1941 officials had detected no contamination but they kept a watchful eye on water quality in anticipation of problems associated with expanding industrial activity and urbanization.[73] Their attention was warranted. In the early 1940s, officials detected an organic chemical that had traveled over fifteen miles to contaminate public water wells.[74] The monitoring effort and attempts to prevent a repeat of the incident reflect significant progress in discerning the linkages between surface waste disposal, subsurface water movement, and public water supplies.

Both public and industrial specialists recognized lagoons and solid waste piles as potential sources of environmental contaminants. A 1930s chemical engineering text warned that impounded chemical by-products could damage down-gradient water supplies. According to a 1937 report, it was possible for arsenic to seep from smelter wastes and taint surface waters or groundwaters.[75] The instances of groundwater contamination at Rocky

Mountain Arsenal in the early 1950s demonstrated the ability of organic chemicals stored in unlined lagoons to enter the water table and adversely affect neighboring wells.[76]

Direct application of toxic chemicals to water supplies also aroused scientific concern. Investigators examined chlorinated benzene but found it posed no significant public health problems when used to control algae and slime growths in water treatment processes.[77] During World War II, anticipating hostile use of chemical warfare agents, water-supply officials concluded that mustard gas, lewisite, and phosgene, when dissolved, would not render water supplies toxic, although unpleasant odors and tastes could result. Nonetheless, the U.S. Public Health Service advised that contamination by arsenical agents was a possibility and they circulated information on analytical methods to detect arsenic along with procedures to decontaminate public waters.[78]

Direct consumption of toxic substances in the form of residues from agricultural chemicals was another form of environmental transmission of hazardous chemicals that became a public issue before World War II. In the late 1920s, studies of arsenical residues showed that apples sprayed in late summer retained harmful residues at harvest time.[79] Although there was debate over the hazard levels, public health authorities called for legislation to protect consumers from spray residues.[80]

Beyond concern with direct consumption of toxic substances, public officials and scientists analyzed indirect means of consumption as well. Scientists began to understand the persistence of metallic salts and also chlorinated hydrocarbons, which facilitated long-distance, long-period movement of these toxins through the environment. The potential for toxic substance bioaccumulation or biomagnification also came under scrutiny. Investigators learned that lead and arsenical pesticides were capable of poisoning livestock and humans when "conveyed mechanically to the victim by adherence of its compounds to food or feedstuffs."[81] With the introduction and widespread acceptance of DDT in the 1940s, investigations into its toxic effects commenced. In a summary of toxicological studies, one investigator concluded that DDT "is a poisonous substance which should be used only after adequate investigations have shown it to be safe for the particular use."[82] Toxicologists noted its persistent qualities in studies that pointed out that mammals store DDT in fat and in the butterfat contained in their milk. Meanwhile, entomologists, at the time, voiced skepticism that DDT use on fodder crops would endanger urban milk supplies.[83]

By the early 1950s, however, toxicologists testified to Congress that the toxic potentialities of chlorinated hydrocarbon insecticides are increased by the fact that the body can store them. Exposure to one subtoxic dose may not produce any detectable damage, but some of the insecticide will be retained in the body fat. Repeated exposures may increase this store until it reaches a toxic level.[84]

In addition to direct human physiological accumulation, the fact that concentrations could increase as cattle ingested DDT on fodder and then pass it on to humans in their milk presented particular concerns.[85] Attention to these pathways reflects the course of scientific inquiry and a recognition that complex hydrocarbon chemicals presented difficult environmental problems that extended far beyond direct consumption or workplace exposures.

Furthermore, the persistence of pesticides raised concern about their ability to enter the food chain. Authorities expressed apprehension about the safe conversion of orchards, where toxic pesticides had been applied, to row crops or pasture.

Some suspicion prevails that such crops might acquire through normal processes of growth sufficiently large quantities of arsenic or lead as to become a source of danger to the welfare of human beings and livestock should they become the sole source of animal food and nourishment.[86]

Experiments indicated instead that the pesticide residue would stunt the growth of fodder or other crops. This fact convinced researchers that farmers would be reluctant to convert their orchards to other commercial uses.

Certainly, while users valued DDT's stability, they had to consider problems with long-lasting toxins.[87] Applications of DDT inside buildings worked effectively against insects for extended periods under experimental conditions.[88] Outdoors, experiments indicated that DDT suffered no appreciable change after long exposure to sun and wind, but rainfall did reduce concentrations simply by washing the residue off.[89] Extensive field tests showed that DDT resisted degradation and produced a residual action "that was similar to the residue problems of the inorganic insecticides in that it carries through to the final consumption of agricultural products."[90] The consistent results of DDT testing indicated it was a persistent chemical in the environment, although other agricultural chemicals, such as parathion and aldrin, were less persistent.[91] These observations did not inhibit, however, either the sale or the increase in the use of chlorinated organic agrichemicals during the 1950s.

On a separate intellectual front, an extensive literature on the biological effects of industrial wastes emerged during the early 1950s. Biologists found that earlier U.S. Public Health Service studies vastly underestimated the potential toxicity of certain chemicals to fish and pointed out that highly dilute concentrations of acids, alkalies, and gases posed a threat to freshwater and maritime aquatic life.[92] Subsequent reviews reported on the threshold levels of toxic salts and also their synergistic effects on aquatic life. Researchers concluded that general effluent standards were difficult to develop because of the varying chemical compositions of receiving bodies of water and the mixture of toxic substances.[93]

Admittedly, investigations into the hazards posed by accumulations of toxic ingredients in public waters yielded conflicting results. Inquiries into the impacts of DDT runoff entering public water supplies, for example, suggested that dilution and degradation would minimize its toxic effect within several days. Furthermore, researchers observed that conventional water treatment methods would remove between 80 percent and 98 percent of DDT from low influent concentrations.[94] Nonetheless, some investigators advised that "the possibility of dangerous contamination of domestic water supplies with the toxicants in question, which may be harmful to human consumers, also deserves attention."[95] Furthermore, application of DDT to public reservoir watersheds disrupted the normal biological balance of microorganisms and caused problems for waterworks officials.[96] The concern was not with the potential toxicity to humans but to organisms that maintained a healthful water supply. In sum, by the early 1950s biologists had joined the researchers familiar with indirect environmental impacts of chemical products and by-products.

Despite scientific recognition of basic environmental processes, as well as the toxic and persistent qualities of chemical residues, by the early 1950s only a few investigations had been reported on the toxic impacts of industrial wastes in water supplies that paralleled the work done with agricultural residues and workplace exposures. The paucity of such inquiries largely resulted from barriers between scientific disciplines.[97] The director of the Ohio River Valley Sanitation Commission complained that

considering the careful study given to potential toxicity of constituents in food and drug preparations, it seems inconsistent to have ignored substances in water, which is a universal food. It appears, in fact, that more attention has been devoted to the toxic effects of chemical wastes on fish than on humans.[98]

The work of E. J. Cleary and scientists at the Kettering Institute in Cincinnati refocused attention on small-dosage consumption of direct releases of toxic substances to public water supplies.[99]

Authorities showed greater concern with land-disposed garbage than industrial solid wastes through the 1940s. With the introduction of sanitary landfills as a favored method for disposing of general urban refuse, investigators evaluated the impact of these waste repositories. Rolf Eliassen reported that settling and methane escape were two problems associated with refuse landfills and warned against using landfills as building sites.[100] Investigators at the USPHS Environmental Health Center in Cincinnati reported on leachate problems found in a landfill operated below the water table.[101] Public health authorities recognized the high probability that pollutants would escape landfills, particularly when disposal took place in standing water, and they issued guidelines for proper landfills that recommended against using locations that lay below the water table.[102]

Sanitation experts saw the potential for groundwater contamination caused by industrial wastes as an issue distinct from that of garbage leachate. In 1944 R. F. Goudey, a sanitary engineer in Los Angeles, cautioned that "land disposal depends on the proper isolation and the adaptability of soil, coupled with the proper type of treatment works, so that no underground water supply is spoiled by underground travel of organic pollution or poisons."[103] Impoundments of industrial liquid wastes posed an even more troublesome problem. Instances of contamination of water supplies by chromium leachate from plating waste lagoons on Long Island and in Michigan illustrate the extent of the problem in the 1940s.[104] In response to an increasing number of incidents, the AWWA investigated the groundwater contamination situation. They reported in 1953 that contamination threatened water supplies nationally and that the proper way to control groundwater pollution was to prevent it from happening. The committee recommended appraisal of disposal site geology and exclusion of wastes from inappropriate locations.[105]

The following year, researchers reported that "applied chemicals" (agricultural chemicals) percolate with groundwater and that chemical pollutants travel farther and faster than bacterial pollutants. These findings acknowledged the linkage between surface application of chemicals and their potential to enter groundwater supplies. They also pointed out laminar flow characteristics, a subsurface condition that minimizes lateral dilution. These basic principles enabled public health officials and waste treatment experts to be aware that land-disposed chemical wastes could enter water-bearing formations and migrate long distances without significant dilution.[106]

Richard Eldredge, a practicing sanitary engineer during the 1950s, claimed that before 1965

> the prevalent view was that simply putting solid wastes in the ground was all the "engineering" required since natural processes such as attenuation and decay were adequate to deal with any problems which might arise.[107]

James Etzel, long-time chairman of the prestigious Purdue University environmental engineering program, concurred and suggested that many companies used land burial for chemical wastes "based on the belief that natural processes would adequately handle all problems."[108] Nevertheless, contemporary knowledge of decomposition rates and leachate mobility did not support these conclusions. Etzel based his statement in part on a 1957 report by D. H. Sharp that advised organic chemical pesticide manufacturers to use "a suitable disused working quarry or other 'hole in the ground'" for waste disposal. This report claimed that "all the organic compounds produced will *ultimately* [emphasis ours] decompose by the combined action of weather, soil organisms, and the like."[109] Yet it was well known that decomposition of organic chemicals took place more slowly when not exposed to sunlight and weather. Furthermore, nonhazardous garbage continued to decompose for upwards of ten years according to studies available at the time.[110] Etzel himself admitted that disposing of "masses" of chemical wastes would have retarded decomposition and that "it would have been almost eons until biological processes could have destroyed them [organic chemical wastes]."[111] Given this background, reliance on the Sharp study to support the notion that indiscriminant land disposal was justified at that time stretches credulity. In fact, the study advises waste disposers to use "suitable" quarries or holes, and at that time "suitable" would have meant sites in materials with low permeability or sites not located above usable water supplies. Furthermore, the term "ultimately" recognized that decomposition was a long-term process and implied that long-term control of wastes was necessary.

Investigations that documented the decay of organic chemical waste toxicity did not get under way until the early 1960s. After decades of examining toxic qualities of oil refinery wastes, researchers in 1961 reported that biological degradation reduced the hazardous qualities of wastes already low in toxicity.[112] Yet other scientists found that natural "purification processes" failed to remove organic chemical pollutants in flowing surface waters.[113] The former observations indicate that traditional waste treatment processes worked on low-toxicity refinery wastes. The latter measurements reflect, however, the inability of streams to degrade toxic chemicals.

The extensive research on toxic substances and their environmental impacts provided a substantial base of knowledge that could be incorporated into waste disposal decisions. Published research results acknowledged processes of bioaccumulation and the resistance of certain chemicals to natural degradation. Summaries of this research appeared in technical, government, and academic publications.

UNDERSTANDING GROUNDWATER[114]

Groundwater is a critical link between hazardous substances and human exposure. Contaminants moving in, or in conjunction with, naturally occurring subsurface fluids can cover significant distances relatively quickly and endanger consumers of well water. Historical analysis of the development of the recognition of these principles has engendered considerable debate. The historian Joel Tarr concluded that before World War II "relatively little attention had been paid" to the threats that municipal and industrial landfills posed to groundwater quality.[115] His work on the subject focused on contamination caused by municipal landfills. Garbage leachate presents a far different threat than toxic liquid discharges, however, and should not be equated with contaminants from chemical production residues. Harry LeGrand, one of the better-known hydrologists in the 1960s, claimed in recent years that "it was not well known prior to 1953 that contaminants would leach into ground water and move in ground water flow from buried waste sites."[116] The historical literature suggests otherwise. By the 1940s there was a substantial body of literature on the movement of underground fluids and the problems posed to land surfaces by liquid discharges. Furthermore, there was an ample number of case studies to demonstrate that land-disposed wastes could leach into the water table.[117] This section will examine the scientific and engineering recognition of processes that contribute to human exposure to hazardous substances in groundwater.

Basic Principles of Groundwater Hydrology

It has long been understood that saturated soil or rock can yield water for human consumption, and scientists have examined the mechanisms that produce this situation in detail for well over a century.[118] Nineteenth-century groundwater research, both in Europe and the United States, resulted from a growing interest in tapping subsurface waters for municipal consumption. Darcy, a leading nineteenth-century French hydraulic engineer, established a relationship between pressure, flow, and medium in the 1850s when he demonstrated that the flow of a liquid through a vertical porous column is proportional to the difference in pressure between the top and bottom of the column and inversely proportional to the thickness of the column.[119] Subsequent investigations provided refinements by showing that both soil and rock are permeable to a limited degree; and large-grained sediments, such as sand, with large pores between individual grains, have a high permeability and allow for rapid transmission of fluids. Fine-grained sediments, on the other hand, have a lower permeability and consequently permit fluids to pass through more slowly.[120]

Hydrologists also recognized that variations in the water table, or level beneath which soil is saturated, could create a gradient for the movement of water. The water table generally follows the contours of the land surface and the areas of lowest pressure are stream courses into which the subsurface flow drains. Thus, shallow zone flow tends towards surface water bodies. Hydrologists and well drillers knew that pumping water from wells lowered the water table near the well and caused artificial depressions in the water table. These areas of lower water table, or "cones of depression," can create a situation in which groundwater, within an area influenced by a well, will deviate from the local gradient, causing water to flow down the "cone of depression" toward a well in directions that may be different from the preexisting conditions.[121]

Together, the notions of pumping- or gravity-related movement and differential rates of movement contingent upon medium supply the foundation for a general understanding of the rate and direction of groundwater flow. By the beginning of the twentieth century, hydrologists were fully aware that fluids moved from points of greater hydraulic head to places of less hydraulic head, such as springs or wells. They used this theoretical and empirical knowledge to forecast well discharges and determine fluctuations in flow. Furthermore, they were able to predict the general direction of underground flow when sufficient geological information was available; and they were cognizant of the influence that pumping wells had on local underground flow.

Turn-of-the-century scientists were also aware of the hydrological processes that facilitated surface fluid infiltration into the earth, thereby creating or mixing with groundwater. The principal source of subsurface water was rainfall that percolated into the soil and worked its way downward to the zone of saturation or the water table. Hydrologists recognized that recoverable groundwater occurred in extensive "sheet" formations, in permeable sediments and rock known as aquifers, rather than in well-defined channels as in surface streams. Groundwater existed in relatively shallow soils and sediments and also in deep layers of permeable rock. Observers realized early on that deep aquifers received their water either by direct percolation of precipitation into beds exposed to the surface or by surface water seeping into a bed in contact with the receiving stratum.[122] Thus, surface liquids were recognized as the source of groundwater.

Sanitary scientists and chemists, who were usually familiar with the basics of groundwater movement, identified several important processes relating to the transport of foreign matter by groundwater before 1900. For example, the practice of "sewage farming" was based on the recognition that sediments could filter out suspended material from percolating waters.[123] The finer-grained soils removed more suspended matter, while the coarse soils permitted larger amounts to pass through.[124] Solution channels in limestone offered little or no filtration for contaminants.[125] Furthermore, chemists and groundwater scientists knew that subsurface water transported minerals in solution. They found naturally occurring metals and acids in water supplies and acknowledged that groundwater leached minerals from the rocks and soil that it passed through and then transported the resulting solute downgradient without any filtering action.[126]

Mainly through the impetus of the U.S. Geological Survey (USGS), substantial studies of groundwater continued through the 1920s and 1930s and produced the foundation for several texts that presented a refined view of groundwater processes.[127] C. F. Tolman, drawing heavily on work conducted by the USGS, reported on the laminar flow concept. He noted that turbulence is largely absent in the laminar flow of underground fluid movement; consequently there is little mixing and dilution of contaminants.[128]

Tolman also reported on longstanding groundwater surface mapping techniques used in western states that reflected an awareness of drawdown due to groundwater depletion and subsurface mounding associated with artificial recharge. Recognition of the mounding of groundwater under influent streams or beneath irrigated fields indicates a knowledge that the introduction of fluids from the surface distorts the water table. In fact, Tolman presented a survey of groundwater recharge programs that had been carried out for nearly half a century and specifically pointed out the mounding effects of surface infiltration of water.[129] Tolman's recharge discussion acknowledged that controlled surface discharges percolated to the water table, creating a mound or ridge that increased the gradient. This indicated to readers that fluids discharged at the surface spread outward from the source.

Discussing the "area-of-influence," Tolman reiterated the early twentieth-century findings of the USGS. He presented diagrams that illustrated the "cone of depression," which is caused by pumping water, and another that illustrated the "area of diversion," or the areas outside a well's immediate groundwater divide, but where the movement of water is deflected as a result of the cone of depression.[130] This demonstrates that it was understood that pumping caused distortions in local groundwater flows and that formulas existed for calculating the impact of water removal.

By the early 1940s, there was a substantial body of literature on groundwater processes. Hydrologists had a clear understanding of the basic theoretical physics of the movement of fluids through porous media; they had experimental data on water movement through a variety of soil and rock types and practical measurements derived from field observations.[131] The accumulated corpus of knowledge about subsurface hydrological phenomena enabled investigators during the 1940s to move quickly to identify sources of contamination and to predict their consequences.

Groundwater Contamination

Even before hazardous industrial effluent first caused widespread public water-supply contamination, public health scientists and hydrologists examined the movement of contaminants in groundwater. The earliest investigations looked at waters bearing disease-causing bacteria. By the 1850s public health officials in England recognized the link between typhoid outbreaks and specific water wells, even prior to the development of the germ theory.[132] U.S. officials also commonly investigated wells as sources of cholera exposure during the 1870s,[133] while a French scientist used dyes to trace the source of contaminated underground water in 1882.[134] The methods used by public health officials reflect the contemporary understanding of groundwater movement and illustrate an awareness of the linkages between surface sources of contamination and well water. This understanding led to widespread acceptance of the notion that wells must be set at a safe distance from sources of contamination, such as privies and cesspools. Public health agencies in nineteenth-century England prescribed minimum distances for separating

wells and privies, and by the turn of the century several state legislatures in
the United States had passed laws restricting the placement of cemeteries
within minimum distances of wells.[135] Furthermore, the USGS advised
against using shallow wells in 1902, arguing that "water in the surface zone
of flow is everywhere exposed to contamination by seepage of impurities
from the surface of the ground, [and] wells in this zone of ground waters are
especially subject to pollution."[136] Early twentieth-century advice focused on
the horizontal separation of wells and privy vaults, although, given the
widespread use of both domestic wells and private sewage disposal systems,
hydrologists encouraged well drillers to sink their shafts deeper in permeable
soils to permit greater filtration.[137] Indeed, one authority claimed that "the
main contamination of wells is through seepage of surface drainage. . . .
There is really no 'safe distance' factor in regard to the location of stables,
privies, etc. near wells."[138] In 1929 a leading water supply journal reported on
well contamination caused by tar, ammonia, and nitrates released from a
newly built factory. It recommended "a protective zone 100 meters in
diameter around wells."[139]

In limestone areas, local health officials considered using solution channels or underground caverns for sewage disposal. USGS investigators tracing chlorine through test channels determined, however, that water moved
readily both horizontally and vertically in the fractured limestone. Sewage,
they concluded, could easily contaminate wells over a wide area even if they
tapped water-bearing strata different from those used as sewers.[140]

As deeper water wells and oil drilling became common in the late nineteenth century, naturally occurring contaminants such as toxic metals, acids,
and brines became a concern. Problems resulted from incomplete knowledge of water-bearing formations, improper sealing of abandoned wells, and
ineffective casing of wells drilled through nonpotable aquifers.[141] By 1910
information on geological hazards had been disseminated to geologists,
hydrologists, public water supply officials, and others with an interest in
subsurface waters.

Over the next few decades, experiments yielded a refined understanding
of biological hazards in groundwater. Careful observations of contaminants
in sandy soils illustrated that the bacteria *Bacillus coli* traveled limited distances horizontally and remained at the surface of the water table.[142] A team
of U.S. Public Health Service researchers observed that a chemical pollutant
(uranin) traveled greater distances, faster. They reported that the most
dangerous location of a well is directly in the path of the "down-hill flow of
the groundwater from the point of pollution." Although they demonstrated

that bacterial contaminants posed a limited threat if well and privy place-ments were considered carefully, they pointed out the serious nature of nonbiological pollutants in water supplies. In a related area, they observed that "deep burial" (in the zone of saturation) of contaminants poses a greater threat than burial well above the water table.[143] This work illustrates an early familiarity with the problems later posed by landfills and lagoons excavated to the zone of saturation. Investigations continued during the 1930s to seek the flow characteristics of pollution in groundwater. E. L. Caldwell moni-tored contaminant plumes issuing from an experimental Alabama latrine field and documented that chemical pollution traveled a greater distance than bacteria.[144]

By the 1930s the basic concepts of groundwater contamination from surface biological wastes were widely accepted. Groundwater texts matter-of-factly warned against the placement of shallow wells down-gradient from refuse disposal sites.[145] State sanitation officials recommended that "earth formations that permit the rapid movement of ground water . . . cannot be considered safe." They also issued a strong warning against locating wells too close to any "possible source of pollution" and recommended that wells be placed "in such a manner as to prevent the contamination of the water by either underground seepage or channels, or by surface drainage."[146] A USGS hydrologist wrote that "the greatest measure of protection to wells tapping groundwater supplies occurring under water-table conditions is afforded by locating the wells as far as possible from all surface sources of contamina-tion."[147] Public health policy largely placed responsibility on those drilling wells and not on those who discarded biological wastes to the land surface.

At the same time, engineers recognized that clays, not being always perfect sediments for preventing groundwater movement, could not guaran-tee a secure barrier between contaminants and potable water. A section on groundwater that appeared in a standard engineering text noted that "boul-der clay" sometimes has a pervious structure and is a useful source of water.[148] Oil producers even used clays as filters in refinery operations. Experiments with artificial clay liners at a San Francisco World's Fair lagoon indicated an unsatisfactory degree of permeability when they were first installed. How-ever, by infusing the leaky clay liner with saltwater, developers were able to modify the clay's structure and seal the lagoon to prevent the escape of water.[149]

The growing use of groundwater recharge projects illustrates profession-als' distinction of biological wastes from toxic effluent. European communi-ties had augmented groundwater supplies by introducing surface water to aquifers and using the soil to filter the objectionable solids. During the 1920s, a German community introduced river water containing biological wastes to the aquifer of its public water supply. After providing primary treatment (passage through a "scrubber" to remove solids), they allowed the sewage to percolate through sandy deposits, where it traveled a horizontal distance of 1,600 feet to the water pumping station. Observations revealed that the distance between the recharge area and the wells, and the presence of ample oxygen in the sandy soil, permitted degradation of the biological wastes.[150]

Sewage recharge practices began making their appearance in the United States in the 1930s, but experimenters allowed only biological wastes that had passed through a reliable sewage treatment plant to be recirculated into potable aquifers.[151] Fearing pollution problems, however, by the mid-1940s both Los Angeles city and county had enacted restrictions on industrial waste disposal in aquifer recharge areas.[152] Several years later the Los Angeles County Board of Engineers specified the need to exclude toxic wastes from recharge waters. Reporting on procedures for reclaiming sewage and industrial wastes, they clearly distinguished between biological industrial wastes and toxic effluent. Biological wastes, they concluded, could be treated and then used as recharge waters; however, they specified that grease, oil, solvents, acids, poisonous compounds, brines, and other troublesome substances should be handled separately and kept out of the recharge cycle.[153]

Contamination of public drinking water supplies by nonbiological wastes had become a chronic concern by the early 1940s.[154] From California to Michigan, to Long Island, examples abound of recognized long-term damage to groundwater supplies. A sanitary engineer in the Los Angeles area described problems created by the discharge of nonbiological wastes in the Los Angeles River basin during the 1930s. He claimed that wastes from tanneries, oil wells, chemical works, and refineries did not cause disease, but created other problems in groundwater supplies. He suggested that the sanitary sewer system could handle many of these wastes, although he recommended piping oily, saline, and acidic wastes directly to the ocean. Examinations of contamination, during the period 1927–1939, indicated that a series of sumps used for waste oil allowed it to percolate rapidly into the sand and gravel aquifer and thereby contributed to the contamination of several private wells. Furthermore, researchers concluded that industries using the Los Angeles and San Gabriel rivers as sewers posed a threat to groundwater supplies when the contaminants percolated into the aquifer underlying the seasonally dry river bed.[155] On the basis of the Los Angeles experiences, one researcher reported to an industrial waste producers' symposium that

> some types of liquid wastes discharged into underground water supplies result in far-reaching damage; gas wastes travel as much as five miles and food product wastes can be conveyed over a mile through the underground water.[156]

In 1945 the notorious "Montebello Incident" forced the closure of eleven public water supply wells located fifteen miles from the manufacturer of a weed killer. Floor washings from a new herbicide factory entered a surface water course used to recharge a local aquifer. "Within 17 days, all of the 11 wells were out of operation. . . . Although the plant was shut down almost a year ago . . . water in the area must still be treated."[157] In an effort to protect its limited groundwater resources from such disasters, the State of California authorized a groundwater monitoring program in 1949.[158]

Other industrial incidents included picric acid contamination in Lansing, Michigan, chromium contamination on Long Island, New York, and organic chemical wastes near Denver, Colorado.[159] A leaking underground storage tank impelled an extensive USGS groundwater investigation and remedial actions in Arlington, Virginia, during the mid-1940s.[160] The range of industrial contaminants encountered before 1950 included organic chemicals, acids, and toxic metals. These experiences provided public health and industrial officials with warnings of the consequences of uncontrolled releases of such substances in permeable soils.

Although authorities relied on soils to attenuate and absorb troublesome wastes, there was never a belief that soils had an unlimited capacity. As early as 1918, the chemist William Mason pointed out the expectation that there were limits to the rate of attenuation. He stated that "with a large and constant flow of polluting material the purifying powers of the soil quickly cease to act."[161] By 1954, a study of chemical pollutants in groundwater concluded that "many applied chemicals can be expected to reach the ground water along with percolating liquids" and that chemical pollutants traveled farther than bacterial contaminants.[162] Sheppard Powell noted that "the soil offers little protection to water supplies against inorganic compounds." In point of fact, "a few hundred pounds of such materials can contaminate millions of gallons of valuable water."[163] Such statements did not support reliance on natural processes to attenuate and absorb unlimited quantities of chemical wastes.

Professional Response to Contamination

The increased incidence of contamination prompted a response in the public health community and among those who had traditionally used the ground for waste disposal. The Committee on Ground-Water Supplies of the State Sanitary Engineers, a national organization, issued an early warning against tapping water sources in industrial areas. Their 1937 report cautioned that well sites "should be avoided which are near industrial developments that have offensive, poisonous, or dangerous liquid wastes that may reach the ground water."[164] Several years later the U.S. Public Health Service issued a manual for "public ground water supplies" with the intent of encouraging "a greater uniformity and a higher degree of safety in the sanitary control of public ground water supplies." The manual called for a minimum distance of fifty feet between a well and a source of potential contamination, but it cautioned that a safe distance was contingent upon several factors, including subsurface material and rate of pumpage. The authors specifically identified limestone and coarse gravel as unsuitable media for a well, and they recommended that other water sources be used when these materials were present or that the water receive treatment before distribution. They also warned that wells supplying large volumes of water should be placed at greater distances from pollution sources than those pumping small amounts of water.[165]

Although professional groups saw the release of toxic liquid wastes in permeable media as a serious threat to public health, there was concern with impacts of municipal landfills as well. Monitoring efforts documented the possible movement of methane gas from landfills,[166] and guidelines for landfills cautioned about the potential threat of groundwater contamination.[167] In response to such concerns, the Illinois State Geological Survey reportedly began conducting geological evaluations of proposed landfill sites in the 1930s to help the Illinois Public Health Department determine if they were secure.[168] The California Department of Public Works also commenced hydrological reviews of proposed landfill sites. They considered the site's geological permeability, the proximity of water supply wells, and the composition of the waste. Although they permitted disposal of "inert materials" such as building materials, they prohibited numerous industrial by-products such as organic wastes, phenolic compounds, oils, toxic salts, brines, acids, and caustics.[169]

Following the widespread occurrence of groundwater contamination during the 1940s, the problem attracted greater popular and professional

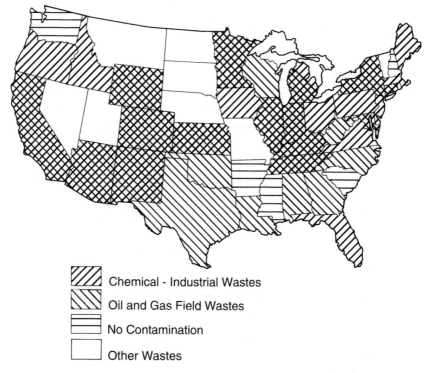

Chemical - Industrial Wastes

Oil and Gas Field Wastes

No Contamination

Other Wastes

FIGURE 2.1. States in which groundwater contamination incidents were reported before 1957, by type of waste. The American Water Works Association inventory of groundwater contamination incidents illustrates that few states had not encountered the problem before 1960 and that a range of contaminants had been detected. Source: Task Group 2450 R, "Underground Waste Disposal and Control," *Journal, American Water Works Association* 49 (1958): 1336.

attention. A consulting sanitary engineer reminded public health officials in 1947 that there was no dilution in groundwater and called for limits on the amount of industrial pollution allowed in prime aquifers.[170] The National Safety Council warned that the disposal of solid wastes containing water-soluble substances on permeable soils could lead to groundwater contamination.[171] Shortly thereafter, a text on groundwater conservation noted the frequency of contamination caused by industrial wastes released into pits and ponds.[172] In addition, a manual for chemical plant managers advised executives to extend their company's research efforts to include the hazards associated with waste products, particularly in terms of surface and groundwater pollution.[173]

The American Water Works Association organized a task force that surveyed state sanitary engineers, which reported that "isolation cannot be provided against those nonbacteriological types of pollution which are not destroyed by passage through the earth materials."[174] At a national level they found the problem unevenly distributed, and they recommended further investigation. In a followup report, they commented on the long-term effects of groundwater pollution and the small quantities of contaminants required to render a water supply useless. The task force also reported that dilution in groundwater was less likely because of the laminar flow of subsurface fluids. While the increasingly sophisticated view of groundwater processes ran contrary to the increasing use of lagoons and deep-well injection of wastes, it brought about demands for more geological information to enable accurate predictions of the speed and direction of underground flow. Although the task force conceded that there were uncertainties about particular movements of underground fluids, largely due to the distortions caused by pumpage and geological irregularities, they concluded that it was necessary to prevent the introduction of contaminants in order to protect public water supplies and that this was a serious public concern.[175] The USGS offered a similar view in 1953 when a spokesman wrote, "It is the general policy of the U.S. Geological Survey to recommend against the underground disposal of sanitary and industrial wastes, because of the difficulty of obtaining adequate assurance in advance that a proposed disposal project will not contaminate currently or *potentially* [emphasis added] usable aquifers."[176]

In arid, western states, groundwater researchers concluded that placing wastes above the water table or zone of saturation would restrict the production of leachate.[177] This principle became ingrained in California's groundwater policy, and ultimately prominent national organizations incorporated this concept into their waste management manuals.[178] They did not point out, however, as the original researcher implied, that this practice would provide greater protection in arid climates than in the humid eastern regions of this country.[179] This principle may have contributed to a false sense of security among waste disposers in humid areas who abided by it.

Trade organizations also advised their members to avoid groundwater contamination. The American Petroleum Institute cautioned against the use of ponds for caustic wastes as early as 1951:

> The ponding of spent caustics is not considered a general recommended practice. . . . The geological formations at the pond location must also be considered so as to prevent contamination of potable water supplies by seepage.[180]

A Manufacturing Chemists' Association pollution abatement manual also discussed the use of ponds as a treatment technique, but warned its members to take precautions against "an escape of the wastes through flooding or porosity of the bottom or sides of the ponds which could contaminate surrounding property or water formations."[181] Chemical producers also began using deep-well injection techniques to sequester toxic wastes in the early 1950s. The basic principle behind this practice was to entrap harmful chemicals in deep impermeable geological formations and thereby prevent future contact with potable water supplies.[182] These guidelines and practices confirm that the issue of groundwater contamination was not restricted to academic or public health circles.

Before the end of the 1950s, additional insights into the movement and control of contaminants were documented. A group of civil engineers reported that "applied chemicals can be expected to reach the ground water along with percolating water," which could cause serious consequences if the concentrations were sufficiently high. They also concluded that chemical pollutants move faster than biological contaminants and can travel several miles.[183] To restrict the movement of contaminants, a petroleum engineer recommended that certain conditions were necessary for oil refinery waste disposal on land. He listed several favorable, although rare, conditions for surface impoundments: low rainfall, remote location, little groundwater, and geologically safe impounding areas. As an acceptable situation for surface disposal, he cited a Wyoming refinery that discharged its wastes into impoundments overlying an impervious geological formation that formed a "blind basin," thereby protecting any groundwater supplies.[184]

Despite a rising awareness among both generators of industrial waste and public health officials, by 1957 representatives from twenty-five states had reported incidents of groundwater contamination by chemical waste (Fig. 2.1). An American Water Works Association committee documented that chemical contaminants had traveled substantial distances (105,000 ft) and that contaminants included toxic metals, organics, and acids.[185] It assigned much of the problem to increasing industrial activity and population densities. A subsequent report found that ponding and surface disposal of wastes continued "to be the practices most hazardous to potable ground water supplies." Nevertheless, the committee found hope in the trend that industry and legislative bodies were becoming more aware of the problem.[186]

A massive study of groundwater contamination, authored by two MIT professors for the U.S. Federal Housing Administration, assembled an impressive number of groundwater contamination studies (over 600) and analyzed the state of knowledge regarding the contamination potential for many different substances.[187] Although the authors called for investigations to define the specific characteristics of many different contaminants, their substantial review clearly demonstrates that an extensive literature existed at the time. The following year, the USPHS sponsored a conference to address the "insidious" problem of groundwater contamination. One of the conference organizers pointed out the reasons for the increasing interest in groundwater quality, namely, greater reliance on subsurface water supplies and a corresponding use of land disposal methods.[188] Attendance at the conference tripled the organizers' expectations, underscoring a widespread interest in the topic.

Responding to the increasing interest of its members, the American Society of Civil Engineers (ASCE) compiled an overview of groundwater basin management practices in 1961. It stated that "many ground water quality problems stem from the fact that man lives and conducts most of his activities on land overlying ground water basins." The report summarized earlier findings that chemicals traveled farther than biological wastes and that they posed the greatest threat. In fact, the ASCE pointed out that underground disposal of industrial wastes is more hazardous than surface discharges "since the resulting degradation is cumulative and long-lasting."[189]

Another extensive review of groundwater contamination appeared in 1963. While it offered little in terms of institutional guidelines for protecting underground water or even a summary of the current level of knowledge, it provided an unsurpassed survey of instances of groundwater contamination that had occurred in the state of Michigan since the 1920s. Most of the case studies that it presented had occurred before 1955 and illustrated a variety of geological conditions and contaminants. Of the fifty incidents summarized, twenty-two had occurred before 1950 (another twelve were undated) and fifteen had resulted from disposal or storage of hazardous materials beneath or on the ground surface. Through his interpretation of historical cases, the author provided a glimpse into the level of hydrological knowledge obtained during the period studied. He demonstrated that there had been a keen awareness of the dangers posed by industrial wastes to deep and shallow wells and of the hazards posed by surface impoundments of hazardous substances that had been installed during the preceding twenty years.[190]

Government action to abate groundwater contamination was hampered by several related factors. As others have argued, the obvious problem of surface-water pollution partially eclipsed attention to subsurface supplies. In fact, efforts to divert wastes from surface waters were a prime reason manufacturers deposited wastes in land disposal sites.[191] Yet government officials were largely unaware of the scale of the problem. The Federal Water Pollution Control Administration reported, on the basis of industry-supplied information, that only 1.5 percent of all industrial liquid wastes were discharged into the ground in 1964.[192] Such numbers would hardly be expected to stimulate extensive control efforts.

Overall, before 1950, practitioners in the fields of civil engineering, public health, and industrial waste management had access to ample information that clearly indicated that groundwater was a potential medium for the movement of hazardous substances from disposal sites to potable water supplies. Although there has been some compartmentalization of knowledge among the sciences and between applied and theoretical communities, there was more than adequate communication across professional lines to disseminate the message that land disposal of chemicals posed a high risk of pollution of groundwater resources.

CONCLUSIONS

During most of the twentieth century there was widespread recognition of the need to separate the general population from dangerous substances. Acting on such knowledge, waste managers explored combinations of physical isolation and engineering techniques to minimize human exposures. In addition, the advent of numerous hazardous chemicals forced manufacturers to apply comparable control measures in the workplace: physically separating workers from harmful concentrations or providing mechanical means to remove fumes, dust, or liquids.

There was also recognition of various pathways by which harmful chemicals might pose an indirect threat to populations via environmental media. Initial attention focused on poisons associated with food products. By the 1930s, various specialists examined the impacts of road oils and other potential toxins in public water supplies. With the advent of more persistent chlorinated organic chemicals such as DDT, the concept of bioaccumulation came into currency. It offered a conceptual framework for anticipating long-term impacts connected with agricultural chemicals, and in association with an emerging field of ecological studies it provided an array of environmental linkages between industrial chemicals and human exposure. Furthermore, analyses of public waters in the early 1950s yielded an increasing understanding of the potential toxicity of minute quantities of toxic substances.

Although much of the research associated with hazardous chemicals centered on products rather than wastes, there was an understanding of the scientific principles and characteristics relating to the effects of wastes as well. In particular, by 1950 the study of groundwater hydrology clearly indicated the potential for movement of liquid wastes from land disposal sites to surface and groundwaters. The overwhelming evidence demonstrates that there was an adequate recognition of the endangerment potential of land disposal of chemical wastes.

Accommodating Hazards

THREE

INTRODUCTION

In practice, chemical waste management during the 1940s and 1950s was an amalgam of science and engineering mixed with heavy doses of convenience and expediency. This mixture produced a national landscape sprinkled with thousands of known hazardous wastes disposal sites, to say nothing of the thousands of as yet undetected sites.[1] It is easy to condemn past actions from a post–Love Canal perspective, but that is not our intent. This chapter will consider the pre-1970 actions taken to control chemical wastes within their contemporary context and in comparison with other related actions. In the light of historical knowledge, many of the waste management decisions before 1970 illustrate both hazardous qualities of wastes and concern for public safety, but reflect little concern with long-term control and trusteeship.

Most early twentieth-century waste control decisions revealed a fundamental desire to either conceal (physically or structurally) any troublesome by-product or to recover marketable products from the waste stream. Segregation included dilution, geographic separation from population, or physical containment. As dilution and geographic isolation became less tenable in the face of population increases, waste producers turned increasingly to various treatment technologies for managing their effluent.

Treatment options included destruction through neutralization, biological degradation, and incineration. Treatment residue or untreatable wastes required additional handling, and this led to more elaborate isolation steps such as containment or deep-well injection. Containment, of course, remained one form of physical isolation, and waste managers had at their disposal numerous devices to encapsulate dangerous substances. The ultimate failure of some or all of these management choices, notably land disposal, illustrates a chronic problem within the industry that never received the same level of attention that industry spokesmen advocated.

MANAGING WASTES TO MINIMIZE RISKS[2]

Isolation or Segregation

One of the simplest and most common chemical waste management techniques was physically isolating the nuisance or hazard.[3] Selecting remote manufacturing locations enabled chemical producers to guard against recognized liabilities—such as off-site property damage risks due to explosions, direct contact by children or unsuspecting adults, or water and air pollution—and acknowledged an endangerment potential. However, traditional economic criteria such as relative proximity to market or raw materials, transportation services, and labor and power costs remained the leading influences at a regional scale, while waste disposal issues contributed to decisions at the local level.

Discussions of geographic solutions for current and future pollution problems permeated the chemical waste management literature of the late 1910s and early 1930s. Harrison Eddy, a cofounder of the prominent engineering firm of Metcalf & Eddy, asserted in 1917 that the selection of a site for a manufacturer producing large quantities of wastes was extremely important. He advised chemical manufacturers to keep in mind that "in no case can one acquire a right, by proscription [sic] or otherwise, to create a nuisance." In addition, he counseled plant builders "to anticipate complaint of objectionable conditions."[4] While promoting his company's services, Eddy's remarks underscore the realization that wastes were offensive and could be hazardous.

Eddy encouraged manufacturers to recognize the severity of pollution problems and to plan for them, although more commonly writers cited isolation, or removal from densely settled regions, as a means to escape nuisance liability altogether. Victor Kelsey, an assistant manager at Corning Glass Works, advised manufacturers to be aware that some communities, after going to great lengths to attract a new factory, found that they also had inadvertently acquired obnoxious fumes, dust, odors, or hazards from fires and explosions as part of the bargain. He claimed that a manufacturer that preceded residential development had the de facto right to continue polluting. If the factory followed residential land uses, then the burden to remove the nuisance should lie with the industry. He concluded a community relations discussion with the statement: "With proper care and foresight so-called undesirable chemical industries can select locations relative to towns or cities that will result beneficially to all concerned."[5]

The possibility of off-site damages prompted the explosives industry to follow an isolation policy. When selecting a site in northern Alabama, the Hazard Powder Company identified seclusion as an important criterion. A contemporary newspaper account (1892) reported:

> In selecting the location Mr. Emanuel was particular to see that the site should be one remote from the city and other industries. . . . There is not a house within a mile of the site, nor a furnace or other industry within three miles. The land is broken, being bounded by mountains, hills and forests. This just suits for a site, as such things break the force of explosions.[6]

Other powder manufacturers also selected sites outside city limits and nestled in narrow valleys.[7]

Discussing petroleum refinery siting, A. D. Smith listed several typical economic factors. The first of his other, noneconomic "important" influences was water supply, which impinged directly on waste disposal. He warned builders to consider whether an effluent might form the basis for a pollution lawsuit and advised refiners to consider local nuisance laws prior to building. He discouraged acquisition of sites in congested territory unless an "*exhaustive engineering study* [emphasis ours], legal advice and general business counsel" suggested there were no liabilities.[8]

Writing for the National Association of Real Estate Boards in 1926, the geographer Richard Hartshorne pointed out waste disposal as an important local consideration in selecting factory sites. He singled out chemical manufacturers as an industry that produced large quantities of unmarketable by-products and noted that these substances needed disposal at a minimum expense. Among the techniques available, he listed liberating gases to the atmosphere and discharging liquids into rivers and streams. Nevertheless, Hartshorne warned that such practices were subject to restrictions, especially if objectionable or poisonous materials were involved. He pointed out that unsettled parts of the country had fewer restrictions on waste disposal practices.[9]

There were obvious limits to a policy of geographic isolation in a country with increasing population densities and economic factors in the siting equation that favored sites near the consuming markets. During the 1920s, rural chemical plants became more common across the country, but remoteness was difficult to maintain. The greatest expansion of industrial activity was in the so-called manufacturing belt (which included the northeastern and midwestern states). As the Department of Commerce reported in 1933, "Despite the general tendency toward manufacturing decentralization . . . the dispersion which has occurred consists principally of expansion into areas adjoining the dominant population and industry centers."[10] Consequently, this pattern thrust industry into urban fringe areas. In 1926 several farmers, for example, sued the Monsanto Chemical Company plant in Illinois for damaging their crops with harmful effluent dumped into the sluggish waters of a floodplain creek.[11]

Furthermore, segregation was often short-lived. Many businesses took an active role in building or encouraging the construction of worker housing near their plants. Across the Mississippi River from St. Louis, chemical and oil refineries along with primary metal processors built new facilities, partly to avoid nuisance statutes in Missouri, and constructed residences for workers in their company towns.[12] As the population density surrounding the plants increased, the risk of nuisance suits rose. Personal injury and property damage suits, as well as nuisance complaints, became commonplace. Local courts frequently found in favor of the plaintiffs, although the appeals courts often overturned the original decision.[13] One nuisance-causing industry won a case in Cleveland, where initially it had located on an isolated tract and argued that later residential arrivals could not complain about a preexisting condition. The court agreed.[14]

A geographic isolation policy permitted pollution to continue, and thereby allowed chemical manufacturers to ignore developments in waste treatment technology and to build plants without pollution abatement equipment. The absence of treatment, even in sparsely populated regions, eventually earned chemical manufacturers a tarnished reputation. Neighbors did not appreciate dead vegetation and unusable water caused by a nearby factory; and when the chemical manufacturers found themselves proximate to populations, they devised strategies to minimize their culpability in pollution cases. The DuPont Company, for example, purchased both property and the right to pollute neighboring properties when it acquired land in Virginia for a containing dyes and metals. Each of these treatment options produced a sludge or semisolid residual; Besselievre argued that by-product recovery from such intermediate wastes might minimize treatment program costs.[23] Recovery could underwrite the additional handling and equipment and meet the concerns of managers during economic hard times. Recovery of silver from photographic film production sludges was touted as one of the more successful examples.[24] Also, the oil refining industry accounted for several recovery achievements: Propane reclamation, converting propylene to isopropanol, and transforming ethylene to a series of solvents were notable accomplishments.[25] Nevertheless, by-product recovery was not a panacea for waste elimination. Poor markets for recovered products and also the expense of developing recovery techniques limited their applicability during the 1930s.[26]

Despite the discovery of several process modification and by-product recovery options, in practice, technologies that simply removed a single offending waste item from an effluent stream became the principal pollution control methods. During the 1920s, vaporization of phenolic wastes and separation of floating oils exemplified this approach.[27]Likewise, for the chemical industry, with its complex waste streams, treatments tended to be selective and generally focused on a single component within a brew of by-products.[28] One of the least expensive treatments available was the controlled release of plant effluent. Relying on dilution, this procedure involved the simple construction of holding tanks or ponds. Impoundments retained offensive liquors on the manufacturer's property until the receiving stream was at a sufficient stage to accommodate a large volume of waste. This method required extensive land holdings, but retention ponds or lagoons served a dual function by allowing troublesome wastes to evaporate—although they also permitted harmful fluids to percolate into the soil and groundwater. In general, lagoons were not viewed as long-term disposal facilities, but as temporary holding basins. Biological degradation, similar to the procedures used in sewage treatment, was another simple waste treatment application. Dow Chemical Company employed trickling filters for weak phenolic solutions.[29] This procedure was not as successful with toxic or acidic wastes, however. Calco Chemical Division experimented with a system of "composting" or blending various wastes in an impoundment to enable it to treat them all in a single process, but this was hardly typical.[30] Adapting well-known sewage treatment techniques to chemical plant effluent was not successful with all wastes or with particularly concentrated materials or unlimited amounts.

During the late 1930s, the sheer volume of industrial effluent and the recognition that toxic discharges caused environmental problems undermined the reliance on dilution. The belief that toxic wastes were beneficial sterilizing additives to waterways with large populations of pathogenic bacteria gave way to a recognition that they were detrimental to aquatic life. Finding ways to secure or sequester toxic wastes without causing environmental damage had become particularly vexing, especially with the introduction of new, more complex, and environmentally persistent chemicals, and in the absence of a universal waste treatment method. By the 1930s, toxicologists pointed out the detrimental environmental impacts of synthetic organic chemicals, and public health experts began to recognize deadly chemicals as serious components of industrial pollution—in addition to the biological wastes that carried waterborne diseases.[31] Biologists singled out chemical manufacturers as major sources of potentially harmful effluent and argued for a reduction in industrial reliance on dilution.[32]

To deal with these problems, neutralization and pretreatment found wider application. Acidic and caustic wastes, common outputs of chemical manufacturing processes, could be mixed to neutralize one another. Where the volume or strength of alkaline wastes was insufficient to offset the effects of acids, manufacturers sometimes added lime.[33] The sediments and sludges produced by primary treatment, or pretreatment, and the new, more complex waste streams fostered segregation and land burial of toxics. Besselievre had recommended using chemical wastes to fill low ground in the early 1930s. While land reclamation or filling was based on traditional "out of sight, out of mind" principles, he warned of possible dangers that might result from "indiscriminate piling of wastes."[34] Monsanto Chemical Company's plant near East St. Louis separated its toxic wastes as early as 1932 to prevent them from entering the Mississippi River. They buried toxic wastes in pits on their property during the 1940s,[35] while at Love Canal, Hooker Electrochemical Company began burial of toxic chemical residues on company property in the same decade.[36] Calco Chemical also relied on land disposal of sludges.[37]

Burial offered chemical producers several advantages. By excluding toxic wastes from waterways, chemical manufacturers evaded scrutiny by state water pollution control agencies. Confining sludges and residues to burial grounds on their own property limited public exposure and kept dangerous substances in areas where workers, usually trained to handle dangerous substances, supposedly would avoid injury or ill effects.[38] Waste management specialists realized, however, that land burial of toxic chemicals was not an absolutely secure system for preventing human exposure. Eldridge advised extra security for sites containing toxic wastes and warned against the possibility that leachate from a toxic impoundment could seep into neighboring wells. Specifically, he recommended fencing impoundments containing toxic liquids and concrete liners where there was a risk of groundwater contamination.[39] Both these measures embodied physical containment principles.

Manufacturers took steps in some instances to segregate reactive chemicals before land disposal. This kept substances that could explode or create toxic fumes from mingling. Hooker Electrochemical in Niagara Falls disposed of some thionyl chloride wastes during the 1940s in this way:

> This material is disposed of by placing [illegible word] the drums
> into a waste pond provided for this purpose at a point some distance
> from the plant buildings yet convenient and accessible. The mate-
> rial is quite reactive with water, so that care must be exercised not
> to dump directly into water. . . . It is advisable to empty them at two
> different points in the pond.[40]

This plan indicates that waste managers viewed waste segregation as essential, no doubt to minimize the risk of incompatible material reactions in this case. It also demonstrates that the company recognized the need to create physical buffers to separate people and valuable real estate from inherently dangerous activities—in this instance dumping a water-reactive chemical into a lagoon.

Incineration of chemical process residues was another viable technology that waste management experts promoted. By the 1930s there was already half a century of experience with incineration technology. New York City had begun incinerating its solid wastes in the 1880s and by the early 1920s 200 municipal incinerators were in operation.[41] It was against this backdrop that the chemical industry created their own array of specialized combustion destructors. Besselievre touted combustion as a means for handling general industrial wastes in the early 1930s and others recommended it as a method for oil and tar waste destruction.[42] The Hoffman–La Roche factory in Nutley, New Jersey, installed one of the first facilities during the 1940s. After the local sewage commission and six land disposal site operators rejected its residue, the company opted to employ an incinerator to destroy its "stink liquor," the waste resulting from production of pharmaceuticals, vitamins, and fine chemicals. The chemical company hired an engineering firm to design the incinerator and burned the stink liquor along with trash and garbage.[43]

Hooker Electrochemical used a primitive type of fluidized-bed incinerator for thionyl chloride process wastes during the 1940s as well. They recognized that it cost more than land disposal, but it removed a long-term containment problem. One employee recommended:

> The author feels that an adequate incinerator for burning all organic residue should be built. It costs about twice as much to burn the residues as it does to bury them, but I feel that eventually we will have a quagmire at the Luve [*sic*] Canal which will be a potential source of law suits [*sic*] in the future.[44]

Hooker may have been one of the first chemical processing companies to build and operate a dedicated chemical combustor, but they eventually chose to resume land disposal of chemical residue, whereas companies such as Dow Chemical installed a rotary kiln incinerator in the mid-1940s.[45]

Despite a number of treatment options available to chemical manufacturers, only a small percentage opted to install treatment facilities. The Manufacturing Chemists' Association (MCA) surveyed its eighty-seven member companies in 1936 and found that among the 230 individual plants only 47 had "installed equipment for trade waste treatment." Although the MCA touted this as an impressive figure, it represented a mere 20 percent of its membership's facilities, to say nothing of the many smaller chemical producers that did not belong to the trade organization and who were unable to afford treatment facilities.[46] Investigators reported that New Jersey chemical plants released 6.8 million gallons of waste into the state's waterways daily. If 20 percent received treatment, the untreated portion stood at about 5.4 million gallons a day in the mid-1930s.[47] By way of contrast, 49 percent of urban sewage received treatment before being released to a waterway several years later.[48] Despite distinct waste streams, even the larger chemical concerns had made less progress toward treating their wastes than had municipalities by the late 1930s.

Following the virtual hiatus in waste treatment research during the war, chemical manufacturers resumed experiments with technologies to render wastes innocuous and harmless. Incineration and deep-well injection were two key components of the renewed interest in waste management. In the late 1940s DuPont adopted a policy that it had recommended a decade previously and proclaimed that all new plant construction would include adequate waste disposal. DuPont proposed to incinerate its organic liquid wastes and inject brines into subterranean rock formations at its Victoria, Texas, plant. Monsanto's new plant in Texas City was to produce styrene, and company specialists proposed to burn all organic wastes. For hydrocarbon wastes they employed a distillation process and used steam stripping to remove acrylonitrile wastes.[49] Koppers styrene plant in Pennsylvania also installed an incinerator to handle its benzene acid sludge wastes and developed a method to burn its styrene still residue, mixed with other fuel, in a heating furnace.[50] Another West Coast styrene producer developed a treatment procedure that separated oils from tar wastes. One fraction served as a fuel for the plant and the other as a weed killer.[51]

Certainly by the 1950s adequate technology was available to offer effective chemical residue incineration. Special refractory lining materials that could withstand high temperatures and corrosive effects of chemical combustion, such as silicon carbide bricks, were available by 1920.[52] Vulcan Iron Works had developed rotary kiln incinerator technologies by the 1940s and even touted twenty-eight customers in the chemical industry.[53] The adoption of incineration by Dow, Monsanto, and other chemical industry leaders reflects the availability and practicality of burning of wastes. A major trade organization concurred and recommended incineration to reduce water pollution by tars, and a 1955 manual noted that steam stripping could minimize excessive smoke emissions. In addition, the 1961 Manufacturing Chemists' Association guidebook described two incineration techniques and advised users to beware of air pollution problems.[54]

Incinerator technology had become cost-effective by this time as well. National Aniline in Buffalo, New York, installed an incinerator on its property to guard against hazards and nuisances created by its former practice of open burning. Furthermore, they reported that it was the "cheapest continuous solution to this problem."[55] Hooker also developed an innovative incineration system to dispose of its halogen-containing organic residues during the early 1950s and installed it in 1961. It used a high-temperature air/steam combustion system that produced gases that could be captured with conventional scrubbers and therefore caused no obvious pollution problems. Company officials reported that "this process is cheaper than most conventional methods (i.e., ground burial) and offers the added advantage of complete and permanent disposal."[56]

Another important development in controlling chemical by-products, particularly highly toxic effluent or saline wastes, was deep-well injection. Drawing on well-known principles that had been used for years in oil fields to control brines, chemical producers began employing this technique with increasing frequency during the early 1950s. Application of a deep-well injection system demanded a preliminary geological investigation to identify suitable rock formations that would (1) hold the intended volume of wastes and (2) prevent contamination of usable water supplies or other natural resources. Additional steps were necessary to ensure that the well itself did not allow contamination of freshwater aquifers that it penetrated. Working with state authorities, several companies put such operations into practice. McCarthy Chemical Company used the method to dispose of a mixture of organic and saline wastes at its Winnie, Texas, plant, while Dow and DuPont used deep wells for saline wastes.[57] Deep-well injection was also chosen for toxic wastes at the Rocky Mountain Arsenal, following the failure of surface impoundments.[58] Although costly, subsurface disposal did serve the purpose of diverting wastes from surface waters.

The MCA pollution abatement committee issued several manuals during the postwar years. Its initial publication encouraged manufacturers to find uses for by-products, and if this course of action was unfeasible, "the research men must develop a suitable method of treatment so that the production of the chemical which they have learned to make will not create a waste disposal problem."[59] If treatment was not a viable option, the MCA listed burial as a suitable means for disposing of valueless oils and tars. Nevertheless, it advised the disposer to investigate the site for possible groundwater and surface-water contamination pathways.[60]

For acidic and alkaline chemicals, the MCA offered traditional neutralization remedies. Although its 1950s advice relied on more sophisticated monitoring techniques, the basic steps of equalization or blending two waste streams with contrasting pH values were in line with procedures recommended during the 1930s. The MCA did, however, encourage its members to consider more sophisticated treatment for organic and toxic chemicals, claiming that neutralization could prove more costly for such wastes.[61] Despite concern over toxics and other hazardous wastes, the MCA manual on alkaline and acidic wastes carried the message that discharges to waterways would continue, albeit in a modified form.

State and local authorities stepped up restrictions on the release of harmful effluents into waterways during the early 1950s and advocated the adoption of primary waste separation techniques. This increased generation of sludge and semisolid residue, which required more land disposal sites. Furthermore, lagoons, evaporation ponds, and infiltration basins became popular inexpensive and low-technology remedies to stream pollution for companies with adequate space for such facilities. A California sanitary engineer even argued that land disposal offered many advantages, particularly in arid regions. There were widespread concerns about the adequacy of such methods, however.

A lone claim that the "soil has the ability to oxidize many toxic and noxious organic and inorganic wastes"[62] simply did not apply to most complex chemical wastes. Certainly, land disposal of domestic sewage had found long-standing acceptance for aquifer recharge, but by the late 1940s, hydrologists, chemists, public health officials, and industrial waste management experts all were familiar with the harmful consequences of releasing toxic effluent into the ground. Groundwater contamination caused by industrial waste releases to unlined lagoons or basins had prompted public health officials to take action in California, New York, and Michigan before 1950.[63] In a major engineering forum, Sheppard Powell warned manufacturers to avoid the use of surface impoundments, cautioning that the use of lagoons might increase the risk of nuisance suits.[64] This advice demonstrated that both water consumers and waste disposers recognized that chemical wastes could travel with the general groundwater flow, without significant dilution or degradation.[65] The MCA acknowledged the possibility of groundwater contamination and warned members to take precautions against the escape of wastes from ponds that could affect water-bearing formations.[66] Nevertheless, low costs and technological simplicity made lagoons a common, although, when used in improper geological settings, suspect, form of chemical waste treatment.[67]

During the 1950s, waste managers called for more elaborate steps to prevent leachate escape from land disposal sites. DuPont proposed a land burial site for inert solid chemical wastes in Genesee County, New York, in 1956. It included the construction of an impervious dike around the burial pit, sealing the top of the filled pit with "clays, asphalt, concrete, or other similar materials," and encapsulation of the wastes before interment.[68] Experts recognized that liners were not infallible and that reactions between the liner and the impounded chemicals could permit leaks.[69] Overall, waste managers knew that liners enhanced security, and in some cases practice reflected this understanding. A survey of waste impoundments indicated that the most common use of unlined surface impoundments was in food-processing operations and involved biological, not toxic wastes. Indeed, the canning and meat-packing industries accounted for more than seven times the number of impoundments as reported by chemical producers (406 compared with 57).[70]

When confronted with the widely recognized high hazards of nuclear wastes, engineers followed a course that paralleled the actions taken in the chemical industry. The initial design and location of government nuclear facilities attempted to blend isolation and engineered security systems. Facilities such as the Hanford Engineer Works initially relied on its remote location and storage of high-level wastes in metal containers. Waste managers dumped lower-level wastes on the ground, relying on the site's isolated location and adsorption of radioactive isotopes by stable elements in the soil.[71] In developing these policies, the Atomic Energy Commission drew on the experience and knowledge of experts who were already involved in waste management practice. After some experimentation with another containment and isolation combination—namely, dumping concrete vaults holding nuclear wastes into the ocean—these specialists helped contribute to a policy used during the 1950s that followed the basic principle of "concentrate and contain."[72] The long half-lives of the high-level radioactive material demanded the establishment of long-term trusteeship arrangements. Arthur Gorman, a long-time industrial waste expert, put it this way in 1953·

> So long as long-lived radioactive materials are being stored underground, there will be a need for supervision over these wastes. Such supervision may be required for generations. Policies, procedures, and products may change but these wastes cannot be forgotten or neglected.[73]

Monitoring at Hanford went on for decades as authorities kept an eye on containerized wastes. The nuclear industry example illustrates the merging of isolation and engineering techniques to store hazardous substances while allowing natural degradation to occur.

Practice Versus Public Positions. The MCA manuals illustrated promising developments in treatment technologies to reduce the hazardous qualities of wastes during the 1950s, but actual practices fell short of the trade group's stated objectives. The absence of an accurate national inventory of chemical waste management practices before 1957, and the disparity between new developments noted in the technical literature and their widespread application, make it difficult to portray the general practices in the early postwar years as enlightened or even reasonable. Many chemical manufacturers employed a mix of treatment technologies, ranging from the most rudimentary dumping methods to sophisticated destructive systems. In general, the use of advanced treatment technology implied that the waste posed a severe pollution problem, suggesting some response to the threat of litigation or regulatory enforcement. For example, Dow Chemical Company's effluent continued to foul downstream drinking-water supplies in the 1940s. Company officials grappled with this situation and other pollution problems at the Midland, Michigan, plant and eventually modified portions of its treatment system.[74] The facility used biological oxidation to treat its phenolic wastes and incinerated burnable tars. It also provided a three-phase treatment for 50 million gallons a day of general organic wastes. The wastes passed through a primary screen and grit chamber to remove solids. A clarifier then removed additional suspended solids, and the wastes passed through an aeration system to reduce the odor and oxygen demand of the effluent. Sludges provided fill for areas not designated as future building sites.[75] While this was one of the most widely touted waste disposal programs in the industry, its design reflects primary concern with traditional measures of water quality (BOD) and the long-standing belief that waterways should be part, albeit a limited one, of a company's waste disposal system. In fact, Dow still used dilution for brine wastes in the late 1940s.[76]

The USHEW inventory of industrial waste treatment facilities yields additional insight into chemical manufacturers' actual practices. The survey relied on state public health officials and is not complete owing to the shortcomings of local record keeping. Nevertheless, fairly consistent data appear for the eastern states. A partial tabulation that includes 419 chemical manufacturers in twenty-nine eastern states illustrates a disparity between available technology and practice. Of the 419 factories, 130 reported *no* waste treatment and another 186 provided only general waste treatment—for example, municipal treatment or lagooning. Only 134, or about a third, employed an "industrial" waste treatment system. The leading type of industrial treatment (54 plants) was neutralization, with regulated discharge (36) and waste prevention (47) constituting the next two most widely reported techniques.[77] A few years later (1968) the Federal Water Pollution Control Administration reported that the chemical industry treated only 15.5 percent of its total effluent before its release to surface waters. For the oil industry, which had been using separators for decades, the portion of treated wastes released to waterways was over 71 percent.[78] Obviously there was much variation among the many waste producers, but the adoption of existing treatment technologies lagged far behind contemporary capabilities.

In the wake of the Love Canal discovery, Congress surveyed active chemical plants in 1979 and identified common pre-1960 waste disposal practices. In Illinois alone, the survey found forty-nine chemical waste disposal sites used before 1960, although none were as serious as Love Canal. Pits, ponds, and lagoons, along with land burial of chemical residues were common disposal techniques.[79] Indeed, many of the reported sites contained mixtures of urban and chemical wastes. With little engineering involved in either site selection or construction, many of these burial sites are now the most severe environmental problems in the state because of unrestricted accumulations of hazardous substances in improper geological settings.[80]

Treatment options during the 1940s and 1950s were not confined to lagoons and dumps; in fact, there were numerous sophisticated technologies available. Process modification was touted as one of the most effective techniques for eliminating wastes altogether, but it was vastly underutilized. Techniques for waste concentration, incineration, chemical alteration, and biological degradation existed, along with catalytic and ion exchange treatments. These procedures were not untested, experimental procedures, nor were they guarded as proprietary secrets.[81] Although many were costly, they were readily available. Furthermore, sufficient hydrological and chemical toxicity information, much of it compiled by industry, was available to permit waste disposers to foresee the potential harmful outcome of land disposal practices.

Another option for chemical manufacturers was to divert their effluent to municipal treatment plants. This allowed them to present themselves as responsible community members, and it transferred final legal responsibility for discharges to the sewage treatment authority. There were numerous problems posed by relying on the typical biological decomposition treatment processes commonly used by municipal facilities. Many toxic or acidic wastes could either destroy the bacterial flora or severely corrode the facilities. Sludges from municipal treatment works that handled chemical wastes often contained concentrations of toxic metals or other hazardous substances not destroyed by the biological treatment techniques. Pretreatment of industrial effluent could minimize the impact of harmful constituents, but frequently manufacturers and municipal officials simply relied on the diluting capacity of the general urban waste stream and regulated the flow of trade wastes to negate the impact of shock loads.[82] Several industries in the small town of Monsanto, Illinois, developed a cooperative arrangement where the community would handle liquid effluent from several manufacturers.[83] Nonetheless, the total volume of chemical wastes handled by municipal treatment works nationwide was only 3.5 percent of the industry's output in 1959.[84] Even the limited use of municipal facilities reflects a choice to defer the costs associated with treatment equipment and services.

The narrow focus of research was one reason behind the apparent lack of enthusiasm for treatment equipment during the 1950s and 1960s. Two major textbooks provided broad overviews of the existing technology, but neither explored the chemical industry in particular.[85] Rudolfs reviewed the status of treatment technologies in the manufacture of synthetic fibers, acids, and explosives, and in oil refining, illustrating the existence of numerous working technologies. Public attention and research dollars during much of the 1950s and early 1960s, however, became fixed on solving the largely aesthetic problem caused by high-suds detergents.[86] Federal funding for treatment research was erratic at best. In the first two years of the Water Pollution Control Act, Congress authorized only a quarter of the research money called for by the legislation. Again in 1956, Congress approved only $300,000 of the $1.37 million research budget.[87] At the local level, public health agencies tended to seek remedies to a single pollution source at a given time.[88] Consequently, while experts worked to resolve one problem, they deferred action on many others.

While concerns over waste management gained corporate-level attention before 1950, the implementation of pollution control measures remained largely a plant-level matter, and not until the mid-1960s did numerous chemical companies appoint corporate-level executives to oversee pollution abatement programs. Even after making a corporate commitment to self-regulation, individual companies found that plant managers resisted pollution control policies owing to cost considerations.[89] Such responses were predictable, given the industry's long-standing posture vis-à-vis government pollution abatement efforts. Both in trade magazines and testimony before Congress, chemical producers sharply contested government statements and presented evidence that solutions to the problem were well in hand.[90] Public relations experts tutored their colleagues to place the issue before the general public in terms that highlighted the costs incurred by manufacturers.[91]

In effect, corporate action during the 1950s and 1960s relied on dilution and isolation technologies. Some companies pioneered development of incineration and other treatment technologies, but these options did not prevail as general practices. For those wastes that were deemed too hazardous for dilution, land burial became the chief short-term means of disposal and protection against liabilities. Manufacturers all too seldom applied internal expertise on toxicology to waste management decisions on chemical wastes, except when public agencies pressured individual companies. According to national surveys, the use of technology to solve chemical waste problems was severely limited through the 1950s. Industry spokesmen claimed they were handicapped by costs, but in cases in which treatment equipment was installed, there were no apparent adverse economic side effects.[92] In fact, by the mid-1970s a survey of organic chemical manufacturers revealed that more than half of their waste received some type of destructive treatment. Incineration accounted for nearly three-quarters, with recovery and deep-well injection accounting for another 10 percent. Only 15 percent received on-site burial.[93] By that late date, and after the formation of a national environmental protection agency, treatment technologies had supplanted, although not replaced, traditional burial.

DISTINGUISHING BETWEEN GENERAL URBAN AND HAZARDOUS WASTE

The fact that many municipal landfills received industrial wastes has prompted some to argue that little distinction has been drawn between general urban refuse[94] and hazardous wastes in regard to appropriate disposal sites.[95] Actually public health and industrial authorities have long distinguished between all forms of general urban and industrial wastes. Sewage and garbage had presented public health problems during the early twentieth century and public agencies had assumed responsibility for them. The general responsibility for industrial wastes, however, normally had fallen to the producer, not the public. The distinctions arise from basic social expectations about private responsibilities and the characteristics of the waste itself. This section will discuss the differences recognized between general urban and hazardous wastes.

Solid wastes have been a perennial problem for urban authorities since the emergence of cities. Associated with disease, putrefying wastes have been banished from densely settled areas for centuries, while paper and other debris have been viewed as simply aesthetically objectionable. As the populations of U.S. cities increased during the nineteenth century, the refuse problem grew. Garbage, defined as kitchen and biological wastes, along with refuse (which included building debris and paper wastes) and ash, to say nothing of the massive quantities of manure left by draft animals, posed an immense removal problem. During the latter portion of the nineteenth century, municipal governments assumed responsibility for removing and disposing of urban wastes.[96] Quite commonly they distinguished between the various types of waste and even provided different forms of disposal. As early as 1873 Chicago ordinances identified a wide range of wastes. Households, restaurants, and hotels were to set garbage, offal, and swill, and in some areas ashes, by the street for city crews to remove. The city restricted "night soil" transport to licensed scavengers, required them to use watertight containers, and mandated that they follow specific transport and disposal guidelines. Contemporary public health policies viewed biological waste as a potential contributor to epidemics, and officials sought to control these wastes to minimize the hazards associated with them. In general, the policy was to remove the waste beyond densely settled regions and generally isolate it in "low" ground. Chicago's ordinances even specified that offal had to be buried under at least twelve inches of earth to prevent nuisance or offense.[97] When a municipality assumed responsibility for refuse removal, it did not extend it to industrial wastes. Chicago's Bureau of Street and Alley Cleaning had the duties of removing "all dirt, filth, litter, garbage, ashes, manure, offal, swill, dead animals, and other material, and to keep such streets, alleys, and public places in a clean and wholesome condition."[98] General nuisance provisions applied to offensive industrial wastes such as offal, tars from coal-gas works, and tannery wastes, but municipalities never took complete responsibility for them.

There was perhaps less distinction between sewage and liquid industrial waste prior to 1900. Cities and factories released untreated effluent into waterways, although municipal ordinances commonly prohibited the discharge of packinghouse and other types of offensive wastes into streams and lakes within their jurisdiction.[99] Public health authorities considered toxic wastes germicidal and therefore not a threat. Overwhelmed with disease-causing sewage, sanitation officials focused their attention on this problem, but nevertheless recognized the distinction between it and industrial wastes.[100]

As many municipalities put sewage treatment plants into operation during the 1930s, new attitudes towards nonbiological industrial effluent emerged. Municipal treatment plants could not adequately handle highly acidic or toxic waste streams, and industrial waste experts recommended that manufacturers provide pretreatment of cyanide, copper, chromium, and chloride wastes before release to municipal treatment plants. One treatment provided for highly toxic wastes was impoundment. Authorities recommended high security around the pond and a concrete bottom to prevent seepage when toxic ingredients such as cyanide were present. Security efforts reflected knowledge that the toxic wastes could cause serious harm to trespassers or seep through the ground and contaminate nearby wells.[101] Ponds for wastes from canning operations or domestic sewage did not require similar precautions, reflecting a long-standing distinction between harmful and nonharmful effluent. Liquid waste treatment textbooks continued to distinguish between industrial and domestic sewage through the 1950s and 1960s.[102]

By the 1940s, cities had begun to adopt sanitary landfills as the preferred means for disposing of garbage. Guidelines for proper design and operation specified that sanitary landfills be designed to contain general urban garbage—not industrial wastes. New York City conducted early experiments with sanitary landfills and used them as receptacles for mixed refuse consisting of garbage, ash, and general urban debris.[103] The U.S. Public Health Service characterized sanitary landfills as facilities to control "garbage, rubbish, and ashes."[104] Following World War II, various professional organizations continued to tout the advantages of sanitary landfills as repositories for municipal refuse. The American Society of Civil Engineers reported on progress in refuse collection and disposal and noted that the sanitary landfill was a promising means to control garbage nuisances.[105] Illinois Department of Public Health personnel issued landfill standards that specified that they were intended for *garbage* and *refuse* interment. They itemized various engineering and site evaluation procedures that included a geological assessment, adequate separation from wells and springs, groundwater monitoring, and leachate collection. Operational instructions called for daily cover and compaction, prevention of ponding of liquids in the fill, and adequate cover to prevent settling.[106] Even with municipal garbage and refuse, engineers recognized potential problems and advised safeguards.

A fundamental change in garbage disposal practices was the shift from isolated dumps toward engineered encapsulation in sanitary landfills. The underlying demand for landfills stemmed from a diminishing availability of remote locations, the increasing nuisance caused by dumps, and the rising costs of transporting garbage. By providing daily cover and compaction, public health agencies ensured that neighbors would suffer less inconvenience and health risk. The very process of sanitary landfilling involved deliberate site evaluation and design considerations typical of other engineered projects. Adequate and acceptable cover was essential, as were suitable substrata to contain the garbage leachate. These considerations have been part of the site selection process ever since the 1940s.[107]

Contemporaneously with the emergence of landfills as the preferred means for handling urban garbage, industrial specialists demonstrated that there were widely accepted distinctions between garbage and hazardous and toxic industrial wastes. The National Safety Council issued a booklet outlining the "complex processes of safe disposal of industrial wastes." Among its recommendations for the disposal of solid wastes, it claimed that solids could usually be disposed of safely in dumps. Nevertheless, it advised that detailed maps of the locations of specific wastes be kept and that the dump sites be secured with fences or other security measures. Furthermore, it noted that toxic, water-soluble, flammable, and other hazardous substances required special attention and handling to prevent off-site problems.[108] A U.S. Army regulation called for trained specialists to manage the disposal of ordnance and recognized that the army held full responsibility for its safe disposal.[109] Likewise, the Manufacturing Chemists' Association advised that burial of tars was an option but warned against polluting nearby water supplies.[110]

Although sanitary engineers frequently addressed the problems of using municipal sewerage systems to handle industrial effluent, there was only limited comparable literature on using sanitary landfills for solid industrial wastes. One particularly significant publication addressed mixed disposal of hazardous industrial by-products and municipal solid wastes. In an address to industrial waste managers, Wilbur Webb defined the wastes that a sanitary landfill was designed to contain: "the type of trash which resembles domestic refuse, such as discarded packaging materials, landscape trimmings, lunch-room garbage, and general refuse." He warned that "if the particular trash considered can be disposed of by a more desirable method, sanitary landfill need not and should not be considered." This comment obviously applied to industrial wastes for which treatment technologies existed. He also specified that the sanitary landfill method should not be used for industrial wastes "if there is any possibility of polluting either surface or ground water supplies." He foresaw potential problems with soluble chemicals leaching from land disposal sites and advised manufacturers to investigate the geology and hydrology of their disposal sites. Furthermore, he clearly stated that wastes sent to sanitary landfills "should not be highly toxic or inflammable."[111]

As an apparent safety measure some of the companies did keep records of waste disposal practices. Monsanto Chemical Company conformed with the National Safety Council's recommendations and maintained maps depicting hazardous waste disposal locations.[112] Many other companies were able to respond to a congressional survey and to identify over 3,300 sites that had been used for chemical waste disposal since 1950 and also characterize their contents. In the face of these warnings, mixing industrial and municipal wastes, or "codisposal," was common among the chemical companies.[113]

A survey of municipal sanitary landfills, conducted in 1961, illustrates a continuing distinction between urban and industrial solid wastes. Over 70 percent of the landfill operations surveyed indicated that they prohibited flammable liquids and that it was common to forbid the use of landfills for industrial wastes where groundwater could be contaminated.[114] However, the growing quantity of wastes during the 1950s, and restrictions on releases to waterways, produced a demand for codisposal sites. Public works authorities in California sought an efficient and consistent method for determining a site's suitability for different wastes and developed a classification system. The system included three types of disposal sites, ranging from insecure sites, for limited types of wastes, to most secure sites, for hazardous types of wastes. Only Class I sites, which fell in a category limited to sites with non-water-bearing rocks or locations over unusable water, had no restrictions on the type of solid or liquid wastes. The classification system identified Class II sites as those in proximity to usable water supplies but above the water table, thereby limiting contamination potential, and Class III sites as affording little or no protection from contamination. The guidelines limited the contents of Class II sites to "household and commercial refuse, . . . decomposable organic refuse, and scrap metal. Class III sites, it advised, could accommodate only "non-water-soluble, non-decomposable inert solids."[115] Although the latter two categories included some industrial wastes, they did not include organic chemical residue or other mobile wastes. When Illinois instituted formal sanitary landfill guidelines in 1966, they applied to general urban refuse and some solid industrial wastes such as "food processing wastes, boiler-house cinders, lumber scraps and shavings.[116] The guidelines specified that the disposal of "hazardous substances" required prior written approval of the Department of Public Health.[117]

Ruling on the Velsicol chemical waste disposal site in western Tennessee, a U.S. judge found that the ASCE and APWA guidelines offered sufficient guidance to preclude dumping of chemical wastes above local aquifers. Through the testimony of expert witnesses he concluded that standards for "industrial or chemical landfills were even more stringent than a sanitary landfill and were referred to as a Class I landfill." He also observed that "hazardous toxic wastes, which can be both [sic] liquid, solid, or gaseous are different than ordinary sanitary landfill wastes."[118]

It is obvious that public health authorities and industrial waste experts have seen toxic, flammable, and otherwise hazardous industrial wastes as distinct from general urban refuse and sewage throughout this century. Although codisposal of these two vastly different types of wastes certainly occurred, the contemporary literature suggests it was not in accord with general principles of public health, groundwater protection, and sanitation.

CONCLUSIONS

During the first two-thirds of this century, chemical producers followed three somewhat distinct phases of waste management. Initially, the policy of physical or geographic isolation appeared fundamentally sound. Given the relatively small quantities of hazardous by-products, manufacturers were sensible to seclude their operations and thereby minimize off-site nuisances and damages. Isolation evaporated as urban land uses encroached, however, and chemical producers turned more and more to waste treatment. New technologies provided some treatment for the most troublesome wastes, and techniques were available for treating or destroying hazardous chemicals by the early 1950s. Nonetheless, installation of treatment equipment ran far behind the available technology. Thus more complete treatment, although feasible and accessible, was an unrealized solution to industrial waste management problems.

During the 1950s, increasingly stringent water pollution laws prompted manufacturers to turn to land burial practices. Sequestering wastes on property they owned and controlled provided a degree of long-term care even in the absence of treatment or destruction. Engineering skills existed to evaluate and modify sites to provide for secure disposal, but seldom did waste disposers utilize the full range of capabilities that were available to them. It is clear that many waste managers did not follow typical site evaluation practices. The number of Superfund sites does not necessarily reflect ineptitude or ignorance, but rather illustrates decisions that embraced low-control options. Because adequate treatment of many wastes would have been more difficult or expensive than the practices actually chosen, those generally employed did not reflect industry's contemporary level of technical problem-solving capabilities.

Regulating Hazards

INTRODUCTION

One view of the history of hazardous material regulation is that legislative bodies neglected it prior to 1970.[1] Yet the historical literature indicates that numerous legal mechanisms existed to address actions seen as hazardous before 1970. This chapter will consider how legal institutions and the industrial community dealt with a broad class of technological hazards before there was a specific legal definition of hazardous wastes. Traditionally, common law provided for redress when noxious industrial by-products caused property damage or personal offense.[2] Twentieth-century legislation has reinforced some common law principles while undercutting others. Nevertheless, over the past century legislative bodies considered and passed laws regulating the safe handling of hazardous chemicals. In addition to the laws, there were enforcement mechanisms in place prior to 1970. State laws created pollution control agencies as early as the 1910s, although insufficient funding and staffing left them unable to monitor either disposal activity or environmental conditions. Consequently, they served at best as a reactive force to address problems after public health emergencies emerged. Furthermore, they followed a general policy of cooperation with industry and had to rely on manufacturers to inform them of their waste characteristics and to produce solutions to problems. Nonetheless, enforcement produced some obvious, although limited, impacts on waste management practices.

Clearly the problems of the late twentieth century reflect poorly on legal accomplishments of the prior decades and this supports the view that legal solutions were unrealized. Yet the situation that precipitated a vigorous legal reaction during the 1970s was born of a complex milieu. Single-purpose laws, the inconsistent public response to perceived environmental problems, the reliance on corporations to solve problems, and the fractured nature of enforcement impeded effective implementation of the mechanisms that existed.

LEGAL RECOGNITION OF PUBLIC HAZARDS, 1900–1960

Nuisance and Statutory Law

Nuisance law provided the framework for initiating legal action against both privately undesirable and publicly deleterious practices at the turn of the century. As part of common law, it relied on the legacy of court decisions handed down over the years. Effectively, a nuisance was defined as "anything wrongfully done or permitted which injures or annoys another in the enjoyment of his legal rights."[3] Nuisance law at the turn of the century adhered to certain fundamental principles that provided legal recourse for damages.[4] These principles were predicated on the broad definition of nuisance that encompassed a wide array of actions, which were not limited to water pollution, but ranged from defiling a neighbor's water supply to dumping offensive waste in the streets, releasing noxious fumes to the air, explosions, operating a brothel, and placing a cemetery too near a neighbor's well. Thus, nuisance law equated a variety of actions, both obvious and invisible, that could result in damages caused by commercial operations. Given this legal context, explosions that damaged neighboring properties were comparable to atmospheric, surface-water, and groundwater pollution. In effect, these actions shared the common characteristic recognized by the law that, whether private or public, they had arisen on private property and could affect neighboring property and might qualify as a nuisance.

At the turn of the century, legal texts offered several important conclusions concerning nuisance law and pollution problems. Legal scholars have agreed that owners of riparian properties had the right to pure water, or at least to water in a reasonable condition so that it could be used for domestic or industrial purposes. From their review of legal decisions, they found that legal nuisances were deemed to have been created by actions that tainted waters and by situations that eventually could cause offensive conditions to arise—such as depositing carcasses in waterways or constructing privies on a water course. In addition, pollution that caused fish kills was a basis for litigation.[5]

Nuisance law also provided a means for taking action against indirect pollution of groundwaters. At the time, courts regarded most groundwaters to be percolating waters and therefore not to fall under riparian common law, which was generally limited to surface waters. Justices turned to the "reasonable use" rule, which held that a landowner was entitled to use of groundwaters under his or her property. Public policies elaborated on this subject:

> The fact that a man has absolute right to the underground waters within his territory, and may abstract those waters entirely, even to the point of draining his neighbor's land, does not give him the right to poison or foul those waters and allow them to pass into his neighbor's land in such condition.[6]

Furthermore, the reasonable use rule prohibited landowners from accumulating substances on their property that could escape and cause harm to a neighbor.[7] This not only applied to manufacturing activities but extended specifically to activities that involved the burial of perceived hazards—namely corpses. "A cemetery association has no right to use property for cemetery purposes when such use will probably, by percolation of water from it carrying disease germs, contaminate the wells of residents in the vicinity."[8] Finally, the fact that a manufacturing or burial operation provided an overall benefit to the community was no defense for pollution. Neither longevity of an operation nor its usefulness to the community lessened the right of the courts to enjoin a nuisance.[9]

Common law had considered many of the issues later incorporated into statutory pollution law, without providing a mechanism for regulation or enforcement. Private citizens could file suit when their personal property was damaged, but individuals did not have standing to file a suit for a public nuisance. To provide a basis for public prosecution, city councils passed ordinances that defined certain actions as public nuisances or restricted specific activities through zoning. These included such workplaces as town gasworks, rendering plants, brothels, garbage dumps, and explosives plants without regard to whether they actually annoyed anyone.[10] State legislatures further clarified the definition of nuisance. In 1905, twenty states had laws that placed restrictions on the disposal of certain industrial wastes into public waters. This was done either by declaring the act a nuisance or making it a

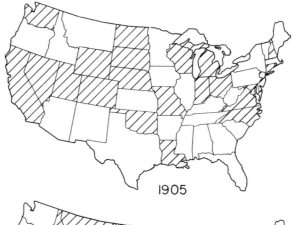

1905

1926

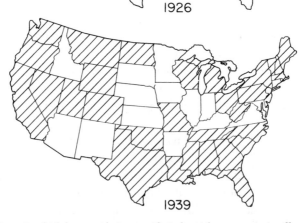

1939

FIGURE 4.1. States in which laws regulating specific industrial wastes were in effect in 1905, 1926, and 1939. As early as 1905 numerous states had addressed the problem of industrial wastes as pollution sources. By 1939 more states had laws that specified trade wastes as nuisance-causing. Source: Edwin B. Goodell, *A Review of Laws Forbidding Pollution of Inland Waters in the United States*, 2d ed., Water Supply and Irrigation Paper No. 152 (Washington, DC: U.S. Geological Survey, 1905); U.S. Congress, *Pollution Affecting Navigation or Commerce on Navigable Waters*, 69th Cong., 1st sess., H. Doc. 417, 1926; and U.S. Congress, House, Water Pollution in the United States, 76th Cong., 1st sess., H. Doc. 155, 1939.

criminal offense. In either form, statutory law augmented common law by specifying certain actions as public nuisances and set a precedent for public regulation of pollution, both of water and the atmosphere. State laws early in the twentieth century outlawed release of such industrial wastes as coal-gas tars, slaughterhouse refuse, bagasse (sugar cane waste), beet pulp, and sawdust into public waters (Fig. 4.1).[11]

Most nuisance litigation stemmed from private actions, and the courts tended to uphold both the riparian and reasonable use standards where the evidence of damage was clear and the burden of abating the pollution was not too onerous. For example, the courts held a Colorado mill owner liable for damages caused to a downstream farmer by introduction of poisonous substances into the stream.[12] In Massachusetts the courts ordered an injunction against discharges by a manufacturer when it determined that the releases caused damage to livestock downstream and that the release of harmful substances was not essential to effective operation of the plant.[13] The case of *Ballantine and Sons v. Public Service Corporation of New Jersey* illustrates the issue of reasonable use. Ballantine and Sons, a brewing company, argued that wastes that percolated from a neighboring gasworks tainted their water supply, thereby rendering it useless for brewing purposes. The court held that the reasonable use rule applied and that the brewer had a right to untainted water.[14] One observer commented that the court's attitude at the time was "not so much a stricter enforcement of the principles of common law, as a better understanding on the part of the courts of the principles of sanitary science. The common law always existed and was always enforced according to the lights of the courts."[15]

The common-law system of pollution control has been criticized for tolerating the polluting behavior of large manufacturers in view of their roles as major employers and influential community members.[16] This view was clearly expressed by the Illinois Rivers and Lakes Commission in 1915:

> Certain manufacturing wastes at the present state of the art of
> sewage purification, are very difficult or impossible to treat with
> satisfactory results in entirely preventing stream pollution. In these
> cases it is a question of allowing a certain degree of local stream
> pollution or of abandoning the industry.[17]

Nonetheless, the historian Christine Rosen contends that judges in several northeastern states found economic arguments less convincing in the early twentieth century.[18] Such rulings, in part, depended on the courts' finding a clear distinction between natural and industrial pollution of a waterway. U.S. Public Health Service attorneys concluded, "Discharging waste from a manufacturing plant or mine into a stream is not a natural use of the stream and if done to the material injury of the lower riparian proprietor, creates a liability for damages."[19] Along the same lines, the Washington Supreme Court ruled:

> There can be no more practical or just rule of liability resting upon riparian owners using the water of a stream for industrial or manu-facturing purposes, and thereby polluting the water with foreign substances, than that damage caused by such use and pollution of the water renders such user liable to a lower riparian owner.[20]

Furthermore, some courts rejected outright the argument of eco-nomic priorities. A federal court held that the importance of a manu-facturing operation to the economy had no bearing on its liability for pollution:

> It is urged that the defendant is prosecuting a business useful in its character, beneficial to the public, and furnishing employment to a large number of men, and that it is conducted with skill and pru-dence, and with the most approved machinery, and, if damage results, it arises from no fault of the defendant, and that in such cases the ancient rigor of the law has been modified in furtherance of industrial progress and development. This contention finds no support, either in principle or authority.[21]

The rulings of the court system, based on turn-of-the-century common law, were that industrial polluters could be liable for damages.

Such general legal principles found their way into specialized law texts. Thornton points out in regard to oil and gas law that polluting substances entering a neighbor's water well constituted a basis for action against oil producers and refiners.[22] Thus, common law, before 1920, forced businesses to consider pollution as a risk or potential cost. In fact, R. L. Kraft, addressing the chemical industry, sent a clear warning to beware of local ordinances and zoning regulations when establishing new facilities. He advised in 1927 that "there is a growing tendency in various parts of the country to stop such pollution by industrial wastes" and observed that the courts had shut down several plants because of groundwater pollution, although he offered no examples.[23]

The liabilities for off-site property damage were well known to chemical manufacturers before 1920, and some operators took protective measures when acquiring new plant sites. E. I. du Pont de Nemours and Co. fought complaints from fishermen and property owners near its Hopewell, Virginia, plant. Neighbors claimed that acid fumes and liquid discharges from the plant damaged crops and the quality of Bailey's Creek, a stream that carried waste from the manufacturing site.[24] DuPont challenged the complaints in court, and in one case produced a contract that released the chemical producer from liability for property damages.[25] In effect, DuPont had purchased the right to pollute from its neighbors, and contested the suits, in recognition of the potential liabilities of common law and in an effort to fend off further suits should one complainant win his case.

The adoption of the *Restatement of Torts* (1939) ushered in utilitarian criteria for evaluating nuisance acts. In what is known as the balancing-of-utilities test, courts were to evaluate actions on the basis of the relative public good of the action in relation to the damages. According to the *Restatement of Torts*, "An intentional invasion of another's interest in the use and enjoyment of land is unreasonable . . . unless the utility of the actor's conduct outweighs the gravity of the harm." This test provided for a defense after 1939 that allowed defendants to demonstrate that polluting behavior engendered greater public benefits than personal costs.[26] The *Restatement* shaped public policy until the pace of legislative activity concerning pollution picked up following World War II.

Legislation

During the 1920s and thereafter, legislative bodies attempted to refine common law through supplementary statutes. By 1924 all forty-eight states had statutes that dealt with industrial wastes. Many of these laws either prohibited certain industries from releasing wastes or declared specific bodies of water off limits to discharges. Conversely, laws provided exemptions for certain critical industries or classified severely polluted streams for waste removal, while protecting less-polluted waterways.[27]

State laws, however, were unable to address interstate water issues.[28] Searches for legal remedies to interstate conflicts took place during the 1920s, and each centered on a single obvious pollutant when conditions were at a perceived crisis level. The U.S. Congress responded to public pressure when it considered legislation to prevent the fouling of beaches along the Atlantic seaboard. After extensive debate and deliberation, the federal legislators accepted the argument that maritime vessels, and not land-based oil refineries, were the major contributors to the coastal pollution problem. Oil industry spokesmen heartily supported the bill that regulated only ocean-going craft, and ultimately Congress passed this legislation (1924).[29] The first federal pollution-control effort, like the various state pollution laws, was extremely narrow in scope and limited in its authority to certain waste producers and to certain bodies of water. This permitted oil and other industrial discharges into inland rivers, even those that served as public water supplies, to continue.

A second major effort to restrict interstate pollution arose along the Ohio River. Rather than seek federal legislation, the major industrial states along the Ohio River formed an interstate compact to motivate coke producers to halt release of phenol into the river. Working with the U.S. Public Health Service and industry representatives, the states of Pennsylvania, Ohio, and West Virginia jointly agreed to enforce the same phenol release policies. This landmark pact produced considerable progress in abating phenol pollution and demonstrated the value of interstate cooperation.[30]

Nonetheless, internal state legislation continued to dominate regulatory efforts, although it focused mainly on surface-water problems during the 1920s. In an effort to augment industry-specific laws with enforcement organs, several states created pollution control agencies by 1930: Rhode Island, 1914; Massachusetts, 1917; Pennsylvania, 1923; and Illinois, 1929. Generally such government bodies were a part of the state public health department and looked upon public water supplies as their chief responsibility. Although they recognized industrial wastes as a threat to drinking-water supplies, municipal sewage was their greatest challenge and received the most immediate attention before 1940. The Army Corps of Engineers bolstered this priority in 1926 when it reported that "domestic sewage, the greater part of which is untreated, probably comprised 90 per cent of the total volume of polluting substances."[31] Except for the particularly troublesome industrial effluents, such as phenols and oils, public health agencies tended to overlook factory effluent in general, despite laws that forbade their release. The emphasis on domestic sewage also derived from professional expertise within the field of sanitary engineering.[32] Nevertheless, there is ample evidence that when particular problems arose, state agencies did take action to remedy the pollution situation.[33]

Legislative action, although it was no part of its intent, effectively undercut the broad principles of common law. By providing special exemptions for certain types of industries and designating specific waterways as waste carriers, statutory law forced a shift away from strict interpretation of common-law principles toward tolerance for job-producing businesses. Both policy-based decisions carried out by state agencies and common-law decisions reflect this trend. The weakness of state law was all too obvious to contemporary observers. Treatment specialists reported, "Laws governing the discharge of industrial wastes into streams have been placed on the books of nearly every one of the United States . . . but unfortunately, the means for enforcement, i.e., finances and police power, are not always adequate."[34] A member of the Pennsylvania Board of Fish Commissioners offered a similar observation about the passage of state laws, but complained that "closer analysis of their high-sounding verbiage usually reveals weaknesses that render them ineffective and inoperative." Furthermore, he reported that industrial interests had been able to defeat pollution control legislation by using the argument that "to require Pennsylvania industries to properly dispose of their wastes would penalize them in competition with those of other states in the open market and thereby put Pennsylvania industries at a competitive disadvantage."[35]

Rose v. Socony-Vacuum illustrates the erosion of common-law principles in terms of pollution.[36] In this case the plaintiff owned a farm in East Providence, Rhode Island, where he raised hogs and hens. For thirty years he had watered his livestock from a well and a stream on his property. The defendant operated an oil refinery on adjoining land and released refinery wastes to basins on its grounds. Leachate percolated from the basins to the stream used to water the hogs and also contaminated the plaintiff's well, causing the alleged death of 136 hogs and 700 hens. The court ruled:

> It is an unavoidable incident of the growth of population and its segregation in restricted areas that individual rights recognized in a sparsely settled state have to be surrendered for the benefit of the community as it develops and expands. If, in the process of refining petroleum, injury is occasioned to those in the vicinity, not through negligence or lack of skill or the invasion of a recognized legal right, but by the contamination of percolating waters whose courses are

not known, we think that public policy justifies a determination that such harm is *dammum absque injuria* [loss without injury].[37]

The appellate decision both showed a lack of understanding of groundwater processes and ran contrary to other decisions regarding off-site contamination. In fact it became the object of several critiques, both from legal scholars and groundwater scientists. Attorneys criticized that "public policy should be more concerned in the protection of individual property rights than in relaxing the ancient rigor of the law in favor of industrial progress."[38] Hydrologists claimed that the court's decision in no way reflected contemporary understanding of groundwater movement.[39] Nonetheless, *Rose v. Socony-Vacuum* ushered in an era of common-law tolerance for industrial nuisances that was strengthened by the *Restatement of Torts*.

Recognizing that surface-water contamination had reached a serious condition and that state efforts were insufficient to abate pollution, U.S. Senator Augustine Lonergan (Connecticut) convened a conference to discuss federal stream pollution control legislation in 1934. The gathering was to craft uniform pollution abatement policy and enforcement measures.[40] Testimony clearly indicated that pollution was widespread, that it was deleterious to aquatic life, and that the federal government possessed authority to enter the arena of interstate pollution control.[41] The conference produced a pair of bills introduced to Congress in 1936. The Lonergan bill (S. 3958) called for the creation of sanitary water districts that would fix standards of water purity within their drainage basins, establish minimum standards for effluent treatment, and enforce these standards. The compromise bill (S. 4627) proposed merely to create a Division of Stream Pollution Control within the U.S. Department of Public Health. It would work with the various state agencies to prepare a plan for eliminating or reducing pollution, promote the enactment of uniform state laws, study pollution abatement technologies, and provide loans to install treatment equipment.[42]

Although Congress twice passed versions of the compromise bill (1936 and 1938), neither was enacted. In 1936 opponents of the moderate measure called it back to the floor at the end of the session and effectively killed it that session. President Roosevelt vetoed a similar measure in 1938, claiming that it circumvented administrative office funding procedures. Congress once more debated similar measures in 1940 but failed to approve them. Consequently federal surface-water pollution legislation languished until after World War II.[43]

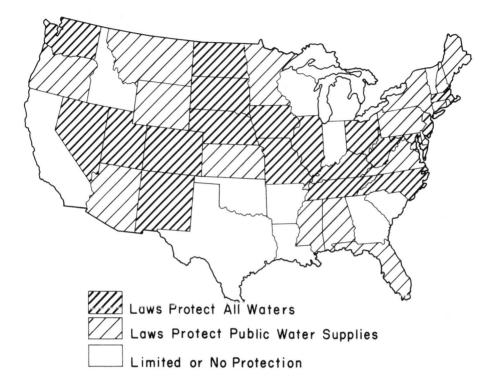

FIGURE 4.2. States having water protection laws as of 1901, by type of protection. An inventory of water protection laws indicates that many states, at least implicitly, included groundwater in the realm of legal authority. Source: J. L. Leal, "The Legal Aspects of Water Pollution," *Public Health: Papers and Reports* 27 (1901): 103–112.

Groundwater had remained a background issue during the 1920s and 1930s. According to one estimate, not quite 17 percent of the total population relied on subsurface water for drinking purposes in 1930,[44] and as might have been expected, the issue received little legislative attention. Nonetheless, states generally had statutes that restricted the poisoning of wells or springs. Furthermore, as early as 1901 several states had had laws that specifically protected "all" waters from pollution and this included underground waters (Fig. 4.2).[45] Although ranging in severity and specifics, these laws recognized the failure of common-law principles to serve the requirements of public safety adequately and represented early steps to enact clearly defined groundwater legislation. New Jersey law, for example, prohibited the introduction of "factory refuse" into any lake, pond, well, spring, or reservoir.[46] Michigan had legislation that made intentional poisoning of a well a felony, while Illinois law simply declared that tainting a spring or other body of water was a nuisance.[47] North Dakota, North Carolina, and Connecticut all restricted the placement of cemeteries in proximity to water wells.[48] Federal hearings and legislation largely ignored groundwater. In part this resulted from Congress's interest in resolving interstate pollution problems—less so in intrastate issues such as groundwater cases.

The courts offered inconsistent rulings on groundwater issues. In 1925 a New York court found that landowners were not required to ascertain the course of subterranean waters before burying noxious substances on their land.[49] In another case, a Texas court concluded that an individual who polluted a neighbor's well as a consequence of polluting his own land was liable for damages.[50] Even the *Rose v. Socony-Vacuum* case provided inconsistencies. The court held that it was the landowner's responsibility to confine noxious material to his own property, but found that the refinery was not liable for causing a nuisance in the absence of negligence.[51] This decision reflected a distinction between riparian rights and the right of an owner to fully utilize percolating waters. By noting the distinction, the decision permitted damages when there was no malicious intent. Consequently, in subsequent cases plaintiffs had to prove intent rather than merely demonstrate damages under the reasonable use rule. This trend did not completely undermine nuisance law's effectiveness in abating subterranean pollution; however, it added to the uncertainty of how a court might rule.

Before 1930 there were only a few state laws that addressed groundwater resources, other than those dealing with wells or springs, but such legislation was typified by the Illinois Sanitary Water Board Act of 1929, which clearly specified that the board would exist to "control, prevent, and abate pollution of the streams, lakes, ponds and other surface and underground waters of the State."[52] It was not until the late 1940s, however, that several other states began to follow up on a series of groundwater pollution incidents and enact laws dealing expressly with groundwater. Michigan, in 1949, created a Water Resources Commission, which was directed to "protect and conserve the water resources of the state and . . . [to maintain] control of the pollution of surface or (and) underground waters of the state."[53] California, likewise, grappled with a series of groundwater pollution incidents during the 1930s and 1940s and passed groundwater protection legislation in 1949.[54] Furthermore, by this time ten states had laws prohibiting the placement of cemeteries within specified distances of water supplies as a public health precaution.[55] Although public attention and congressional action were largely attuned to the obvious surface-water problems, state legislatures showed increasing concern with subsurface waters. By the late 1940s legislative action had addressed groundwater protection from a variety of perspectives, illustrating that the concepts of groundwater pollution certainly were not foreign to either specialists or legislative bodies. These cumulative actions all point to laws that relocated responsibility for protecting water supplies from the user to the producer of noxious wastes or deleterious conditions. They explicitly called for measures to be taken by waste producers to provide some degree of protection against natural resource destruction.

Underlying pollution control regulations was the public agency view that manufacturers were ultimately responsible for preventing pollution. The Illinois Sanitary Water Board issued a general policy in 1946 that stated, "The industry is responsible for the solution of its problem."[56] Likewise, the International Joint Commission, a cooperative Canadian-U.S. commission that confronted transboundary issues, assigned responsibility to industry in 1951. While assessing the impact of industrial pollution in the Niagara region, they concluded that "it is a recognized fact that the correction of industrial waste pollution is the responsibility of industry."[57] Legislation merely formalized a preexisting understanding.

Federal involvement in water pollution finally gained congressional enactment and implementation in 1948 with the passage of the Water Pollution Control Act. It contained many similarities to earlier federal legislation and largely provided funding for research on water pollution problems, loans to support installation of municipal treatment facilities, and power to federal authorities to step in when states did not take action to halt egregious pollution. Amendments in 1956 to the 1948 law changed federal funding from loans to grants for sewage treatment systems and encouraged states to establish desirable water quality levels. The legislation still relied largely on voluntary action on the part of both states and polluters and had little effect on actual discharges. In an attempt to improve water quality, Congress passed the Clean Water Act of 1965. It required states to establish water quality standards and to develop plans to enforce them. Although more powerful than its predecessors, the 1965 act was unworkable in many respects. It created an adversarial climate among states, which, depending on their commitment to pollution control, could court manufacturers by offering less vigorous enforcement than their neighbors. Thus, immediately prior to the passage of what is generally considered the first effective federal water pollution legislation (the Federal Water Pollution Control Act of 1972), little progress had been made in establishing an effective federal pollution control program.[58]

Related Legal Issues

In addition to water pollution legislation, numerous related issues forced society to consider the hazards of chemical substances and to develop means for ensuring public safety. The principal sources of exposure to hazardous chemicals were chemical additives to foods, agricultural chemicals, and workplace exposure. Legislation impinging on these technological hazards indicates that the discovery of these problems long antedated the publication of *Silent Spring* (1962), the acknowledged wake-up call of the environmental movement.[59]

By the end of the nineteenth century, most states had passed laws to regulate food adulteration, and the U.S. Congress followed suit in 1906 with the passage of the Pure Food and Drugs Act. The state statutes and the federal legislation sought to protect consumers from food modified with either poisonous substances or nonfood ingredients. These measures came following the Department of Agriculture's Division of Chemistry exposé of food preparation practices that included the introduction of aniline dyes into candy and toxic metals into canned vegetables. The use of additives had proliferated with the advent of chemical discoveries that allowed food producers to enhance products by manipulating colors and flavors. Enforcement of the 1906 act became mired in political wrangling that rendered the measure ineffective; nonetheless, the bill's intent was to protect consumers from inadvertent consumption of relatively small quantities of toxic substances.[60]

The environmental linkages between toxic chemicals and humans were acknowledged by federal agencies and public health bodies during the interwar years. Between 1919 and 1929 the use of lead arsenate on high-value crops increased two and a half times and residues on fruit and vegetables became associated with both acute and chronic health problems. This prompted concern within the medical profession and among workers at the Food and Drug Administration (FDA). Fueled in part by yellow journalists, popular fear of toxic residues heightened during the 1930s.[61] Despite public concern, the FDA could do little to tighten its standards during the Great

Depression. Following a lengthy battle between fruit growers and the medical community, Congress finally passed the Food, Drug, and Cosmetic Act of 1938, which gave the FDA statutory authority to establish tolerance levels, or presumably harmless levels, for toxic residues on consumer products. The administrator of the Food, Drug, and Cosmetic Act approved new tolerance levels in 1940, but the introduction of DDT largely eliminated the concern with lead arsenate as a residual threat to consumers.[62] Again, in 1958, Congress acted to protect unwitting consumers when it passed the Food Additives Amendment to the 1938 legislation. This new measure sought to establish tolerance levels "at a presumed no-effect level" for both food additives and pesticide residues and to set the tolerance level for cancer-inducing ingredients at zero.[63]

Safe-label legislation reflected another area of concern with low-level exposure to hazardous chemicals. Attention toward both worker and consumer safety prompted efforts to alert users to the dangers inherent in certain products. In 1927 Congress passed the Federal Caustic Poison Act, which required precautionary labels on eleven chemicals. It soon became apparent that this list of chemicals did not cover a sufficient number of substances, and by 1935 the Surgeon General had approved a uniform labeling method for about a dozen individual compounds and classes of hazardous chemicals.[64] The rapid expansion of synthesized chemicals and the increasing unfamiliarity of workers with the products that they worked with prompted the Manufacturing Chemists' Association to develop a more extensive labeling system in the mid-1940s. In addition, the Federal Insecticide, Fungicide, and Rodenticide Act of 1948 directed manufacturers to label hazardous products and to supply directions on their use that "are necessary and if complied with adequate for the protection of the public."[65] In 1960 the Federal Hazardous Substances Labeling Act became law and initiated a period of further refinement of product safety labeling.[66] Thus, legislation has progressively called for manufacturers to alert users of toxic substances to their dangers.

Worker exposure to hazardous chemicals was another issue on the legislative agenda. New acts modified common law and revised worker compensation policies. Turn-of-the-century common law allowed employers to erect three effective defenses against suits filed by workers injured on the job. They could claim that the employee assumed the risk knowingly, that the worker's negligence contributed to the injury, or that a fellow worker caused the accident. By 1915, however, labor organizations and their supporters had introduced workers' compensation ideas to employers, insurers, and politicians. Effectively, workers' compensation allowed all employees to contribute to a monetary pool and in the case of an accidental injury, excluding willful misconduct, the injured would receive assistance with medical and unemployment expenses.[67] Congress added coverage of diseases to the federal occupational policy in 1924, and individual states also had statutes that extended coverage from accidental injury to illness caused by long-term exposure to hazardous substances.[68] By 1946, thirty-two states or federal territories offered fairly extensive policies for occupational disease; and they included coverage for either acute or chronic exposures.[69] In general, the state laws offered lists of "compensable" conditions that arose from worker exposure to harmful substances, whether gases, liquids, or solids. Following the passage of these laws, many manufacturers in conjunction with their insurers began to institute safety measures to prevent or at least minimize employee exposure to occupational hazards.[70]

The legislative process up through the 1950s placed on the manufacturers the overriding responsibility for identifying which chemicals were hazardous and for providing safeguards. Basic common-law principles of negligence made the supplier of toxic substances potentially liable for damages caused by their products, under reasonable circumstances. That is, "a manufacturer must provide products that are reasonably safe for the foreseeable use."[71] Chemical producers recognized that their liability for personal harm caused by hazardous chemicals started in their production facilities, extended to other industrial settings where the chemicals were used in the manufacture of other products, included uncontrolled releases of by-products, and culminated in consumer use of the products.[72] Both federal and state legislative bodies enacted laws that attempted to provide workers with protection from unsafe doses of hazardous chemicals and other workplace hazards and to provide them with a means of compensation should they fall victim to either acute or chronic toxic substance exposures. Furthermore, the common law and legislation that applied to hazardous substances between 1900 and 1960 recognized the environmental linkages that could expose populations to dangerous materials. The rule of reasonable use allowed groundwater users to seek damages for contamination of their wells by noxious waste disposal practices, and public laws specified certain types of undesirable land-use activities in the recharge area of domestic and public wells. By the 1930s, legislative bodies were grappling with the problem of exposure to small quantities of toxic residue on food. Although the legislative process came to regard chemical industrial wastes as a subject for specific laws only in the late 1970s, the major components of the toxic waste issue had been dealt with by specialists and legislators by the early 1950s.

Guidelines for Safe Handling of Hazardous Substances

In addition to specific legal restrictions on the use of hazardous substances, government agencies provided guidance on proper and safe handling of potentially dangerous materials. While some of these guidelines were voluntary, others were required when companies were engaged in filling government contracts; this was particularly true during wartime. This section examines the role of government agencies in establishing protocols for safe handling of hazardous chemicals.

During World War I, there were numerous injuries and fatalities in the explosives industry. Fatal poisonings in the production of trinitrotoluene and other explosives exceeded five hundred, with nearly twenty thousand cases of nonfatal poisoning. This disrupted production and caused serious morale problems. At the outset of mobilization for World War II, the War Department sought to avoid similar problems caused by mishandling toxic chemicals. In cooperation with the Army Surgeon General's Office and the U.S. Public Health Service, the Occupational Health Division was formed to survey industrial hazards and to institute safeguards. In addition, the Office of the Chief of Ordnance activated a Safety and Security Division in 1942. It supplemented the Occupational Health Division and distributed information to installations on both industrial hygiene and "environmental sanitation." Furthermore, it recommended specific practices and assigned the Ordnance Industrial Hygiene Branch responsibility for making inspections.[73] Government inspection policies applied to most government-owned/company-operated facilities. Although direct civilian worker supervision was not the program's intent, federal agencies actively provided financial assistance, consulted with local and state agencies, and promoted similar industrial hygiene standards for war-related industry.[74]

The Division of Industrial Hygiene released a substantial industrial hygiene manual in 1943. It summarized extensive research by experts from several federal public agencies and from insurance companies. The manual offered diagnostic and treatment advice for occupational maladies and also presented engineering solutions to workplace exposure. Included was a list of "toxic limits" for numerous chemicals and compounds typically used in the production of wartime materials. The list included toxic metals, organic solvents, and other materials known to pose a threat to workers' health.[75] In reference to stream pollution the authors warned that "the *dumping of industrial wastes* into our rivers and streams is an unjustifiable although time-honored practice which should be discontinued." It added, "While the dumping of obnoxious but nontoxic wastes may have to be condoned, the dumping of highly toxic matters may produce fatal consequences."[76] An extensive survey of liquid wastes from munitions manufacture concluded that numerous diluted wastes were not toxic and that with minimal treatment, such as neutralization for acids, they would pose no serious public health hazard.[77] Such reports appeared to sanction continued release of industrial wastes. Nonetheless, guidelines for military installations called for base commanders to "change the sewage or any products of treatment so the receiving waters or land is not damaged." Undesirable side effects of military installations included public or private water-supply contamination, property damage, creation of offensive conditions, and damage to fish, livestock, or recreational areas.[78]

In addition to concern with domestic threats to public water supplies, the Civil Defense worked with public health agencies to develop methods for determining if belligerent states had poisoned public water supplies. The effort provided analytical techniques for detecting small concentrations of specific chemical warfare agents and warned the medical community of their effects.[79]

The U.S. Public Health Service also offered advice on general refuse disposal. It pointed out that open dumps were unsatisfactory for garbage and advocated the "sanitary fill" method—disposing of garbage, rubbish, and ashes in a pit and immediately compacting and providing cover.[80]

Management of specific hazardous chemicals, particularly those produced by private manufacturers for the Chemical Warfare Service (CWS) involved direct guidance by the CWS or cooperative programs between the government and private sector. Generally, guidance followed standard manuals or guidelines.[81] In certain cases, the Chemical Warfare Service issued specific directives to chemical manufacturers. In 1945, for example, it advised all CWS arsenals and depots to dispose of all drums that formerly contained certain chemicals, including arsenic trichloride or thionyl chloride, in a particular manner. The notice specified that the drums should be drained into a pit lined with bleach or lime to neutralize toxic liquids; that additional decontaminating agents should be poured over the liquid wastes and the empty drums; that the contents should be covered with eight feet of dirt; and that the owners should post the site.[82] The CWS sought advice on waste treatment from private waste treatment companies and chemical producers as well. Hooker Chemical Company sold a process used to recover small quantities of chlorine blow gas to the CWS.[83] In reference to other ordnance plants, the army provided guidance on the construction and operation of TNT plants. Although waste treatment systems were designed by private consultants, the army maintained some authority on the specific systems installed, and in some instances inspection teams enforced the army's decisions.[84]

In sum, the federal government possessed a great deal of influence, whether statutory, contractual, or merely implicit, in the management of industrial wastes during wartime. This acted, at the very least, to offer more uniform waste management guidelines than the state regulations and raised expectations for safe chemical waste disposal.

ENFORCEMENT

Common law provided legal means for abating nuisance-causing pollution, but public enforcement procedures were largely absent until the 1910s. For the most part, prosecution sought to obtain compensation for private property damages, or public agencies responded to citizens' complaints to obvious nuisance conditions. The development of state agencies with pollution abatement responsibilities provided a means to approach polluting industries and municipalities as well as personnel to document environmental degradation. The central mission of these agencies was to protect public water supplies, but they did not maintain ongoing water-quality-monitoring programs. Rather they responded to problems as they arose with whatever authority legislative bodies had delegated to them. In general, they possessed the authority to forge agreements with polluters to prevent future pollution, but prosecution was the responsibility of the state legal officer—generally found in a separate agency. Thus, enforcement was a dual responsibility, and ineffective enforcement was in part a product of the fractured authority.

At the turn of the century, local public health officers held primary authority for abating pollution. Operating under the authority of local nuisance ordinances, they had the power to call for prosecution of offending parties. As long as local manufacturers chose to release their effluent downstream from local water intakes, there was little call for legal action.[85] Downstream water users might object to both municipal and private waste discharges and they could take legal action. Missouri, for example, contested Chicago's diversion of its sewage into the Mississippi River drainage basin. It argued before the U.S. Supreme Court that Chicago's sewage would deliver deadly diseases to its water intakes. After hearing extensive expert testimony, the court ruled that Chicago could use the inland rivers to transport its sewage.[86] Most commonly fish kills or damage to livestock prompted private citizens to take legal action.[87] Decisions favoring fishermen and farmers did not always deter further pollution. The large volume of municipal sewage and the mixture of industrial wastes complicated the identification of specific culprits and in effect permitted industrial discharges to continue unabated.[88]

State conservation authorities also had a limited role in policing waterways. Most states had a fisheries or wildlife commission that sought to uphold laws affecting natural resources. One of their responsibilities was to protect freshwater and marine aquatic life from pollution. Despite expressed concern with pollution problems, they were frequently powerless to demand that industries or municipalities halt releases that were deleterious to fish. The Illinois Board of State Fish Commissioners lamented:

> We are frequently in receipt of complaints of fish being killed by the introduction of refuse from different manufacturing or other establishments, which is being turned into the rivers and streams. . . . We have found also that, no matter how flagrant the case appeared, we as fish commissioners, having no authority further than that of any citizen . . . could only point out the sole means of relief, a suit for damages by nuisance.[89]

Their appeals for additional legislative protection went unheeded for years. Pollution, in the absence of more stringent enforcement powers, damaged many inland fisheries.[90]

As industrial pollution became more apparent, states recognized they needed to bolster their enforcement powers, and they began to establish pollution control bodies during the 1910s. Illinois's Rivers and Lakes Commission had the duty to "prevent the unlawful pollution of streams."[91] Unlike the state public health department, the Rivers and Lakes Commission had the authority to arbitrate pollution disputes. They heard complaints at public hearings and handed down binding orders to abate pollution. In 1916, for example, they ruled on twelve complaints involving industrial wastes. In seven of the cases, they issued cease-pollution orders.[92] Clearly, authority was available and sometimes it was exercised.

Cooperative efforts among states along the Ohio River effectively forced manufacturers to divert their phenolic wastes from the waterway in the

1920s. By enacting similar pollution standards, the states convinced steel makers and coke producers to alter their disposal practices and volatilize wastes on land.[93]

The cooperative approach was generally regarded by state public health officials as the most effective available enforcement tool. Unlike current practices in which regulatory agencies monitor water quality conditions, state authorities responded to specific complaints and sought solutions that fit the situation. For example, in the early 1930s, following local complaints the Illinois Sanitary Water Board convinced oil refineries along the Mississippi River to install separators without taking legal action.[94] They worked with other manufacturers as well to secure agreements that would ensure treatment of industrial wastes prior to their release to waterways of the state.[95] In Michigan, when toxic wastes from metal platers killed livestock near the community of Bronson in 1939, the state and the manufacturer solved the surface-water problem, at least temporarily, by the construction of liquid waste impoundments for the effluent.[96] Long Island officials deferred action during World War II, but immediately following the war they met with aircraft manufacturers who were causing groundwater pollution and secured agreements to modify their release of chromium wastes.[97] By the mid-1940s, the expressed policy of the Illinois Sanitary Water Board was that "the industry is responsible for the solution of its [industrial waste] problem."[98]

The oil industry preferred this approach and jealously guarded its exclusive responsibility in the area of waste management. It fought off federal regulation of oil releases to inland waters in the 1920s and argued that most oil pollution came from floating craft and not land-based industry.[99] The American Petroleum Institute began publication of a series of waste treatment manuals during the 1930s and argued that the industry could control pollution through internal guidance and self-policing.[100] Likewise, the Manufacturing Chemists' Association formed an internal committee to consider stream pollution issues during the 1930s and lobbied against federal stream pollution legislation.[101] In effect, they sought to exclude government involvement in specific waste management practices and thereby assumed responsibility for implementing pollution control systems.

Their record as policemen is not impressive. Although the MCA claimed success with its policy of internal control, only about 20 percent of its members' facilities had treatment equipment in place in the late 1930s.[102] By the 1950s, a federal survey of pollution control equipment revealed that approximately 36 percent of the reporting chemical plants in the Northeast, Midwest, and Middle–Atlantic states had some form of "industrial" waste treatment. Although impressive at first glance, the chemical plants listed as having industrial treatment equipment in the 1957 survey represented only 2.9 percent of the regional totals for chemical manufacturing facilities.[103] Adequate treatment equipment remained a rare fixture at most smaller plants.

Legal action was a viable option for public agencies when the cooperative approach or internal policing failed to protect public water supplies or wildlife. Officials in Lansing, Michigan, obtained a court order that forced a munitions manufacturer whose picric acid wastes had tainted public ground-water supplies to find another waste disposal method.[104] In Texas, the Game, Fish and Oyster Commission deployed wardens to monitor wildlife and also water quality in the vicinity of oil production areas and major manufacturing districts.[105] Following World War II, they began prosecuting polluters who openly violated state laws and collected modest fines from those convicted.[106] Michigan officials took industrial polluters to court following the overflow of plating waste lagoons in Bronson. When toxic liquids ran down streets, bubbled up through manhole covers, tainted at least one domestic water well, and threatened public water supplies, the state Water Resources Commission, under the authority of a new state law specifying their jurisdiction in groundwater matters, filed an action against several companies.[107] Although the principal defendant, a metal plater, fought off the suit on procedural grounds, the case illustrates the efforts of state authorities to supplement the efforts of industry trade groups to abate pollution.

California law, as in many other states, required manufacturers to obtain permits for waste disposal. Following the "Montebello incident," a situation in which spills of an agricultural chemical (2,4-D) tainted public groundwater supplies over fifteen miles away from the source, public health officials required modifications in the waste treatment systems proposed for new plants. In this arid region where groundwater supplies were extremely important, officials took greater steps to protect potable water supplies,[108] such as establishing a groundwater monitoring program in 1949.[109]

Postwar regulation efforts arose at the state level and Congress followed with a federal act. Most states passed new legislation during the 1940s in an attempt to make enforcement possible. Yet their efforts had little effect according to contemporary observers, and Congress finally passed the Water Pollution Control Act of 1948 to assist states in controlling the pollution of interstate streams. This act yielded little legal action because of inconsistent funding and the intent of the bill to simply support the adoption of treatment equipment, rather than prosecute polluters.[110] In the absence of federal enforcement and with pollution continuing, states continued to revamp their laws in response to the persistent use of waterways for the removal of factory wastes. This produced a perception of stepped-up enforcement during the 1950s. Industry groups complained that governmental agencies were hounding them, but the dominant abatement policy remained the cooperative or voluntary approach.[111]

One exception that ultimately laid a foundation for much of the enforcement action of the early 1970s was initiated by the U.S. Army Corps of Engineers in the early 1950s. Seeking to force several major steel producers to contribute to dredging costs, the Corps of Engineers took action under the provisions of the 1899 Refuse Act. The government argued that discharges from the steel plants contained sediments that settled to the bed of the sluggish Calumet River and formed shoals, and thereby interfered with navigation. After years of litigation, the U.S. Supreme Court ruled in 1959 that the deposits were obstructions and that the government had the authority to issue an injunction to block their creation. This opened the way for additional litigation against manufacturers in regard to release of "all foreign substances and pollutants" into waterways, and this interpretation became a key tool for contesting pollution.[112]

On balance the enforcement of state pollution laws did little to diminish industrial pollution. Many specific factories modified treatment techniques, but such actions did not prevent the continued release of impurities to the land or water. In one overview of court decisions, the assistant attorney general of Wisconsin reported that "the courts seem to be less ready to award injunctive relief than to award damages."[113] As long as fines were minor costs, pollution continued. In addition, statutory limitations blocked consistent, statewide enforcement programs. In 1969, the Illinois attorney general, in a partisan proclamation, complained that the traditional cooperative approach had undermined enforcement. He argued that fines levied against small factories or mines downstate did little to control the industrial pollution around Chicago and redirected prosecution to the major pollution sources.[114] Much of the inequity he pointed out stemmed from state laws that prohibited the state from enforcing its laws in the Chicago metropolitan area. Such administrative restrictions remained as obstacles until the enactment of the National Environmental Protection Act.

Government enforcement of related hazardous substance laws, regulations, and standards was also inadequate. Regulations to control human
exposure to agricultural chemical residues, it has been argued, did little to
affect use, but rather impinged on marketing. Although laws required reg-
istration and labeling of hazardous chemicals, they did not preclude their sale
or application.[115] Despite investigations into the potential toxic effects of
chemicals such as DDT, their use continued into the 1960s.[116] Thus, widespread use of agricultural chemicals encountered little direct legal opposition during the 1950s.

State agencies generally inspected workplaces for safe conditions. The
inspectors' mandate was to spot any of a wide range of conditions that might
pose a hazard to workers. Such personnel generally were not toxicologists
and lacked special skills and equipment. It was likely that they would identify
only the most obvious exposures to unsafe toxic chemicals. In spite of trade
organizations' encouragement for manufacturers to employ physicians to
monitor worker health internally and thereby prevent costly illness to its
work force,[117] industry received harsh criticism for leaving the issue of
workers' health to government and insurance companies.[118]

In respect to public water supplies, county public health agencies and
municipal water delivery agencies maintained water quality testing programs to ensure safe drinking water. They relied on the U.S. Public Health
Service drinking water standards[119] that adhered to a bacteriological standard and sought to identify biological contaminants, placing less emphasis
on physical and chemical characteristics. While these standards included
permissible limits for toxic metals and several other chemical contaminants,
identification of disease-causing bacteria or their surrogates remained the
central concern of public health agency monitoring through the 1960s.
When conditions fell below safe levels, the water supply could be shut down
or diluted with pure water to restore it to an acceptable condition. Remedial
actions against the source of pollution rested in the hands of the local
authority and could include either legal action or modification of waste
disposal practices in agreement with the public health agency.

Finally, the military inspected government facilities and privately operated munitions plants. The intent of the inspections was to encourage
compliance with government guidelines or regulations with regard to waste
management. Inspectors in some cases cited inadequate practices and recommended improvements.[120] Through this procedure, government leader-
ship promoted standards of care that encouraged at least minimal conform-
ance with local laws.

IMPACT OF LEGISLATION AND ENFORCEMENT

There were several concrete impacts of legislative and enforcement efforts. During the first two-thirds of the century, under the threat of common-law nuisance suits, many offending industries migrated to locations at the peripheries of cities. Beyond the city limits and the purview of municipal ordinances that specified which type of industries were nuisances, chemical producers, coke works, local gasworks, and rendering plants operated with less opposition.[121] While there were other reasons to move to marginal locations, the threat of legal action certainly was a significant influence.

As statutory law refined the definition of nuisance or outlawed certain waste disposal practices outright, manufacturers of noxious wastes diverted waste from waterways to land or atmospheric sinks.[122] The adoption of quenching techniques for phenolic wastes in the 1920s and the use of separators by oil refiners reflect this pattern. Chemical companies also monitored their effluent releases more closely to assure "adequate" dilution. During the 1930s, for example, Dow Chemical installed various treatment, containment, and incineration facilities at its Midland, Michigan, plant to control the release of offensive waste and avoid excessive shock loads of noxious substances to the stream.[123]

In response to increasing enforcement action in certain states, some larger chemical companies adopted forward-thinking waste management policies. DuPont initiated an extensive effort to investigate potential waste discharges and install adequate treatment equipment at its new plant in Victoria, Texas, in the late 1940s.[124] In general, the chemical industry claimed that it was spending $40 million a year to control pollution in the early 1950s, mostly at new facilities.[125] However, there was little effort directed toward retrofitting existing plants. The Chemical Manufacturers Association's internal committee published several manuals on chemical waste treatment and encouraged member firms to follow these guidelines, but few companies, especially the smaller ones, hired qualified personnel to manage wastes. Frequently the development of waste treatment facilities was contracted out, and the chemical industry sustained criticism that they did not use their best staff to investigate and solve pollution problems. Sheppard Powell, a long-time waste management consultant for chemical producers, argued that manufacturers assigned production tasks to their top engineers and delegated pollution control matters to the least qualified personnel.[126] Furthermore, some manufacturers saw pollution as a public relations problem, not a technical one.[127] Although companies reported a fear of prosecution,[128] it was not until the late 1960s that some of the major chemical companies appointed corporate-level staff to coordinate pollution control efforts.[129]

The 1979 congressional survey indicates that the chemical industry had disposed of over 760 million tons of wastes since 1950.[130] Of the on-site and off-site disposal methods, pits, ponds, and lagoons were among the most common, despite availability of more sophisticated treatment technologies. On-site disposal was extremely common and reflected concern with liabilities. The American Petroleum Institute's manual on solid waste disposal advised that

> the philosophy of "out of sight out of mind" does not hold. The refiner may still be responsible for wastes after they leave the refinery property. Therefore, the refiner should be certain that wastes are handled in an acceptable and responsible manner.[131]

The fact that respondents to the congressional inquiry reported disposing of more than 90 percent of their wastes on property they owned suggests a concern with minimizing legal risks from off-site exposures.

Overall, the net environmental impact of legislation and enforcement during the years leading up to 1960 were negligible. Early twentieth-century legislation had limited effects, but it did occasionally move industry to less objectional sites and later shifted wastes from one environmental sink to another. Nonetheless, the enactment of numerous laws relating to industrial wastes and hazardous substances during the 1960s and 1970s reflects the inadequacies of previous efforts and a public recognition of and revolt against their environmental consequences. Industry expended a portion of its efforts lobbying against legislation and seeking public relations solutions, while in many cases deferring costly technological solutions to pollution problems.

CONCLUSION

At the turn of the century the burden of pollution enforcement, as defined by common law, largely lay with neighbors and private property holders. Court rulings often backed up the right of property owners and downstream riparian water users to untainted water supplies. As this century progressed, statutory law broadened the investigation and enforcement responsibility to include public agencies created to protect natural resources, including public waters. In the absence of adequate funding or specific water- or air-quality standards, these government agencies relied on a co-operative approach that was supported by industry. In fact, major trade groups struggled to retain responsibility over their waste disposal practices. Thus, the explicit and implicit burdens for controlling hazardous wastes resided with the creator of the wastes. Furthermore, laws concerning exposure to hazardous chemicals, whether as residue on or in food or in the workplace, placed the responsibility for prudent management of these chemicals on the producers of hazardous substances.

Working with Existing Knowledge

INTRODUCTION

Waste management decisions, at either the corporate or plant level, have been a product of many interrelated factors. Economics and external priorities certainly have played an important role, as have corporate ethics and public liability. Knowledge of the hazardous qualities of waste and their potential threat to workers and neighbors was a fundamental factor as well. Before knowledge of potential hazards had become recognized, little thought was given to considering the economics of wastes, exercising control over wastes, or isolating wastes either geographically or technologically.

A previous chapter has demonstrated that chemical manufacturers had become aware, during the first two-thirds of this century, that their products and by-products presented dangers. This chapter will examine the extent of that awareness and how it guided the decision-making process. It will tie management personnel to actual decisions about waste disposal practices, demonstrating a familiarity with the waste control issue. It will review the various forums and mechanisms by which technical staff and management could and did acquire information about chemical hazards, examine the techniques available for collecting and analyzing data, and consider the process by which those in responsible positions responded to hazardous substance management problems.

DECISION MAKERS

Personal Knowledge

Individuals with backgrounds in chemical production, not business administration, generally ran the chemical industry in the early twentieth century. The historian David Noble convincingly argues that chemical engineers guided this industry's transition into a large-scale, high-volume, mass-production enterprise.[1] Leo Baekeland, for example, patented the first plastic, Bakelite, in 1907 and launched the General Bakelite Company to produce it.[2] Likewise, breakthroughs in petroleum refining came from entrepreneur/scientists like the Dubbs family, which developed a continuous-process cracking still in 1913.[3] Typically, management at the time depended on a working knowledge in the fields of chemistry, engineering, and business, although sometimes without a formal education in any of them.

The outbreak of World War I, in 1914, severed U.S. access to many coal-tar intermediate chemicals—formerly purchased from Germany. Consequently, U.S. companies scrambled to fill the void and began manufacturing these products. There were few U.S. businesses with experience in production technologies for these coal-tar chemicals, forcing manufacturers to experiment with new equipment and processes. Nonetheless, chemical producers, working with seized German patents, successfully adapted the European technology to their needs and the demands of the U.S. market. Experimentation with unfamiliar technologies required research staffs to direct the effort. This to a degree removed management from research and development and created an initial buffer between them and the new technologies their companies used.[4]

After the war chemical production underwent a so-called revolution. Corporate research staffs shifted their attention from adapting German technologies to U.S. production wants to the development of new chemicals and uses for them.[5] Product diversity became the mainstay of the industry,[6] and by the 1930s companies redirected 3–4 percent of profits back into research. This required hiring chemists and engineers dedicated to research and development projects and to coordinate the many processes required to transform raw materials into finished products.[7] An inevitable result was a separation of management from the laboratory and the factory, but still most managers rose from the ranks of chemists or chemical engineers. In fact, the name of the main trade organization—the Manufacturing Chemists' Association—reflects the technical background of industry leaders.

In addition, the nature of corporate structure at the time allowed upper-echelon decision makers to participate in discussions involving the related issues of product liability, workplace hazards, and waste management. E. I. du Pont de Nemours and Company provides several good examples. It first hired an occupational health physician in 1904. He investigated the effects of acids and toxic gases on workers and helped DuPont avoid some of the occupational health problems other manufacturers faced during World War I. Along these lines, DuPont abandoned the use of benzene following the death of two workers from exposure to the solvent. Likewise, after employees exposed to tetraethyl lead died and following the discovery of toxic qualities of tricresyl phosphate (an ingredient of cellophane), DuPont took precautions to prevent worker and public exposure.[8] Disasters or fatalities prompted high-level officials to become involved in efforts to reduce exposure. Willis F. Harrington, a senior vice president for DuPont, received reports on hazardous qualities of chemicals. The head of the medical division advised him against locating a tetraethyl lead plant in the vicinity of St. Louis, given the high incidence of "medico-legal racketeering" there.[9] His files also contain extensive discussion on the toxicity of freon and methyl chloride, as well as notices from the Manufacturing Chemists' Association reporting on the safety of methanol as an antifreeze.[10] Furthermore, Harrington directed the president of Lazote Incorporated (DuPont's ammonia subsidiary) to respond to an inquiry from a leading trade periodical, *Industrial and Engineering Chemistry*, regarding the company's knowledge of methanol's toxic properties.[11] Harrington's direct involvement in decision making is apparent and his files indicate, at the very minimum, that he had a general knowledge of the toxic nature of several products.

In the late 1930s, when the Manufacturing Chemists' Association formed its stream pollution abatement committee, the president of DuPont, Lammot du Pont, took on responsibility for deciding whom to appoint as his company's representative to the committee. His initial inclination was to assign a staff person from the company's legal division, but he opted to delegate the responsibility to an employee with a background in chemistry.[12] Fred C. Zeisberg, a research chemist, received the appointment and kept his superiors informed of the committee's activities. Lammot du Pont also wrote directly to the secretary of the MCA and encouraged the organization to push for the passage of "reasonable" pollution abatement legislation.[13] Again, officials within DuPont, at the highest levels, concerned themselves with matters of chemical hazards and pollution. They delegated direct technical responsibility to specialists, but concerned themselves with the subjects from an administrative and legislative perspective.

DuPont management felt toxic substances warranted careful study and considered a plan to open a medical research lab in 1933. In a proposal presented to Willis Harrington and other company officials, George H. Gehrmann reminded his superiors of the tetraethyl lead incident and the problems presented by benzol. He argued that it was essential for the company to investigate the hazardous qualities of process chemicals and products.[14] Two years later at the opening of the toxicology lab Gehrmann stated, to an audience that included DuPont corporate executives, that the Haskell toxicology facility was established to "develop accurate information on the toxic action of chemical compounds on the human organism."[15]

When the American Petroleum Institute issued its first waste treatment manual, it stated that the manual had been "prepared for the use of executives in deciding questions of expenditures for disposal equipment and operation, for the use of refinery managers in deciding questions of refinery equipment and operation," and "for the use of engineers in designing disposal equip ment."[16] Corporate-level officials in some companies certainly were aware of minute details of waste management practices. In 1932, the Illinois Sanitary Water Board surveyed industries in the village of Monsanto (now Sauget), Illinois, to collect information on toxic chemicals discharged into village sewers and from there to the Mississippi River. F. B. Langreck, an assistant vice president for Monsanto Chemical Company, responded for his firm. He reported that plant effluent consisted mainly of cooling water, but conceded that occasional acid spills occurred. He maintained that the company conducted hourly sewage analyses and responded to any abnormalities. He also reported that "no sludges or highly toxic materials" left the plant with normal discharges.[17] These comments indicate that a corporate official expressed an in-depth knowledge of waste management practices for that particular plant.

Hooker Electrochemical Company officials directly observed disposal practices and recommended changes in procedures. A Hooker yard employee, Stephen Witkowski, mentioned in an affidavit that Mr. Klaussen and Mr. Murray, both key corporate officers, once came to watch workers dispose of thionyl chloride wastes at Love Canal and passed out coffee and doughnuts to the men. Witkowski recalled, "You had to puncture the drum before rolling it into the dammed-off area. When the drum hit the water it would make a lot of smoke and would scoot along the water." While Klaussen recommended a method that would produce less smoke, Witkowski stated that the workers abandoned it soon afterward because it was too slow for efficient disposal of large quantities of waste.[18]

The chemical processing industry had a wealth of toxicological information available to it; furthermore, staff toxicologists shared critical information on worker exposure problems. One vehicle for disseminating toxicological information was the Manufacturing Chemists' Association (now the Chemical Manufacturers Association) *Chemical Safety Data Sheets*. These multipage publications capsulized physical and toxicological information on specific chemicals and offered guidance on safe handling, storage, waste disposal, human exposure response, and other aspects of product handling and use.[19]

When Hooker Electrochemical experienced an outbreak of chloracne among workers exposed to dioxin impurities in the herbicide 2,4,5-trichlorophenol in the 1950s, information sharing among plants working with the same basic chemicals went into action. Chemical company officials corresponded with one another about their experience, although some sought to limit public knowledge of the problem.[20] J. Wilkenfeld, Hooker's assistant technical supervisor, wrote about a meeting with a German firm's representative: "Dr. Kudszus also requested that we not publicize this information since it might have an adverse effect on the end product uses. They are passing this information on by word of mouth to interested persons." Wilkenfeld also pointed out that the same chemical product posed long-term contamination problems for I. B. Farbin company. He reported:

> The troubles they and I. B. Farbin have had in decontaminating buildings point out that in cases of major spillage they renew all insulation, chip off all the old paint and even tear up and relay the floors in the building since the material will absorb and sublime from concrete and paint surfaces.[21]

Hooker took several steps to minimize worker exposure, thereby underscoring the existence of internal expertise and procedures to deal with dangerous substances.

The Manufacturing Chemists' Association advocated corporate-level involvement in waste management as early as 1948. In its first water pollution manual, it proclaimed that "pollution control must be considered at every step in industrial development, from research, through design and plant operation." It went on to describe the general composition of waste management that was considered advisable at the time.

This job [pollution abatement] might be assigned to a vice president, who would then select a competent person to serve as specialist on industrial waste disposal, and to direct and coordinate all activities within the company having a bearing on pollution abatement.[22]

The manual further recommended that the waste manager have broad experience within the company and that, depending on the size of the corporation, this individual should have a staff of engineers and chemists. Such a structure would have given management a direct role in pollution abatement decisions through appointment of personnel.

A handbook also advised chemical company officials to take a responsible position towards managing chemical wastes. It called for company officials to organize a waste disposal group that included personnel with appropriate expertise and to establish a cooperative relationship with regulatory agencies.[23] Through the 1950s, many waste management actions remained plant-level decisions, although not all reflected existing knowledge. Dwight Metzler, a public health official during the 1950s, testified at the Love Canal trial:

It was well known that these wastes [the contents of Love Canal] were in general toxic to humans and to animals and that they should be placed in a container or in a place where neither animals nor humans could get to them, and once you found that out then you don't need to argue about toxicity levels. . . . The problem is that these wastes are [sic] bad news, they ought to be put someplace where they'll not come in contact with humans and that is what happened with a few human failures along the way.[24]

Few chemical companies had corporate-level waste management specialists during the 1950s, but by 1966 six major chemical companies had assigned internal waste management decisions to experts who held high-level positions.[25] Nonetheless, implementation remained a plant-level activity, and cost perceptions continued to stymie compliance in spite of expressed corporate and industry goals.[26]

In their academic training and in actual practice, corporate officials encountered chemical hazards and waste disposal issues. While they were not directly involved in all aspects, they had access to information and could make informed decisions on it, and in certain cases they took part in crucial decisions.

Corporate Expectations

There were several reasons for corporate concern with hazardous substances: avoiding lawsuits for property damage or personal harm, controlling insurance costs, maintaining a good public image, and preventing government interference with internal operations. Failure in any of these categories had implications for reducing profits—either through increased costs or reduced sales. In general, such concerns provided ample motivation for taking hazardous wastes seriously and for initiating actions to minimize the risk of exposures both on site and beyond the factory grounds.

Plant location choices consistently incorporated public nuisance and property damage considerations. Selection of suburban or rural sites underscored decisions that recognized the potential for offending or harming neighbors, possible legal complications, and the desire to avoid such consequences. The practice of isolating chemical plants and their associated wastes, therefore, minimized the risk of lawsuits, legal expenses, and damage payments. This reflected a knowledge of hazards potential.

Insurance companies offered policies to protect against the costs of certain hazardous events—namely, fires, explosions, and sudden or accidental releases of hazardous chemicals. By purchasing property damage and general liability insurance, chemical manufacturers were able to offset some of the risks posed by the hazardous chemicals they handled. Liability insurance coverage protected manufacturers from claims following accidents when there was no intent to cause damage and due care was exercised. Although the purchase of insurance protection might encourage laxity or negligent behavior in respect to hazardous substance use, the courts generally excused a negligent party's insurer.[27] Furthermore, trade organizations frequently developed safety standards. If manufacturers followed these standards, such as fencing a disposal operation, they might qualify for discounted premiums. Hooker Chemical, for example, sought to extend its liability coverage to the Love Canal site and provided its insurance carrier with information about the site fencing and operation.[28] By conforming to existing guidelines or providing prudent safeguards, a company enjoyed some comfort that it would be indemnified in the event of an accident.[29] Accidents, however, were not equated with long-term releases of chemicals to land disposal sites or chronic disregard for safety. One insurance industry spokesman argued that when a company had previous experiences with adverse outcomes of hazardous substances releases, "there is no unexpected event; there is no accident."[30]

Through the 1940s there were no specific industry standards for chemical waste disposal other than local laws; but companies received the advice that mere compliance with the law did not guarantee that they would escape liability in the event of accidents.[31] Insurers, meanwhile, accepted the industry argument that waste management was process-specific and general standards were impossible to institute.[32] The closest approximation to standards was guidelines offered by trade organizations such as the American Petroleum Institute, the National Safety Council, and the Manufacturing Chemists' Association. Each of these trade organizations, at least by the early 1950s, had offered warnings that land disposal of hazardous chemicals could cause off-site damages, thus informing manufacturers that there were well-known liabilities associated with such practices.[33]

By the early 1950s, water pollution had become a highly visible public issue, and in their defense manufacturers advocated a policy of public education concerning their expenditures on pollution abatement. This, they suggested, would maintain a good public image.[34] In addition, public relations staff encouraged industries to inform host communities of their efforts to control wastes and to distinguish between harmful wastes and those that would not damage natural resources.[35] Central to this public relations position was the notion that manufacturers were already hard at work solving pollution problems and that they were attentive to community interests. The public relations discussion centered on obvious surface-water and atmospheric pollution and seldom included land pollution issues.

In developing waste management policies, a final corporate expectation was to minimize government interference in production and business operations. Chemical producers saw regulation of pollution as unwarranted government involvement in internal matters. The MCA consistently supported the status quo—or no federal involvement—when testifying before Congress. In 1936 the MCA argued that state regulations could adequately serve the country's pollution control needs. Two decades later an industry spokesman again asserted that pollution control was an issue to be decided at the state level and argued that a voluntary control program would produce satisfactory results.[36] In addition to forcing change, industry feared that government inspections would allow technical secrets to escape and thereby undermine corporate security and eventually profits.[37] At the most basic level, they objected to the potential costs that pollution abatement equipment would entail and the fact that government would be dictating business decisions. Although the MCA and individual companies publicly supported the concept of clean air and water, they fiercely resisted federal regulation, which, as they saw it, was interference. Implementing a pollution control strategy still fell to a company's management, whatever the position taken by the trade organization.

Delegating Research

Corporate efforts to acquire adequate knowledge about the relative hazards of industrial substances varied dramatically both within companies and across the industry. The initial emphasis on toxicology spawned an internal corps of industrial physicians and specialists, as well as university-based researchers. DuPont formed its research lab in the 1930s; other companies also had toxicologists on staff by the 1940s.[38] At the same time, manufacturers encouraged studies by the government to spread the costs.[39] Meanwhile, they continued to support internal research and contributed to independent, industry-supported labs that conducted pollution control and toxicity research. Before the early 1950s, attention focused on worker exposure to toxic substances and the impacts of liquid wastes on aquatic life. Beginning in the early 1950s industry supported an admittedly belated research thrust into human toxicity of wastes.[40] Thus, during the 1950s government and independent labs supplied additional information to industry specialists, supplementing internal and trade-group efforts along similar lines.[41]

In addition to toxicologists and their concern with the effects of hazardous wastes, an increasing number of manufacturers employed engineers to develop waste treatment systems. During the pre-1950 period, many of the published discussions of chemical waste management emanated from private consultants with backgrounds in sanitary engineering.[42] Dow Chemical Company employed a sanitary/civil engineer to supervise the waste management practices at its Midland, Michigan, plant in the 1930s. When an independent laboratory that employed chemists and engineers began to investigate chemical waste treatment techniques, a technical advisor to the pulp, paper, and paperboard industry hailed its opening.[43] Likewise, the head of the Atlantic Refining Company's pollution control laboratory had training in both chemical and sanitary engineering.[44] Not surprisingly, abatement procedures employed at chemical plants consisted of modified municipal waste treatment devices and controlled release of phenolic wastes.[45]

Apparently appointment of adequately trained personnel was exceptional. Sheppard Powell, a waste treatment consultant, castigated the chemical industry in 1947 when he claimed that industry tends to concentrate the ablest minds on production problems relating to cost and quality of plant output. Too often industrial waste problems are delegated to less experienced personnel who do not receive the support, guidance, and financial aid necessary for carrying out a successful corrective program.[46]

In the ensuing years things began to change, particularly after the passage of the first federal water pollution abatement legislation, when more and more chemical engineers published findings on waste management techniques, reflecting a gradual delegation of authority to or at least involvement of qualified personnel.[47] This was of course in accord with the recommendations of the Manufacturing Chemists' Association.[48]

To address the problem of industrial wastes, the MCA organized a pollution abatement committee in the 1930s. One of the committee's fundamental purposes was to share waste treatment technologies within the industry. In 1936, when Lammot du Pont was pondering the selection of a staff person to serve on the MCA committee, H. C. Haskell, an assistant director of the DuPont legal department, recommended the appointment of D. C. Carmichael of the engineering department on the basis of his previous work on pollution problems.[49] Ultimately, however, as noted above, DuPont assigned the task to chemist F. C. Zeisberg. In May of 1936 the committee held its initial meeting with representatives from DuPont, Dow (I. F. Harlow, a sanitary engineer), American Cyanamid (W. S. Landis, a metallurgical chemist), U.S. Industrial Alcohol, and Merrimac Chemical. Initially they surveyed chemical producers "to ascertain whether at the plants of the members steps had been taken either by modification of process or by installation of waste treating equipment to render liquid waste products discharged from the plants less objectionable."[50] DuPont's representative to the committee regularly reported on the committee's action to the company president and recommended additional staff, including engineers and chemists, to attend other meetings.[51] In 1947 and 1948 the committee hosted two-day meetings. At the latter gathering, eighty-four company representatives "exchanged technical data on the treatment and disposal of chemical wastes."[52] Hooker Electrochemical Company's technical representatives filed internal reports following the 1948 meeting of the MCA committee. They noted that the 127 attendees discussed various treatment technologies and considered the toxic effects of industrial wastes. In addition to the two Hooker employees, DuPont sent sixteen representatives and Allied Chemical another fifteen.[53]

By the early 1950s the MCA pollution abatement committee reported to the National Technical Task Committee on Industrial Waste that it had eleven members, "all of whom are professional industrial waste men." The committee spokesman, Lyman Cox of DuPont, testified that the MCA committee brought knowledgeable people from individual companies together and they shared technical information on pollution abatement technology, with the authorization of management.[54] Although some of their efforts were directed toward legislative matters, the committee produced several manuals on waste management that reflected a cooperative engineering effort. A review of the committee's fifth conference in 1951 summarized one of the committee's objectives this way:

> It has been decreed by those high up in the chemical industry that stream pollution abatement and waste treatment is not to be allowed to fall into the category of competitive enterprise. This decision opened the door for the establishment of pollution abatement committees and conferences for the free exchange of information and "knowhow" within the chemical industry.[55]

Furthermore, the MCA sponsored basic research on stream maintenance at the Philadelphia Academy of Natural Sciences, broadening the contacts of its waste treatment specialists with the science community, including the famed aquatic ecologist Dr. Ruth Patrick.[56] Finally, university specialists served as consultants for numerous companies and thus facilitated linkages between the corporate and academic worlds.[57]

Delegation of responsibility did not stop at the professional level. The American Petroleum Institute manuals on waste disposal claimed to be prepared for executives, managers, and engineers, but also for the use of drainage supervisors and for instructing men who operated equipment and facilities. In a similar vein, the MCA's first manual noted that a pollution abatement policy should be made clear to everyone in the company and that the waste treatment supervisor should have adequate assistance in discharging his duties.[58] Upon opening a new plant in Port Lavaca, Texas, Union Carbide Chemicals Company advocated a training program that extended from department heads to all technical and operational positions.[59] This type of organization indicates that there was more than mere advocacy of training personnel to be alert to waste disposal problems.

Management of the larger chemical concerns assigned professionals within the company to develop and manage waste treatment programs. This arrangement, at the very least, demonstrated an awareness of the problems associated with chemical waste pollution and an effort to take responsibility for the problem. Within the ranks of the major chemical producers, and the profession as a whole, there existed a body of expertise in handling chemical wastes and management-level awareness of the problems associated with wastes and hazardous substances.

AVAILABLE INFORMATION

A factor related to the capabilities and awareness of decision makers was the more basic matter of what information was available and how widely it was disseminated. Within any professional community there is a vast reservoir of knowledge. It is fed by the many discoveries of individuals working on specific problems and is tapped by those who encounter similar problems within interpersonal communication networks. There are also larger systems that work to distribute information from that reservoir to a wider body of users. Technical publications and conferences offered by professional organizations served this purpose in the case of industrial wastes. Although some observers have suggested that information was sequestered within small circles of experts, the overwhelming contemporary evidence indicates the channels of communication, while not perfect, were open and functional.[60] This section will examine the technical information that was available to waste management experts and the networks by which that information flowed through the industry.

Technical Literature

The most accessible forum for the dissemination of information about chemical waste management was the technical press. Numerous monthly and sometimes weekly periodicals were available to chemical company personnel—such as *Chemical and Metallurgical Engineering*, *Industrial and Engineering Chemistry*, and the *Engineering News-Record*. They contained a mix of industry news items and technical articles written by practitioners. Articles reported on new developments and techniques in manufacturing and kept readers abreast of economic, social, and legislative issues within their field. They also reported on promotions and transfers, enabling individuals to maintain contact with their peers and also watch the social dynamics of the profession. Far from being obtuse, theoretical discourses, these publications served as a vital part of the knowledge pool for practicing engineers and chemists and were read widely.[61]

In 1931 *Chemical and Engineering News* ran a special edition devoted to industrial wastes. The editor claimed that he hoped it would serve as a symposium "on the best of American practice in waste disposal and byproduct recovery" and that it would "prove the forerunner of a greatly enhanced interest on the part of the chemical engineer."[62] It contained a series of articles addressing industry-specific waste problems, particularly techniques available for treating wastes from coal-gas works and oil refineries, as well as other general waste management issues.[63] An underlying theme was that chemical engineers could contribute to solving the pollution problem. This optimistic viewpoint found unabashed expression in the remarks of E. B. Besselievre, one of the most respected waste treatment specialists of the day. He claimed that "it is a matter of record, based upon the handling of many industrial waste problems over a period of years, that there is no waste discharged for which there is not a treatment."[64] The appearance of the special edition in 1931 was a response to public concerns with the largely uncontrolled pollution of the 1920s.

A second review of the field followed several years later. This time (1939) *Industrial and Engineering Chemistry* compiled a special edition on industrial wastes in response to federal legislative efforts of the 1930s. The volume contained a series of papers presented to a group of practitioners belonging to the Division of Industrial and Engineering Chemistry of the American Chemical Society and presented a variety of solutions to waste treatment problems. The authors examined several specific industries, including chemical plants, iron and steel, pulp and paper, and petroleum refiners. Although there was a consensus that treatment solutions were problem-specific, there was also general agreement that sound engineering could conquer pollution problems, and the publication presented several examples thereof.[65]

Both special editions represented major industry self-examinations. They revealed concerns with public pressure to alleviate water pollution and an industry-oriented mechanism to distribute information about waste treatment technologies. In addition, they illustrated that applied professionals exchanged waste treatment research findings with one another. Although there were lapses in utilizing available expertise, this does not diminish this knowledge reservoir's significance and industry's ability to mobilize and distribute the information when necessary.

Basic reference books also presented chemical engineers with waste treatment information. One of the first U.S.-published texts on trade wastes appeared in 1913; it offered an extensive discussion on treating one of the most troublesome wastes of the day, namely those from coal-gas works.[66] E. F. Eldridge summarized much of the sanitary engineering literature through the 1930s in his text on industrial waste treatment in 1942. His work included chapters on coke-plant and oil-refinery wastes.[67] This publication suggests that a commercial press saw a market for a synthesis of the dispersed technical literature on trade wastes. In addition, the basic texts on industrial chemistry provided cursory discussions on waste treatment.[68] Passage of the federal Water Pollution Control Act (1948) stimulated additional publications in the early 1950s. Willem Rudolfs, a sanitary engineer with extensive industrial experience in New Jersey, edited a volume that summarized techniques available for a range of industries including the petroleum industry.[69] Edmund Besselievre, the Dorr Company engineer, chose a thematic presentation, but included flowcharts and tables depicting treatment options for chemical plants.[70] These major technical summaries drew on the existing technical literature and reflected a growing, albeit specialized, audience for trade-waste information.

In addition to the published findings, there were numerous opportunities for specialists to exchange information first hand at professional conferences and meetings devoted exclusively to trade-waste topics. In 1931 the National Safety Council held a special gathering on the "hazards to life and property that sometimes result from inadequate waste disposal."[71] E. B. Besselievre presented the featured address. He noted that industrial wastes have a "definite effect on the health and comfort on those resident nearby." He suggested that "judicious" disposal of solids was useful in reclaiming wetlands, but argued that manufacturers should remove all pollution from their effluent before releasing it to waterways.[72] The American Institute of Chemical Engineers focused on industrial wastes at their meeting that same year. The 1939 edition of *Industrial and Engineering Chemistry* presents the results of another such gathering. Several years later, the Pennsylvania Chemical Society hosted a symposium on the Chemist's Responsibility in the Control of Industrial Wastes.[73]

Starting in 1944 Purdue University sponsored an annual conference devoted to industrial waste problems and solutions. Far from serving just as an academic forum, it became a place for practitioners to meet and learn about developments in the field. Attendees included public health and sanitation officials, private consultants, army engineers, and industry specialists. Chemical companies also sent representatives to these meetings: In 1944 only one was present, but seven attended the 1947 conference, and six the

1949 assembly.[74] Although the proceedings dropped its attendees listing in 1949, chemical and oil company representatives presented papers, indicating both their presence and the corporate view that information exchanges were beneficial.[75] Regional conferences also assembled industrial waste specialists in the Southeast and Pacific West, further enhancing the opportunities for exchange.

The Manufacturing Chemists' Association stream pollution abatement committee was a central player in information dissemination. As previously mentioned, it proclaimed that two of its central functions were to prod chemical manufacturers to undertake responsible waste treatment and to promote free information exchange within the industry. One member reported the committee's work this way: "The chemical industry as a whole is organized to study and solve this problem for its wastes. . . . The aim of these committees is primarily on the sound and effective coordination of application by individual member companies."[76] Toward this end it sponsored meetings attended by appointees from the major chemical companies. In 1951 researchers from DuPont, the Chlorine Institute, Johns Hopkins University, the Kettering Laboratory, the U.S. Geological Survey, the Dorr Company, and Oldbury Electrochemical presented talks on specific waste disposal problems or technologies.[77] Furthermore, it produced a series of technical publications dealing with establishing pollution control programs and treating insoluble wastes, oils and tars, and acidic/alkaline effluents.[78]

There was apparent information exchange among company specialists, facilitated by the military during World War II. Mr. Gilcrease of Hooker Electrochemical Company, for example, visited the Lake Ontario Ordnance Works in 1942 to meet with the engineer in charge of waste disposal. They discussed various treatment methods and the effect of phenolic wastes discharged into waterways, and the potential for TNT wastes to pollute groundwater. From the ordnance works, Hooker's representative proceeded to the consulting firm of Metcalf and Eddy for further discussion of treatment technologies.[79] Metcalf and Eddy's expert in this field reported that evaporation/incineration methods were the treatment adopted by producers discharging effluent to public water supplies.[80] Hooker also dispatched its toxicologist to the Haskell Laboratory to discuss the effects of volatile organic compounds.[81]

Government bodies also compiled technical information and made it available to industry. The Bureau of Mines and the U.S. Public Health Service concerned themselves with occupational hazards during the first half of the twentieth century. While Congress deliberated the Oil Pollution Control Act, the Bureau of Mines inventoried waste treatment technologies employed by oil refiners.[82] Beginning in the 1920s, the Public Health Service initiated extensive studies of water quality, with an eye to the impact of industrial pollution, on both the Ohio and the Illinois rivers.[83] The Ohio River investigations culminated in the release of a series of industrial waste guides, including coke works and oil refineries, in 1944. These guides summarized the waste streams of these industries, described the pollution effects, and recommended remedial measures.[84] While somewhat cursory, they indicate that a number of recovery and treatment techniques were available and they made this information public. The bibliographies indicate that government researchers relied heavily on industry expertise and helped further circulate information already available to professionals both inside and outside industry itself.

At the regional level, ORSANCO (Ohio River Valley Water Sanitation Commission) vigorously sought industry participation in promoting pollution control within the Ohio River watershed. It formed a series of committees

> to promote within the ranks of their specific industry an apprecia-
> tion of the need to minimize pollution of wastes; to assemble facts
> and make an appraisal of the waste-disposal problems of their
> industry; and to consult with the Commission in the establishment
> of water-quality objectives and waste treatment requirements.[85]

The cooperative program resulted in the publication of a series of waste treatment manuals during the 1950s, several of which were re-published by the Water Pollution Control Federation, a national trade organization.[86]

Following the passage of the 1948 Water Pollution Control Act, Public Health Service personnel conducted additional investigations of industrial waste problems in certain industries. An initial round of investigations focused again on coke works and steel mills, along with beet sugar plants,[87] while subsequent inquiries looked into oil refinery wastes.[88] Industry, in general, welcomed federal expenditures on waste treatment research.[89] As with previous government programs, one intent was to make the information more readily available to industry, particularly smaller firms without research staff.

Ability to Collect and Analyze Data

Commonly, those who have claimed that past disposal practices were in keeping with contemporary standards posit that there was neither a recognized risk associated with the practices nor analytical methods to detect hazardous levels of contaminants.[90] Nonetheless, it is essential to consider past waste disposal practices and analytical methods as they related to hazards that were recognized at the time. In this section we will examine the methods available for collecting and analyzing contaminant information. This discussion will consider three related questions regarding site and disposal practice: How suitable was the site for waste disposal? How would leachate be detected? How would the information come to the attention of the proper authorities?

Site Evaluation. The ability of a land disposal site to contain wastes, without engineered enhancements, depended in part on the permeability of the strata on which it was situated (as well as the waste and soil chemistries). During the 1920s and the 1930s, the U.S. Geological Survey (USGS) compiled a tremendous repository of soil permeability information. Survey scientists had collected over 2,000 soil samples and, based solely on soil characteristics, measured the permeability coefficient for each. Their coefficient values for more than 1,300 samples served as bases for extrapolating coefficients for similar soils. This information permitted applied hydrologists, such as well drillers, to predict the yields for water-bearing formations and the rate of fluid movement within specific formations. In addition the USGS reported on field methods for determining the velocity and direction of groundwater flow. From the USGS studies, engineers could examine a soil sample and calculate the rate of movement of liquids through that matrix. For example, the USGS considered that a clayey silt, with a permeability coefficient of 0.0002 and a gradient of 10 feet to the mile, would allow a fluid to move only 0.0004 inches a year or 1 foot in 30,000 years.[91] By the early 1940s these methods provided reasonable tools for determining both the integrity of waste disposal sites and the rate of movement of leachate.

Field methods for determining the geological suitability for various engineering works had achieved professional standardization by the 1930s; they indicate an ability at that time to collect data necessary for calculating site security. Wherever major engineering works were planned, professionals agreed that geological exploration and material testing were essential prerequisites to construction. These were fundamental steps for highways, dams, bridges, and buildings, and by the late 1940s for municipal sanitary landfills as well.[92] Soil and geological assessment helped determine if design changes were warranted or additional features needed to be added to a structure to accommodate inherent physical shortcomings. The American Society of Civil Engineers (ASCE) manual on the subject called for an engineer to supervise sampling and to determine the suitability of the sub-surface for the project at hand. It also recommended that seasonal ground-water levels and chemical composition be considered as factors affecting the structure's design.[93] The ASCE and other professional organizations recog-nized that subsurface explorations were essential to a structure's survival and to protection of neighboring property. They took cognizance of soil type, soil and groundwater chemistry, and depth to bedrock. Following standard-ized procedures, they were able to sample and analyze these natural features sufficiently to avert massive roadway, bridge, dam, and building failure.[94]

In general, the standards granted latitude for professional discretion. The 1952 American Standards Association manual called for soil and rock explo-rations "at sufficiently close intervals to insure, insofar as practicable, that pockets or nonconformities of substrata are disclosed."[95] An engineering text suggested that for a "normal-sized" (undefined) building, four borings, at the corners, would suffice.[96] By the 1960s more specific guidelines had appeared. The ASCE's Committee on Sampling and Testing by this time called for the pattern of geophysical profiles (core samples) to ignore a "rigid pattern." Rather than sampling at building corners, it recommended a pattern de-signed to collect the "necessary" data. As a rule of thumb, it suggested one boring for every 10,000 square feet for airports, highways, and dams. When erratic subsurface conditions were encountered, it advised tighter spacing or one boring for every 600–2,500 square feet.[97]

The American Society for Testing Materials (ASTM) standards for soil testing called for examinations based on structure and grain size—features that determine permeability. For roadbuilding purposes, the ASTM called for soil boring to a depth at least three feet below grade line and, in areas of soil borrow, to the maximum depth of excavation.[98] A later ASCE study encouraged that reconnaissance explorations "be carried to fully adequate depths" and that borings penetrate "all deposits which are unsuitable for foundation purposes."[99] By the 1940s it was possible to extract soil or bedrock samples from depths of several hundred feet, permitting adequate sampling for extremely heavy loads. Professional organizations recognized the impor-tance of detecting inconsistencies that could cause structural failure. Fur-thermore, this indicates that adequate engineering knowledge about site sampling existed to identify undesirable conditions and professional codes called for sufficient sampling to detect any site failings.

It was also a common design goal to accommodate extreme events, such as floods, heavy downpours, and high groundwater conditions. As early as 1907, the ASCE offered a guideline for designing storm-water sewers. It reported that surface runoff during a storm represented about 40 percent to 54 percent of the rainfall and recommended that designs accommodate a maximum of one inch per hour rainfall.[100] By 1947 an engineering text tutored engineers to consider a host of factors such as the extent of impervious areas within a drainage basin and the long-term record of intense precipitation in a locale. It recommended designing drainage systems to accommodate a ten- to fifteen-year runoff maximum in commercial areas, whereas a five-year high sufficed for residential property.[101]

Through the leading professional organizations, site analysis became a requisite step in the erection of any engineering work. The sampling techniques included the basic tests—soil, groundwater, climate, and bedrock characteristics and location—associated with the evaluation of a land disposal site. On the basis of analysis of site conditions, which involved a knowledge of soil science, hydrology, and soil chemistry, design engineers modified the structure and/or designed in other safeguards to prevent failure. Certainly by 1950 a well-exercised protocol existed within the engineering profession for detecting environmental conditions that would present problems for long-term structural viability. Furthermore, the U.S. Public Health Service and the major engineering organizations shared the view that basic engineering principles should guide the selection and development of land disposal sites.[102]

Leachate Detection. The second element of identifying disposal site hazards was detecting leachate off site. This involved two complementary procedures: chemical analysis of the leachate and source determination through groundwater monitoring. It is indisputable that the primary concern of public health officials, such as the U.S. Public Health Service, through the 1930s was bacterial contamination of drinking-water supplies.[103] But this does not suggest that it was their only concern and certainly does not indicate that sensitive analytical methods for detecting known toxic substances were lacking. The 1925 USPHS standards offered health-related limits for lead, zinc, copper, iron, and magnesium and listed recommended methods for analysis, as proposed by the American Public Health Association.[104] In 1941 a toxic water contaminant discussion indicated that available tests could distinguish between the harmless trivalent and the toxic hexavalent chromium, and could detect 4–7 parts per billion of lead, and 10 parts per million (ppm) of arsenic.[105] The updated USPHS drinking-water standards (1943) also reported on methods for detecting contaminants such as arsenic and several metals.[106] In its 1946 drinking-water standards, the USPHS noted that hexavalent chromium in excess of 0.05 ppm rendered water unusable.[107] A two-part review of the toxicity of industrial wastes revealed an extensive arsenal of analytical methods that could be applied to metals, acids, and inorganic gases. These reviews focused on the toxicity of industrial wastes to aquatic life, which had far lower thresholds for most toxins than humans, and they therefore called for analytical methods that could detect extremely low (for the time) concentrations of contaminants.[108]

Synthetic organic chemicals present one of the greatest concerns today and their detection in groundwater dates to the 1940s. In the mid-1940s, California officials detected traces of 2,4-D, an organic chemical herbicide, in eleven water wells. The herbicide was highly diluted and subjected to municipal sewage treatment before its release to the local drainage network. In this way it eventually percolated through unconsolidated sediments to wells over fifteen miles from the manufacturing plant in a span of only seventeen days.[109] Ultimately, officials detected it in well water. Hooker Electrochemical officials expressed concern with analytical measures used by the International Joint Commission (IJC) when evaluating their phenol discharges to the Niagara River. Hayes Black, the IJC inspector, used the "Gibbs test" and detected phenols at 358 parts per billion.[110] Investigators seeking to determine the nature of contamination of groundwater near the Rocky Mountain Arsenal in Colorado in 1954 relied on sensitive analytical chemistry methods to identify a 2,4-D type of chemical.[111] Furthermore, tests to determine the toxicity of DDT in water supplies were able to reveal 0.05 ppm in 1951.[112]

In a survey of analytical methods, Morris Jacobs offered a variety of techniques for identifying trichlorethylene at levels of 20 ppm, an order of magnitude more precise than that required to detect the 200 ppm considered hazardous at the time.[113] In 1949 investigators used similar methods to detect trichloroethylene in well water at estimated levels of 18 ppm. This discovery alerted public health officials to the solvent's persistence in groundwater and led them to warn that even at low levels, measured by existing analytical methods, it could be toxic.[114]

In addition to organic chemicals, there was substantial concern with inorganic contaminants. Long Island officials detected hexavalent chromium at levels ranging from 0.2 to 1.1 ppm in 1947.[115] Michigan officials noted the presence of picric acid during World War II,[116] and analyses detected chloride leachate from the Rocky Mountain Arsenal in Colorado in the early 1950s.[117] By 1955 laboratory techniques existed to detect a variety of toxic salts, metals, and organic chemicals at levels considered harmful.[118] A broad survey of contaminants in groundwater summarized much of the published literature that existed in 1960. It demonstrated abundantly that there was an established body of knowledge on organic and inorganic chemicals in groundwater and methods to detect them.[119]

Harry LeGrand, a government hydrologist, has argued that there was very little knowledge about the movement of groundwater contaminants prior to the 1960s.[120] While he refers to published studies, field methods used by organizations such as LeGrand's employer, the USGS, indicate that theoretical knowledge of groundwater processes served as the basis for techniques used to identify the source of contaminants. In early 1947 Arlington, Virginia, authorities asked the USGS to conduct a hydrological study following a massive gasoline leak. They mapped the locations of gasoline tanks and basements where fumes occurred, then established a grid of wells to determine the path of migration and trace these paths to the source. From the placement of the sampling wells, the possible sources of the gasoline leak, the contaminant sites, and the direction of groundwater movement, they were able to pinpoint the location of the leaking storage facility.[121] The quick and effective application of this method in an emergency situation suggests that the hydrologists were familiar with techniques for characterizing subsurface contamination and identifying contaminant sources.

Other sampling strategies demonstrate the ability to locate a contaminant plume long before LeGrand's earliest publication on the subject (1965). Groundwater contamination on Long Island led to the sinking of ninety test wells in the late 1940s. Samples from these wells permitted hydrologists to map the passage of a "slug" of chromium and cadmium contamination between 1949 and 1958.[122] In addition, USGS hydrologists responded to contamination incidents near Rocky Mountain Arsenal in Colorado. Their initial sampling strategy included a total of twenty-two surface and subsurface points either within the waste disposal system or down-gradient.[123] A 1956 report by university researchers plotted water table elevations for the Rocky Mountain Arsenal area and predicted the "area of influence" of contaminants.[124] In effect, the maps of the Long Island "slug," the Colorado "area of influence," and the Virginia gasoline spill represent early efforts to plot contaminant plumes. While much remained to be learned about specific pollutants and their particular behavior in groundwater, sampling methods existed to map the location and movement of leachate and to establish its point of origin. Furthermore, USGS scientists at the Hanford Nuclear Site in eastern Washington had begun a substantial groundwater monitoring program around waste disposal sites in 1948. Their monitoring effort reported in 1949 that there was a gradual movement of radionuclide leachate toward the Columbia River.[125] The extensive work by the USGS in response to various contaminant incidents depicts a set of methods and techniques that were readily applied to emerging problems. In each case, the researchers mapped the extent of the contaminant plume and documented the rate of movement.

In addition, a massive review of groundwater contaminants prepared for the Federal Housing Administration considered movement characteristics of many different chemicals in the subsurface. In general, the authors, two highly respected professors at MIT, observed that more knowledge was desirable, but they concluded that the ability to predict the movement of particular contaminants existed. They reported that the prevailing view was that organic chemicals could travel several miles and that discharges to the ground would lead to probable contamination downgradient from the point of release.[126] Even Harry LeGrand conceded that "even the uninitiated in hydrology can get a general idea of the gross direction of movement of groundwater in humid regions."[127]

Bridging Disciplines. Despite the availability of methods for determining the viability of a waste disposal site and to identify leachate, one problem remained—linking the user with the information. It can be argued that there were knowledge "vacuums" in or gulfs between the skills and/or responsibilities of individual practitioners. Professional specialization and internal hierarchies created divisions of labor. An analytical chemist could perform one set of tasks and be unfamiliar with toxicology testing methods; likewise, engineers concerned with the load-bearing capabilities of soils could have been uninformed of proper landfill methods. Sanitary engineers, who dealt primarily with domestic sewage, were often unprepared to develop methods for treating toxic wastes.[128] Indeed, the U.S. Public Health Service claimed that "relatively few sanitary engineers have the necessary technical background to deal effectively with all the problems that arise in dealing with refinery wastes. The problem is primarily one for the technologists of the petroleum industry."[129] The blinders created by specialization may have stymied information exchange; nevertheless, research institutes such as the Kettering

Laboratory worked to bridge the gap between toxicology and ecology. Even chemical companies such as DuPont and Monsanto assigned staff to consider the environmental impacts of toxic wastes by the 1950s. Furthermore, early efforts to dispose of toxic wastes by deep-well injection forced waste management specialists to enlist those familiar with groundwater processes, thereby bringing together geologists, hydrologists, toxicologists, and others. The contaminant problems discussed in this section, like many others, aroused cooperative, interdisciplinary efforts and thereby offered a context to overcome the barriers of knowledge vacuums and to foster interspecialty communication.

RESPONDING TO NEW INFORMATION

How did professionals respond to new information, to discoveries of dangers and methods for containing hazards? Certainly the desire to overcome interspecialty blockades demanded a means to assimilate new information, to incorporate new concerns in planning and research. Both the level and the pace of responses to new information indicate that when an industry recognized a serious hazard, it responded with determination, if not speed.

The historian Alfred Chandler suggests that new developments in management and technology provided the means to eliminate the hazards of head-on collisions. Following a series of disastrous accidents in 1841 and a legislative investigation, the Western Railroad instituted precise timetables to prevent deadly encounters between trains. Subsequent technological innovations, such as the telegraph in the late 1840s, further reduced risks for passengers.[130] In less than a decade several measures provided much greater safety on the Western line and these provided a model for safety on the rapidly expanding national rail network.

Legislation and internal consensus-building committees provided the means for dealing with technological hazards. An increasing number of boiler explosions in the early nineteenth century prompted substantial public and professional reactions. As early as 1817, the City of Philadelphia recommended a bill to the state legislature that would institute boiler strength tests, use of appropriate valves, and monthly inspections. The city's effort and subsequent investigations by the Franklin Institute reflected a growing public concern with boiler failures on steamboats and in factories. Nonetheless, the problem continued to grow; between 1816 and 1848 there were a reported 2,563 fatalities due to boiler explosions. By the 1890s numerous states had passed inspection laws and claimed that boiler accidents declined as a direct result. Ultimately, manufacturers and mechanical engineers developed standards that in conjunction with the legislation dramatically reduced the number of boiler explosions during the first two decades of the twentieth century.[131]

Henry Petroski argues that engineering is based on a trial-and-error process; that is, when a design fails repeatedly, new and improved ones follow. The history of boiler incidents certainly provides an example of this protracted process, but other cases illustrate a much more expeditious response. When an iron bridge at Dixon, Illinois, collapsed, the ASCE formed a committee that offered remedies to the problem in 1875.[132] In the twentieth century, as highway fatalities increased, road builders incorporated various design features such as broad and gentle shoulders to give speeding cars a safety zone in which to decelerate when forced off the road. As highway speeds and traffic loads increased, there have been constant adjustments such as the development of limited-access highways and safer roadside structures.[133] Although there has been a lag between safety demands and the delivery of adequate designs, even in the area of long-term infrastructure, the trial-and-error process has produced continual modifications that reflect ever changing demands. For everyday engineering projects, consensus-building mechanisms existed within professional organizations to permit the ready flow of information among practitioners that would allow them to remedy design flaws that were creating public hazards.

In the absence of direct and near-term fatalities associated with projects carrying risks similar to those posed by environmental pollution, how effective were professional organizations? One case study involving invisible and chronic risks stands out. In the late 1940s, the federal government sought to encourage utility companies to embrace nuclear power as a source for electricity. Initially, producers stuck with coal-fired power generation, expressing a wariness about the liabilities associated with the still unfamiliar technology known best for its devastating explosive capabilities.[134] Yet the very industry that acted coolly toward a new power source was one of the most technology hungry industries. Richard Hirsch claims that "one-upmanship" became a common operating procedure in the utilities business, and individual companies constantly sought newer and larger technologies to awe their customers and competition during the postwar years.[135] Nonetheless, the fear of accidents delayed this innovation-seeking industry's acceptance of nuclear power until a series of government-sponsored demonstrations and the enactment of the Price-Anderson Act, which limited liability, finally warmed them to the new technology during the 1960s.[136]

In several of the best-known professional responses, loss of human life or major calamities were necessary to impel decision makers to empower the involved profession to develop more stringent standards. Bridge construction and boiler design reflect the ability of the engineers to respond to unacceptable consequences of design or equipment failures. Internal toxicology lab development following workers' deaths in the 1930s, and aquatic toxicity testing by the early 1950s, provide a parallel example in terms of industrial wastes. Yet it was not essential that death precede precautionary measures. When developing a disposal system for caustic wastes at the Rocky Mountain Arsenal, the U.S. Army corresponded with two private firms that discussed the potential for groundwater contamination. The communications indicate both companies were familiar with caustic disposal problems. After learning of these two firms' experience, the army took precautions to prevent leachate from its caustic pond.[137]

Fatalities caused by air pollution in Donora, Pennsylvania, stimulated a series of studies and eventually contributed to federal legislation that contained a public health, rather than aesthetic, approach. Even though it took several years to pass the federal law, studies by the state, the federal government, and the Kettering Laboratory encouraged the adoption of a warning system based on meteorological forecasts and air quality measurements to prevent a repeat disaster.[138] The reaction to disaster illustrates that during the 1940s and 1950s there was a public expectation that pollution problems needed to be solved and that there were effective means to reduce public risk.

The ability to control emerging technical challenges is quite distinct from taking remedial action following a disaster. The emergence of environmental activism earned the enmity of many within the engineering profession, and this hampered effective responses to problems associated with pollution. One reason can be found in the economic arguments proposed by sanitary engineers for treating water rather than sewage.[139] In addition, industrial engineers were trained to be loyal to their employers, and many rose to the ranks of managers during the first half of the twentieth century. When the federal government first debated stream pollution abatement legislation during the 1930s, the American Engineering Council staunchly opposed it.[140] This fundamental opposition to pollution control efforts remained a perspective of many industrial engineers through the 1960s. Engineers, as devoted company employees, argued that pollution control did not make good business sense and claimed that it was largely a matter of aesthetics.[141] This type of response only produced delays in realizing, but did not stop adoption of, policies and practices designed to adequately control hazardous wastes.

Even within the area of sanitary engineering, there was an inexplicable reliance on principles that experience had demonstrated were inadequate. The basic concept that keeping land-disposed wastes above the water table would prevent groundwater contamination was a commonly accepted practice in the early 1950s.[142] California authorities developed this engineering principle in an area with about fifteen inches of average annual precipitation and in a test period when there was no appreciable rainfall. The author of the study specifically warned that his results must be applied with caution in other locations, but within a matter of years professional organizations adopted landfill design principles developed in the arid regions to the entire country.[143]

Despite the private-sector hesitancy to include environmental considerations in management decisions, public-sector organizations were able to make major strides in this direction. The Corps of Engineers, a construction-oriented agency staffed mainly by engineers and technical personnel, underwent a major transformation during the early 1970s. The passage of the National Environmental Policy Act (1969) forced the Corps to incorporate environmental quality considerations into their planning. Although still criticized for environmental insensitivity, they eventually injected a strong environmental program into their public works mission. This transformation indicates that change is possible even within one of the most tradition-bound organizations.[144] Likewise, when confronted with serious environmental problems, chemical companies subsidized research internally and at institutes such as the Kettering Lab during the 1950s. This involved a commitment from the highest levels and participation by plant-level personnel.

CONCLUSION

At three different levels during this century, there was substantial knowledge for guarding against unsafe disposal of toxic industrial wastes. The first level was that of corporate decision makers. Corporate officials had a working knowledge of the hazards of chemical products and faced increasing external regulation of toxic products. Corporate officials had an obligation to shareholders to minimize liabilities stemming from public hazards, and they faced increased costs when they did not provide engineered safeguards. Furthermore, staff specialists were among the best-informed on the particulars of chemical toxicity, and they participated in a well-integrated system for information exchange, backed by management.

As to information available to decision makers, tools and techniques were available for minimizing the release of hazardous substances from disposal sites. A widely circulated technical press alerted specialists to the problems associated with industrial waste disposal. Certainly by the 1940s, contamination incidents caused by land-disposed chemical wastes should have provided ample evidence to practitioners. Procedures for analyzing a site's suitability for specific uses existed and were known to waste managers. In fact, the standard practices for most engineering works called for a far higher level of assessment than was commonly employed at many waste disposal sites.

Finally, the very nature of the engineering enterprise provided mechanisms for responding to failure to meet these standards. Professional standard-setting committees, in particular, represented an ability of organizations to address and correct obvious problems. Although engineers, as staunchly loyal company employees, may have resisted pollution abatement policies, it was extremely atypical for them to ignore public hazards.

Influencing the
Decision Makers

SIX

INTRODUCTION

Throughout this century those responsible for industrial waste disposal have operated within the framework of existing scientific and technological capabilities, as well as responding to fundamental legal requirements. But adopting existing technologies, assigning qualified personnel to supervise waste management operations, and taking steps to conform fully to government regulations involved additional considerations. This chapter will examine variables that we refer to as waste policy sensitizers and attenuators (fig. 1.1, left side). By this we mean pressures from both external (social) and internal (corporate) sources that prompted waste generators either to adopt more complete control measures or to follow a less cautious course.

External pressures included public liability or the threat of legal action—by this we mean the possibility of enforcement or adverse judicial rulings and not just the existence of codes, statutes, or regulations. Enforcement levels and court decisions fluctuated over the first half of the twentieth century, creating an inconsistent external pressure. This fact caused the degree of liability to change over the years and with it concern for costs associated with creating hazardous conditions. There were also internal considerations, such as the desire of a corporation to follow ethical practices and to preserve a favorable public image. These two pressures filtered through constantly changing attenuators or "desensitizers." External political pressures to expedite production during wartime or to maintain national security during the cold war served as convenient excuses to diminish concern about industrial wastes. Likewise, downward economic cycles produced recurrent incentives to avoid waste treatment expenditures. Finally, the size of a corporation affected its ability to absorb expenses associated with waste management. Waste managers did not operate in a static environment. They faced constantly shifting expectations within a context of changing technologies, financial resources, and corporate commitment to responsible behavior.

SENSITIZERS

Public Liability

Legal scholars have argued that during the mid-nineteenth century courts granted greater latitude than previously to new land uses, such as railroads and nuisance-causing factories, as a matter of course. This tendency was an outgrowth in part of a doctrine that saw economic development as the best possible use of land. Unlike previous doctrines that placed a legal priority on existing uses of property, the new doctrine called upon jurists to impose a balancing test on the polluting behavior (usually the new use of the land) and the cost of damages to proximate landholders. This line of judgement tolerated pollution when the greater economic good lay with the nuisance producer. By the mid-nineteenth century, the courts increasingly permitted actions that caused damage to a neighboring property, if conducted in a nonnegligent manner, or if done in a safe and reasonable way.[1] Theoretically this doctrine minimized the public liability of chemical plants generating hazardous wastes. Yet the business historian Christine Rosen argues that by the late nineteenth century, judges in several northeastern states were ruling against polluters because of new public perceptions of the cost of pollution versus the costs of abatement.[2] Consequently, the number of nuisance suits in the early twentieth century was sufficient to arouse concern among manufacturers.[3] Furthermore, chemical producers continually viewed themselves as subject to onerous judgments, so much so that trade literature continuously warned chemical producers to beware of legal culpability for reckless waste disposal.[4]

During the first third of the twentieth century public intolerance of nuisance-causing activity produced a rash of municipal nuisance laws. These statutes defined nuisances and prohibited certain actions within corporate boundaries or prescribed certain land uses through zoning ordinances.[5] By the 1920s they had, in conjunction with several other factors (discussed in

Chapter 4), effectively excluded most new nuisance-causing industry from locating within the existing city limits and prompted others to relocate when they needed to expand. Particular targets of this type of legislation were coal-gas works, meatpacking plants, and chemical producers. Although municipal ordinances often excluded existing industries, there were examples of cities policing them and acting upon complaints, thereby assuming a degree of responsibility and sensitizing manufacturers to the potential costs imposed on those who employed offensive or unsafe practices.[6]

Driven beyond the limits of municipal authority, chemical manufacturing and other enterprises that produced nuisances represented a new competing land use in formerly rural areas. In the early years of the century, courts still held chemical plants and similar industries culpable for damages caused to neighboring properties. Private suits such as *Ballantine and Sons v. Public Service Corporation of New Jersey* presented a viable means of discouraging the creation of noxious conditions. In this suit, a federal appeals court ruled that a gasworks had no right to permit the negligent percolation of wastes into the well of a neighboring landowner.[7] DuPont faced numerous suits when it began operating a munitions plant in rural Virginia during World War I.[8] In Illinois, farmers won a damage suit when Monsanto Chemical Company permitted its effluent to flood their crops,[9] and an Illinois appeals judge ordered an injunction against an oil refiner when a neighboring landowner alleged the defendant damaged the plaintiff's lake.[10] These few examples are far from a complete inventory of actions against nuisance causers, but they indicate that a viable legal means still existed to restrict off-site damages caused by the release of manufacturing wastes during the 1930s. While damage awards may have been minor, they represented a deterrent that could be used against nuisance producers.

At the time, however, there was virtually no state or public prosecution of nuisance-causing activities. One of the earliest effective pollution control agencies was the Illinois Rivers and Lakes Commission, which did order manufacturers to install treatment equipment, but this type of aggressive public enforcement was exceptional.[11] Most statutory efforts restricted the kinds of activity that occurred in places with high population densities. Several states created water pollution agencies during the 1910s and 1920s, but they concentrated their attention on biological wastes and ignored many chemical pollution problems—with the exception of phenolic wastes in major rivers.[12]

An inversion in nuisance liability effectively began with the Restatement of Torts (1939), which called for a balancing of utilities in nuisance cases.[13]

The balancing-of-utilities doctrine gave greater momentum to an emergent trend in the courts whereby those causing a nuisance were granted greater leeway if no law excluded their action and if an injunction would cause greater public harm (through loss of jobs, for example) than the actual damage they were causing. Decisions such as *Rose v. Socony-Vacuum* reflect this legal tolerance of nuisance-causing activity. In that case, the judge ruled that a farmer who had experienced damages caused by a neighboring polluter should expect such consequences when living in an industrialized district.[14] Implicit in the decision was that the greater public good was served by petroleum refining than hog farming. In effect, this granted a license to pollute—thereby reducing public liability. Such decisions effectively desensitized manufacturers to the consequences of polluting behavior. In the absence of police action, there were few threats of litigation by the late 1930s.

The courts may, however, have been lagging behind the rest of society. The restatement and subsequent decisions occurred at the same time that chemical engineering literature began to issue regular warnings about the threat of injunctions for polluting behavior. A consulting engineer warned: "Now that there is a growing consciousness of the evils of stream pollution and an increasing amount of legislation on the subject, new plants that have waste products will do well to investigate the subject thoroughly."[15] One industry apologist argued:

> As in England, [the movement to halt water pollution] begat some rascally offspring, smart neighbors who discovered that nuisance suits against chemical and metallurgical corporations made a strong appeal to any jury in the land, and unscrupulous local politicians who learned that threats of injunctions or municipal ordinances were heavy well-spiked clubs to swing at the managers of such corporations.[16]

Perhaps the increasing public attention to pollution during the 1930s and the expansion of public agency involvement in pollution control increased fear on the part of business of prosecution, despite diminished liability exposure in court. An invigorated government presence was a function of increasingly active public health agencies that grew during the 1930s and sought to reduce pollution of waterways. State agencies, trying to work cooperatively rather than as antagonists, mainly challenged municipalities releasing untreated sewage and industrial polluters that discharged biological wastes into rivers. In conjunction with the rise of public health organizations, the federal government injected funds into sewage treatment systems during the 1930s. This brought about a vast reduction in the total amount of untreated urban sewage that found its way into the nation's rivers, leaving industrial effluent as a more obvious problem. Ensuing debates over federal pollution control programs during the 1930s took aim at industrial wastes. Although federal laws did not become a reality until the late 1940s, they prompted an industrywide organization of waste management personnel who became increasingly aware of the issue. Starting in the late 1930s, the Manufacturing Chemists' Association formed an internal committee to stay abreast of legislation and to present the manufacturers' position on waste management concerns to Congress.[17]

Federal appellate courts showed limited interest in imposing liability on manufacturers following the Restatement of Torts. A thorough review of the federal appellate decisions on surface and groundwater litigation reveals no decisions involving chemical plants between 1906 and 1956. Several oil refineries and other chemical-using industries were defendants, however. The total number of nuisance suits against all manufacturers decided by federal appeals courts fell from four cases in the decade 1926–1936 to zero for the twenty-year span from 1936 to 1956.[18] While impressionistic, this suggests the Restatement of Torts did reduce the number of appeals cases involving polluting industries and thereby corporate liability for polluting behavior.

The absence of appellate cases does not mean there were no legal steps taken against chemical polluters. From the 1930s through the 1960s, most pollution cases were handled by state and local authorities on a case-by-case basis. There was very little proactive monitoring or litigation, however. Clarence Klassen, a nationally recognized sanitation authority and the technical secretary for the Illinois Sanitary Water Board, expressed his agency's position this way: "The policy of the Board has been through cooperation and education to first endeavor to secure voluntary action to abate pollution."[19] Although Klassen reported that litigation was threatened in several cases, up to that time (1936), no cases had been turned over to the attorney general. This changed by 1954, when the Illinois Sanitary Water Board recommended that the attorney general take action against National Petro-Chemicals.[20] The courts awarded the state an injunction against National Petro-Chemicals' use of a stream for waste disposal. This ultimately led to modification in the waste treatment methods employed by the manufacturer. Overall, this action was one of only a few handled by the state each year, and despite legal action the final agreement involved an informal negotiation between company and state officials.[21] Nonetheless, a standard text on chemical engineering warned: "The states are becoming more and more strict in this regard [pollution enforcement] and an adequate waste disposal system is an absolute necessity."[22]

The International Joint Commission (IJC) also initiated steps to reduce pollution in the Great Lakes. In early 1949, under the supervision of the highly regarded U.S. Public Health Service engineer Hayse Black, the IJC surveyed the waste discharges of industries along the Niagara River. They found effluent from Hooker Electrochemical to be very acidic (pH = 2), and measurements revealed that Hooker's waste releases contained 350 parts per billion of phenols (seventy times the recommended standard). Following their investigation and a series of hearings, the IJC called for effluent standards for all discharges to the boundary waters, and they recommended that "adequate protection should be provided for these waters if substances highly toxic to human, fish, aquatic, or wildlife are eliminated or reduced to safe limits." While the IJC did not set forth "safe limits," it is clear the commission believed that removal of phenols from the waterway was the most appropriate approach.[23] In effect, they were pushing industry, albeit gently, to install treatment equipment.

The sanitary engineering professor Harold Babbitt took a six-month tour of eastern states to interview waste generators and pollution control authorities in 1950. In the course of his travels, he found that although industrial users of streams had inconsistent attitudes about pollution, they commonly recognized legal liability. At numerous manufacturing facilities he asked managers, "Why are you treating your wastes?" Replies included: "The law requires it" and "Damage suits must be avoided."[24] Obviously there was a perception among plant managers that states were prepared to take action against objectional releases.

At the federal level there was only one enforcement action under the federal water pollution law of 1948, but the 1956 Federal Water Pollution Control Act gave rise to a more "realistic enforcement authority." By 1963 the U.S. attorney general had initiated nineteen additional enforcement actions. Of the total between 1948 and 1963, ten cases came at the behest of states and another ten resulted from inaction on the part of states.[25] While not on a pace with post-1970 litigation, this indicates there was a modest federal enforcement threat during the latter half of the 1950s and early 1960s.

In 1968 an attorney for the Metropolitan Sanitary District of Greater Chicago argued that the lack of pollution enforcement was due not to

ineffective laws, but to apathy. He claimed that industries within the jurisdiction of his agency had been discharging pollution into waterways with
impunity until an aggressive enforcement program had begun in 1967. His
staff obtained an impressive response when they took procedural actions
against polluters and only had to file court papers against five companies
among sixty-nine polluters. The favorable response among industries, he
claimed, was because large corporations do "not welcome being a defendant
at Administrative Hearings or in lawsuits."[26]

By 1970 the Illinois attorney general followed Chicago's lead and argued
that the traditional informal method was no longer satisfactory:

> It became apparent that the great bulk of antipollution action
> within the State over the years had been based on a conference
> approach, government meeting with industry with voluntary
> agreements as to installation of control equipment. In many
> instances these agreements were not being kept, or installation
> deadlines provided in them were being freely extended. It was
> therefore decided to proceed against polluters in court, where the
> promise of the polluter to remedy the wrong would be binding and
> the circumstances of the case open to the public."[27]

The more litigious stance of the attorney general suggests that legal action
had not been an imposing threat to waste managers, at least in Illinois, from
the 1930s through the 1960s. Illinois's enforcement posture was not unchar-
acteristic for the time. California authorities reported in 1951 that "surprisingly few suits have been brought by the local district attorneys or the
attorney general to enjoin a public nuisance."[28] New York state had an
enforcement plan in place by 1949 and was taking action against polluters by
the early 1960s, although their most frequent targets were communities
rather than industries.[29] In Wisconsin the assistant attorney general re-
marked in 1956 that recent court decisions reflected "an increasing awareness and sensitivity to the problem by the courts as well as the various state
legislatures."[30] These states represent major players in the pollution control
enterprise, and the few cases in which the state took action against polluters
indicates there was little effective pressure for manufacturers to abide by
existing laws before the late 1960s. As a reflection of this situation, a Shell Oil
Company vice president commented in 1960 that some companies continued to abuse streams by overloading them with effluent, thereby forcing
"close controls on industry."[31]

Ethical Considerations

According to industry spokespersons, most manufacturers chose to follow fundamental social ethics. Although a few nineteenth-century manufacturers placed formaldehyde in milk, toxic metals in canned vegetables, aniline dyes in candies, and copper-green on pickles, these unethical acts brought about massive changes in how companies distributed harmful substances.[32] As early as the 1930s the Manufacturing Chemists' Association began cooperating with government agencies to provide safe labeling for toxic substances[33] and thereby demonstrated sensitivity to basic corporate responsibility or ethical considerations. Although often couched in terms of public relations, good neighbor concerns, or cooperation, managing wastes in a way that does not disturb neighbors, at a fundamental level, is a matter of public responsibility, and choosing to conform with the law is basically an ethical behavior. James Tobey, a lawyer for the American Institute of Baking, placed ethical pollution behavior at the level of fundamental human rights: "When legal principles are applied to the perennial problem of industrial wastes, they involve the right of every individual to the reasonable enjoyment of life, liberty and property."[34] Since the 1910s, the literature has contained a steady stream of statements endorsing and advocating ethical waste management.

In 1917 Harrison Eddy, a noted waste treatment consultant, advised chemical and metallurgical engineers that even long-term practice did not justify the creation of a nuisance. He further counseled that prudent manufacturers should institute policies and procedures to avoid downstream damages and that this would help them avoid costly litigation. Eddy added, "More important than this [litigation], however, is the fact that by maintaining the water in a reasonably satisfactory condition the hostility of lower riparian dwellers may be avoided."[35] While rooted in legal principles, these statements emphasize that practitioners envisioned adverse economic consequences related not just to legal decisions, but to public attitude.

Good will was an important consideration for manufacturers, especially chemical producers. R. L. Kraft advised: " It is good policy for the executives of the plant to take a lively interest in the local community. . . . Good will developed in this way may prove to be a valuable asset in time of trouble."[36] Fred Hartford, an engineer with a large steel company, reminded manufacturers that "even kindly disposed neighbors usually object strenuously when such matter [offensive wastes] is deposited on or above their premises."[37] Besselievre argued that "modern economic teachings" advocated "intelligent cooperation" between manufacturer and governments in order to maintain "good will." "The cardinal and terminal principle in waste treatment," he claimed, "is: cooperation, courage, and common sense."[38] Vilbrandt recommended to chemical engineering students to be alert to a prospective host community's attitude. He warned that if ill will toward chemical manufacturers existed, a company would be well served to locate elsewhere, even if no law prohibited its operation.[39] These views suggest that corporate decision makers encountered opinions both in the trade literature and on their staffs that promoted going beyond simple adherence to the law.

Industry often used the term *cooperation* to indicate its desire to maintain public good will and to conform with acceptable behavior. James Emery of the National Association of Manufacturers portrayed manufacturers as typical citizens in 1936. He testified to Congress that "nobody desires to pollute the streams or the sea, and manufacturers, both as citizens and as industrial producers, has [*sic*] as deep an interest as anyone else in the preservation of the local purity of waters."[40] In a later session Sheppard Powell, speaking for the Manufacturing Chemists' Association, itemized instances of chemical companies installing treatment equipment worth hundreds of thousands of dollars. He added that "there are many more cases which might be cited to illustrate the cooperative spirit exhibited by industries attempting to correct existing or predicted water pollution."[41]

In 1939 U.S. industry was emerging from a crushing economic depression and entering an era of technological discovery and expansion. At the same time, manufacturers were mindful of heightened legislative interest in pollution control. In response to the public attention directed toward water quality, a major trade publication carried an extensive discussion on the subject and industry's responsibilities. The editor expressed an industrial viewpoint:

> The manufacturer is slowly but surely realizing that disposal of wastes is a necessary manufacturing cost. Pressure from outside is forcing industry to clean up its sewers. More often than many suspect, the process yields a profit. However, whether profitable or profitless, utilization or disposal, waste elimination should be undertaken.[42]

This surge in civic responsibility found expression in decision making within the chemical industry. R. Briggs of Hooker Electrochemical wrote a report on chlorine emissions to the Niagara plant chief engineer, T. Lyster. Briggs had investigated various air pollutants and their permissible release limits.

Although he found no specific standard for chlorine emissions, he stated:

> No quantitative data is [*sic*] available to the writer on the permis-
> sible chlorine content of the atmosphere, but it is obvious that there
> is a *moral restriction* [emphasis ours] due to the fact that there are
> several plants at Niagara which produce chlorine and under certain
> circumstances variable quantities of chlorine may escape to the
> atmosphere.[43]

Clearly, as industry entered the 1940s, there was a growing recognition of a moral, if not standard-based, responsibility to the public and to workers to protect them from harmful substances, including wastes.

World War II temporarily disrupted the growing concern with industrial wastes, but interest reemerged after peace returned. The Pennsylvania Chemical Society hosted a symposium, "The Chemist's Responsibility in the Control of Industrial Wastes," where one speaker argued that waste treatment should be considered a fundamental cost of doing business. Shortly thereafter, in a special issue of *Industrial and Engineering Chemistry* devoted to waste management that was circulated to all congressmen, the editor stated that chemists and chemical engineers wished "to abandon the tradi-tional ivory tower of the past and join with others in concerted efforts to find solutions to the pressing questions that confront all."[44] Such pronounce-ments reflect the belief, of at least a few individuals, that chemical producers bore an underlying social obligation to properly manage their wastes. The Manufacturing Chemists' Association released its first waste treatment manual in 1948 and confessed that "in too many cases, industries and towns have discharged their wastes without regard for the effect such wastes would have on the water. As a result, aroused public opinion has compelled states and legislative bodies to pass laws to protect the natural resources of the country and the public health and welfare."[45] While pointing out that manu-facturers were not the only polluters, the MCA acknowledged their partici-pation in problems and expressed a sensitivity to public will. Also, it reflected a recognition that lax waste control led to undesirable legislation and govern-ment interference.

Companies indeed internalized concern with good-neighbor issues, with-out legal restrictions on surface-water pollution. Following a visit to an MCA pollution abatement committee meeting, Hooker Electrochemical Com-pany staff reported that one of the central issues of the meeting was the industry's voluntary efforts to be a good neighbor.[46] Several years later company officials "were convinced that it was desirable to abandon this property [Love Canal] for use in burying chemicals in view of the close proximity of residences which have been recently constructed."[47] A report from the general manager of Hooker's Eastern Chemical Division listed several reasons for converting from land disposal to incineration; among them were encroachment of residential land uses, the risk of children's trespassing at a landfill, and complaints from downwind neighbors. Significantly, he notes that these problems had been plaguing the company for years.[48]

H. W. De Ropp, of DuPont, reported in 1951 that his employer had "adopted a policy of not authorizing new plant construction until adequate provision for waste disposal had been incorporated into the design." After espousing this policy, DuPont undertook extensive investigations prior to a Texas chemical plant construction project that included developing a waste treatment process to satisfy both the company and public agencies.[49] In the late 1950s DuPont chose not to produce a butadiene polymerization product at its Newark, Delaware, plant, because they were unable to perfect a waste disposal process that met their internal standards.[50] Such practices earned DuPont a reputation among waste management professionals as the "bellweather of environmental regulations within the whole chemical industry."[51] Testifying at the Love Canal trial, former DuPont engineer George Amery claimed that his employer tried to follow state-of-the-art disposal practices. In response to a question about contamination caused by a DuPont operation he stated:

> I can assure you that the corporate responsibility was always there, and we would never have considered an operation or a disposal [method] state of the art if we knowingly knew that it was going to be a detriment to the health at the time that we did it.[52]

Such remarks indicate that some firms considered ethical questions in addition to the financial bottom line.

Willem Rudolfs continued the call for responsible waste management in the 1950s. He wrote: "All responsible, progressive and law abiding companies are interested in abating pollution."[53] In a similar vein, H. L. Jacob advised chemical plant managers to

> develop a forward-looking policy in regard to stream-pollution abatement. A policy of obstruction may succeed for a time but will

result ultimately in bitterness, bad public relations, and in more restrictive regulations imposed by the enforcement agency. On the other hand, public relations will be enhanced by a policy of cooperation and sincerity.[54]

The trade literature continued to echo this basic position into the 1960s. W. F. Bixby claimed that industry had "an important responsibility in maintaining a wholesome atmosphere."[55] A spokesman for Cities Service touted the installation of a complex waste treatment facility at a refinery in Ontario as a demonstration of its "good neighbor policy."[56] In a 1960 commentary before a national water pollution conference, K. S. Watson of General Electric claimed that "in recent years industry has been more and more motivated by the responsible citizenship concept." He illustrated this credo by citing such actions as providing adequate waste treatment equipment and thereby preventing serious pollution problems.[57] These sentiments clearly indicate that manufacturers realized there were social costs to their polluting actions, that bad-neighbor actions could result in adverse outcomes, and that legislation, litigation, and regulation were inevitable public responses to irresponsible behavior.

Numerous events heightened public interest in corporate responsibility for their wastes and thereby increased public perception of risks. Although not always directly in line with chemical waste control, there were numerous campaigns to restrict pollution that undoubtedly spawned public attention and awareness of the problem. There was a massive public outcry over oil wastes during the 1920s, and this led to federal legislation and the development of internal procedures for reducing oily effluent.[58] Also during the 1920s, public attention briefly focused on phenolic releases, particularly on the Ohio River. Once public attention focused on this issue, manufacturers took steps to minimize their phenol releases to the river.[59] During the 1950s and 1960s, as attention focused on polluted waterways, one of the central attractions of public scrutiny, legislative attention, and research funding was detergent suds in rivers.[60] Although considered little more than an aesthetic problem at that time, it came to epitomize the surface-water pollution topic and caused greater public participation in pollution issues. In any case, public organizations gave extensive attention to toxic substances during the early 1950s, and chemical producers had to consider their responsibility for toxic discharges and ingredients.[61]

Corporate Security

A fundamental concern to manufacturers operating in a competitive market was maintaining security over chemical formulas and unit operations. When German patents were distributed among U.S. producers during World War I, it became obvious that keeping control over patented products was extremely important. Furthermore, with greater and greater investments in corporate research, chemical producers did not want to turn over new products to a competitor. With so much at stake, corporate security became an obstacle to government inspection of waste management practices and monitoring of plant operations. Corporate officials did not want secrets to leak out through government inspectors, nor did they wish competitors to be able to analyze their waste streams or records of their waste discharges in attempts to determine production processes. Although federal programs during the 1950s supported government researchers who helped develop treatment technologies, the industries that cooperated with this effort were not chemical producers.[62]

Richard Eldredge, a long-time and highly respected Public Health Service official, reported that "prior to the mid-1960's, few industries shared knowledge of waste disposal technologies or experience with competitors or regulators, believing that such an exchange would compromise trade secrets and reveal production capacity."[63] Likewise, Clarence Klassen claimed that "it was my experience that industry normally did not share information about their wastes with regulators unless compelled to do so." He recalled that "during the 1940's and 1950's, chemical residue waste were [sic] not normally disposed of at municipal or other public landfills by large chemical companies." He observed that rather than risk industrial espionage, and "to safeguard trade secret compounds," chemical companies disposed of wastes on property they owned or controlled.[64] W. B. Hart, of Atlantic Refining, put the same point in industry terms: "Many industrial people . . . feel that they know their own problems best. They prefer to solve these problems themselves—to have freedom either to treat the wastes or eliminate them."[65] Discussing the reluctance of some chemical producers to respond to a waste treatment survey, Harold Babbitt, a prominent sanitary engineer during the 1950s, concluded that "the attitude of fear and secrecy was not directed toward governmental stream pollution authorities, but was directed toward possible competitors and the possible careless or unwarranted misuse of the information collected."[66]

These views underscore that although some corporate officials may have resisted government inspection for pollution abatement, they were prepared to go to even greater lengths to guard against scrutiny by their competitors. To permit wastes to be discarded in a manner that allowed general public access would have undermined security efforts enacted at other levels of production. Thus, concern over security would have acted to heighten sensitivity about control of waste products.

Government Training and Advice

The U.S. government provided training and expertise to the staffs of chemical producers that alerted them to the hazards of toxic chemicals and raised their sensitivity to product and waste management liabilities. Furthermore, there was ongoing exchange of both information and personnel between agencies such as the Chemical Warfare Service (CWS) and private corporations. This, without question, exposed chemical company staff to information about toxic chemicals and current expectations about handling safety, particularly during and after wartime. Also, the conscription of public health officials during wartime and their efforts to manage military wastes fostered exchange of crucial information about industrial waste hazards.

During World War I, the army sought to acquire chemical stocks for its chemical warfare branch. According to an Edgewood Arsenal history, private manufacturers refused to supply the chemicals because of "their highly toxic character." Consequently, the army set up plants to manufacture a variety of chemical agents.[67] They drew upon existing chemical manufacturing technologies and privately trained personnel at the time. Following the war, many of the Chemical Warfare Service staff returned to private industry, where they regularly received a CWS bulletin apprising them of chemical warfare innovation.[68] It reported on such topics as how to protect workers in the chemical industry, how to detect toxic gases, and how to safely store chemical munitions in a way that would not permit their escape.[69] In fact, some of the bulletin's articles were simply reprints of items drawn from the technical publications available to the chemical engineering community. Furthermore, it noted that there had been long-standing relationships between the CWS and private industry. The American Chemical Society, it reported, appointed a committee of qualified experts to assist with solving CWS problems and many civilian chemists worked as consultants to the CWS.[70] Such interaction exposed private-sector researchers to the safety concerns associated with highly toxic chemicals and contributed to heightened sensitivity to waste management strategies.

In order to justify its existence during peacetime, the CWS undertook investigations into civilian problems produced by hazardous chemicals and nonmilitary applications of toxic chemicals. The commander of the Edgewood Arsenal proclaimed that the CWS was "especially equipped and designed to study problems of this nature [toxic exposure] occurring as peacetime hazards in industry, or from various other causes." This comment appeared in a report that detailed the CWS's role in determining the cause of 125 chemical-related fatalities in a Cleveland hospital. A CWS investigation team found that the calamity had resulted from fires and explosions attributed to chemical decomposition of improperly stored x-ray film.[71] The CWS claimed its research team was prepared to solve "any peacetime problem involving the use of, or protection against, poisonous materials." Along these lines they discovered beneficial "by-products" of the chemical warfare program such as substances to control boll weevils and marine borers and a new type of gas mask to protect against industrial poisoning. General Fries concluded that "it is believed that the contributions of the Chemical Warfare Service to industry alone have more than amply justified the sums devoted to research."[72] Such comments underscore the role played by the CWS in direct collaboration with private industry; and much of that interaction centered on the hazards associated with toxic chemicals.

There were also explicit instructions available for the safe handling and storage of toxic chemicals. The Chemical Warfare Service followed existing Interstate Commerce Commission guidelines on such matters. These guidelines included procedures for proper labeling of extremely dangerous poisons, instructions to limit storage to sparsely populated areas, and specifications for secure containers that would resist corrosion or leaks.[73]

During World War II, private businesses took on many of the contracts for chemical warfare feed stock and they had to follow government standards for safety and waste management. At the outbreak of the war, the government anticipated hiring 2,000 chemically trained inspectors to monitor private plants.[74] CWS staff conducted inspections of chemical plants supplying feed stock or chemical munitions and thereby pointed up the government's expectations. Inspection reports from Monsanto, Illinois, Midland, Michigan, and Niagara Falls, New York, called on the private companies to shut down an unsatisfactory waste incinerator and to develop an adequate sludge removal system.[75] Colonel Munchmeyer, another CWS staff member, issued specific instructions for safe burial of arsenic trichloride and thionyl chloride following World War II. He advised disposers to have a CWS officer present during disposal operations, to excavate a pit deep enough to bury containers beneath eight feet of cover, to line the pit with a neutralizing agent, and to consider future land uses of the area.[76] In addition to specific instructions to chemical warfare contractors, general guidelines regarding chemical wastes from munitions manufacturers and military base sewage treatment increased sensitivity among private and public organizations that were exposed to these documents either during military service or when dealing with military bases.[77] Perhaps as much as any other organization, the CWS contributed to a higher level of sensitivity to the dangers of highly toxic chemicals and their wastes.

WASTE POLICY DESENSITIZERS

Given the number of sensitizing forces, it appears that there would be little justification for managing wastes in a casual or negligent manner. However, a variety of countervailing influences acted to offset the sensitizers and incline businesses to justify lower standards. Wartime imperatives placed production on tight schedules and diverted personnel and resources away from adequate attention to waste treatment. Following the cessation of World War II, cold war tensions fostered clandestine actions in the interest of national security and encouraged casual waste disposal practices. Economic cycles, which caused periods of less than capacity production and tight profit margins, justified—in the eyes of some producers and regulators—a relaxation of ongoing investigations into proper waste management technologies. One industrial waste treatment specialist summed up conditions in 1948:

> Little in the way of industrial waste treatment was provided for in this manner—not enough, all told, to make even a ripple on the surface of existing pollution conditions. . . . Then came World War II, and the conditions that were bad enough before the war became much worse. . . . Then came the deluge—the country-wide enactment of antipollution legislation. . . . This gave rise to the problems—right along with the problems of reconversion, readjustment, jockeying for postwar markets, labor strife, and material shortages. . . . The establishment was busy expanding the variety of its

products, extending its markets, and increasing its production. Least of all was it giving any thoughts to its wastes.[78]

Although his portrayal was extremely dismal, it illustrates some of the influences that offset sensitivity to the problems of waste disposal.

Like the sensitizers, the desensitizers or attenuators did not exert consistent influence over time, nor were they exclusively negative factors. Wartime imperatives were an important external desensitizer, but they had both a positive and a negative influence. On the negative side, the priority given to production at all costs deferred interest in and expenditures on waste treatment equipment. During World War I, there was little done in the way of chemical waste treatment as industry expanded to meet wartime demands. Yet according to trade publications, this led to pollution problems and injunctions against plants.[79] Expansion of chemical manufacturing capacity for World War II called for the rapid training of about 4,000 chemists to design and operate munitions plants.[80] They worked feverishly to see that new plants were functioning in a relatively short time, and they placed an emphasis on production, not pollution control. The *Engineering News-Record* summarized the wartime experience:

> The most important [reason for delays in pollution control] is the serious interruption of the war years, when materials and money for such work were scarce, and when the patriotic duty of turning out materials for the United States war machine seemed far more important than stream clearance, and many abuses and omissions were overlooked.[81]

Both Dwight F. Metzler and Wesley E. Gilbertson, long-time public health practitioners, specifically pointed out the sacrifices made in normal public health practices during World War II. Metzler, who was professionally active during the 1940s, reported that

> the government made major new product demands upon all industries, including the chemical industry, in support of the war effort. Mobilization required plants be built and put into operation promptly. . . . As new products were manufactured, new industrial waste liquids, solids and sludges were generated, some of which were complex. Liquid wastes were often disposed of directly into

watercourses, and solids were settled out in ponds or stored or
buried or dumped.[82]

Wesley Gilbertson reported that "public policy directed maximum effort
toward World War II goals. Both public and private activities were affected."
He suggested that industry felt forced to focus on production at the expense
of waste management, while communities were unable to maintain their own
sewage treatment facilities because of shortages of materials.[83] Hayse Black,
chief of the industrial waste section of the U.S. Public Health Service
laboratory in Cincinnati, stressed the diversion of materials from sewage
treatment to other uses. "This era of advancement in sanitation was disrupted by war scarcity of building materials and high construction costs."[84]
Other government action also reflects less stringent standards involving
hazardous substances. For example, the adoption of maximum allowable
concentrations by the Public Health Service largely ignored long-term
effects of workplace exposures to toxic substances.[85]

While pollution issues were not overlooked entirely, wartime expediency
overrode most other considerations. In developing its plans for constructing
the Indiana Ordnance Works for the government immediately prior to U.S.
entrance into the war, DuPont staff considered several typical siting factors
such as transportation, raw material supplies, labor force, and the site's
structural geology. Site planners expressed concern over the karst topogra-
phy—a geological condition characterized by underground caverns and sink
holes—and the ability of the site to support structures or preclude hazardous
emission of fumes. A site evaluation determined that these factors did not
pose a hazard and construction proceeded. Another question raised was
whether natural drainage features should be used for the removal of untreated wastes. Legal staff concluded that DuPont could be held liable for
damages resulting from injury to livestock or property, and that even if the
releases were not harmful, the possibility of an injunction existed.[86] As a
consequence of expediency, these conditions did not deter waste releases to
surface features. Some months later, when a neighbor objected to odors and
physically harmful fumes, he attributed it to drainage from the powder plant.
Company personnel promised to look into the problem.[87]

Several other examples also illustrate the priorities of wartime exigencies
in practice. Aircraft manufacturers used surface ponds for disposal of toxic
metal-plating wastes in Long Island, New York. When these wastes leached
into the porous aquifer beneath them, public officials permitted the practice
to continue until the conclusion of the war.[88] Fumes from a waste lagoon

offended neighbors of a large tannery in Hartford, Illinois. When the nearby residents sought legal redress for the nuisance, the judge ruled that "the hum of industry and the whir of busy wheels so vital at this time of our national defense" would cease if injunctions were handed down against offensive manufacturers, and he refused to grant the motion.[89] In Rochester, New York, a war-related chemical plant expansion resulted in the release of hydrochloric acid fumes and chlorine gas. The Chemical Division of the War Department had ordered a plant renovation in such a way that gases escaped. In ruling on a nuisance complaint spawned by the situation, the judge concluded, "To the extent that the common good assumes national proportions, it becomes by just so much a stronger factor; and when that factor involves the power of the federal government to equip armies, no undue interference with it will be tolerated."[90] These rulings and judgments showed a toleration for actions taken by manufacturers during wartime even though they resulted in public health problems or personal property damages. Obviously, jurists stretched their tolerance limits during wartime, and patriotism overshadowed other ethical considerations. This implicitly desensitized industry to waste management concerns.

Even with the cessation of hostilities, much of the wartime mentality lingered if not expanded, especially with the rise of cold war suspicions. Those who have researched the relationship between government and industry during the cold war have characterized the context of product development and production during the period as a state of "urgency."[91] This fueled a transition in the relationship between industry and pollution control officials. Cold war imperatives, and the need to protect national as well as corporate secrets, justified restrictions on government inspectors. Although there still was concern with maintaining control over waste products, the outside inspectors posed a risk to security. By their exclusion from observing waste management practices, the potential for enforcement, at a time of stepped-up legal efforts (1960–1970), was minimized. Thus, as long as companies participated in defense-related work, they gained confidence that their waste management practices would not be scrutinized. In 1948, 62 percent of all government research dollars flowed through the Department of Defense; by 1960 the total had reached 80 percent.[92] Although it is very difficult to calculate the proportion of chemical development supported by the U.S. military, it was important and thus contributed to desensitizing industries working on government contracts.

Perception of what constituted a public hazard has changed over the years and the absence of risk recognition steered waste management decisions toward less control. It has been argued that "in the 1940s and 1950s, knowledge of these possible risks [hazardous wastes] was held almost entirely by a few experts from the various scientific disciplines concerned with waste disposal, water quality, and public health."[93] Perception of risks tended to focus on surface-water pollution during the 1950s, but there was an active discussion in professional circles over groundwater pollution as well. As an attenuator, risk perception appears to have been a minor influence because the very people who were invested with responsibility—namely producers—were the best-informed and in the best position to predict the outcome of careless behavior and they would have had to face any negative consequences of inadequate controls.

Another important factor behind corporate resistance to adopting waste treatment technologies was the cost. This issue has remained a central theme in industry's public statements opposing pollution control legislation throughout this century.[94] Manufacturers generally have shared the view that pollution control is a nonproductive cost and reduces profits. Opposing views have been offered, however, including the observation that foul water costs manufacturers when they have to pay to purify it for production uses.[95]

The actual cost of controlling pollution is hard to quantify. The National Resources Council estimated that it would cost $900 million to provide practical treatment, where the technology existed, for active manufacturers in the late 1930s.[96] After World War II, when treatment options again were being promoted, Thomas Parran, the surgeon general of the U.S. Public Health Service, offered a 1942 estimate of $160 million to install treatment equipment at plants discharging untreated effluent into waterways.[97] A few years later the Public Health Service presented a revised estimate of $4 billion for industrial waste treatment equipment to satisfy needs by 1960.[98] Trade groups became testy about pollution control costs, especially during the 1950s. The MCA claimed that the chemical industry spent about $40 million a year on treatment equipment, and that this represented between 2.5 percent and 4 percent of all construction costs.[99] Yet, although the chemical industry had become the chief generator of hazardous wastes during the postwar period, their annual expenditures on pollution abatement represented only about a tenth of what was needed to reach the U.S. Public Health Service goal of $4 billion by the end of the decade. Certainly expenditures on treatment equipment, even minimal ones, would impinge on profits, but the same could be said for worker safety or advertising. Nonetheless, Walter Lyon, a public health official from Pennsylvania, argued that this was not a valid excuse to defer installing pollution-control facilities. He claimed that "the enforcement of pollution abatement laws may play a part in some business failures, but there is little evidence that this is a significant cause for failure." He reviewed a study of business failures for 1959 and found that the vast majority collapsed because of poor management, not because they diverted investments to pollution control equipment.[100]

Another facet of the cost issue was a desire to recoup expenditures in treatment equipment by developing marketable products from wastes—also known as waste recovery—and industry frequently flirted with this approach. During World War I, manufacturers inaugurated steps to conserve limited raw materials as a form of waste recovery.[101] During the 1930s waste recovery efforts accompanied efforts to squeeze additional profit from a beleaguered market. It became cost-effective to assign engineers the task of finding new uses for wastes when there was no market for the current line of products.[102] Once production picked up to serve the war effort during the 1940s, by-product recovery programs waned. As the economy tightened up during the period 1949–1954, manufacturers resumed their exploration for waste recovery options. Harold Babbitt, a leading authority on treatment engineering, stressed that "the search for profit should be the first step in the solution of the problem of the disposal of industrial wastes."[103] By investigating waste recovery programs, manufacturers, whether successful or not, delayed research and expenditures on existing treatment technologies.

Beyond direct costs for treatment, there was the cost of trusteeship of residues—whether untreated or the product of primary treatment. With increasing installation of treatment technologies, the resulting sludges and other solid residues demanded disposal. How much extra would it cost to discard such wastes in a secure location and to maintain some level of security? One very cheap method was to use wastes to fill property owned by the manufacturer and to encircle the wastes with company operations or fences. In contrast, the bare essentials for off-site trusteeship were secure burial and enclosure within a fence. Insurers and company managers looked at fencing as an expected practice for waste disposal sites.[104] Such expenditures would have been minimal compared with treatment apparatus.

The size of a company directly affected its ability to capitalize the costs associated with developing and installing waste treatment equipment. During the initial push to encourage oil refineries to install separators, one contemporary observer noted that "most of the large refineries were found to have complete drainage systems and efficient separators for recovering the oil. . . . Other refineries, particularly some of the smaller ones, were not adequately equipped for recovering lost oil."[105] Much of the early progress in implementing waste control systems took place among the industry leaders such as Dow and DuPont. Indeed, the members of the MCA's pollution abatement committee were a fairly exclusive club of the major producers and their participation facilitated dissemination of information at least among its members. Nonetheless, by sharing information in the trade literature, in government reports, and through personal site visits, the industry leaders enabled smaller operators to have access to the results of their research and development. Babbitt even argued that "the big fellows" were not alone in making progress in treating their effluent.[106]

Another way to address the cost problem was to challenge legal action and basic social expectations and hope that litigation expenses, if they were encountered, would be less than pollution control. Early in the century this approach may have been generally viable. DuPont found this to be true during World War I when it estimated the costs of installing treatment equipment at its Hopewell, Virginia, plant. The anticipated expense for constructing several holding ponds and dredging a polluted riverbed exceeded the documented fines and legal fees incurred in resolving the cases.[107] Dow Chemical, however, elected to install treatment equipment in Michigan during the 1930s when facing local complaints.[108] By the early 1950s, Babbitt argued that "it is frequently less costly to solve the problem through sewage treatment than to attempt to solve it through litigation."[109] Pollution control programs by major firms such as the one undertaken by DuPont in the early 1950s reflected an acceptance of this doctrine, but the actions of the industry leaders were not always followed by the mass of firms. In 1957 about 69 percent of chemical plants in twenty-nine states reported some form of treatment equipment. Only 36 percent of the total were classified as "industrial" waste treatment facilities—that is, provided with equipment more sophisticated than a pond, lagoon, or domestic sewage treatment system.[110] Installation of equipment suggests that a heightened sensitivity to possible litigation costs had impelled manufacturers to divert earnings into nonproductive treatment equipment. Nonetheless, a 1957 U.S. Department of Health, Education and Welfare (HEW) survey indicates the most equipment in use was not specially designed to treat complex chemical wastes. The HEW inventory suggests that waste treatment expenditures on basic, not specialized, treatment facilities offered some protection from public liability while doing little to abate pollution.

Another cost associated with wastes was insurance. Insurance costs could be reduced by following guidelines accepted by the insurer, but securing protection against liability could contribute to laxity in waste management practices. Conforming to insurance conditions in respect to chemical waste treatment involved taking steps to guard against damage to adjacent or nearby property or harm to trespassing children. Although the National Safety Council, an organization that developed safety guidelines that insurance companies encouraged clients to follow, advised that it was safe to discard solid wastes in pits, it recommended that plans of the disposal site should be made that should depict exactly where each waste was discarded. Furthermore, it specified that "dumps be fenced off or otherwise guarded." It also advised that all waste disposal activities be "examined for possible sources of personal injury (either in the plant or outside), property damage, or nuisance."[111] None of these costs were exorbitant, but they could erode profit margins. Nevertheless, safe practices could earn manufacturers lower insurance rates and therefore reduce the cost of coverage.[112] While insurance provided some financial security against adverse liability lawsuit outcomes, it still worked as a sensitizer because of underlying expectations that manufacturers were to follow safe practices.

CONCLUSIONS

Sensitizers and attenuators—those forces that prompted waste managers to provide safe disposal or that lessened concerns with waste safety—worked in opposition throughout the twentieth century, but with varying intensity. In the legal arena, there was a greater risk of private nuisance suits until the 1930s. Overlapping with this was a period during the 1920s when government agencies and public groups called for the elimination of specific types of water pollution. Thus, the 1920s, a time of peak industrial production and pollution, saw the greatest public opposition and government enforcement effort. This pressure came at a time when industry could best afford to divert profits to "nonproductive" equipment. Again during the late 1960s, government agencies stepped up pollution law enforcement. Public opinion favored strict regulations and tough enforcement. As during the 1920s, this reinvigorated public response occurred during a period of economic prosperity and high industrial output. Sensitizers could be said to have peaked in the late 1920s and again in the late 1960s.

Wars diverted attention from well-recognized pollution control problems and produced the most pronounced periods of desensitization, although there were some long-term effects to the contrary. World War I stimulated the first major expansion of the industrial chemical industry, and years passed before manufacturers showed much concern for the toxic effects of their wastes. Rapid mobilization for World War II focused attention on production capacity, not waste management. Most sanitary engineers were conscripted to serve in the military and could not tend to municipal waste treatment equipment during a period of unprecedented pollution. During the conflict, courts showed leniency toward manufacturers who contributed to nuisance conditions or caused property damage while fulfilling military needs. Wars produced troughs of proper waste management sensitivity.

Nonetheless, military service introduced many scientists and soldiers to problems of waste disposal and also proper handling of toxic chemicals. Although wartime demands sometimes did not allow complete adherence to government guidelines, those who had military training in safe handling and disposal of hazardous substances certainly carried these lessons back to civilian jobs that involved waste management decisions.

Economic depressions produced an odd complex of sensitizers and attenuators that offset one another. Periods of low production stimulated experimentation with waste recovery and by-product marketing. When effective, these efforts contributed to an overall reduction in the volume of industrial wastes. Nevertheless, these investigations were not impelled by government regulations or enforcement, which were at a low ebb during recessions; rather, they were done largely independently of pollution issues. For this reason they did not apparently engender long-term pollution abatement programs. In general, economic troughs coincided with government support for municipal waste treatment systems, and this activity reduced the offensive qualities of urban sewage, leaving industrial wastes more obvious, particularly as production picked up.

This uneven level of sensitivity was influenced by an ever evolving level of knowledge, a dynamic legal context, and growing public understanding of risks. Nonetheless, the discourse found in the trade literature offered a constant reminder of the need to handle industrial wastes with care. Within this complex framework, corporate officials, managers, and plant personnel continued to make choices about levels of control for their wastes that reflect both corporate and social influences on their decisions.

Outcomes

SEVEN

INTRODUCTION

Thousands of Superfund sites bear testimony to half a century of largely uncontrolled chemical waste disposal. What treatment systems were used seldom completely destroyed toxic wastes, and many disposal sites failed to contain hazardous chemicals for a variety of reasons. Three fundamental causes stand out: (1) inadequate stewardship and engineering, (2) deviance from industry or government guidelines, and (3) transfer of trusteeship—although not one of them is singularly responsible at any given site. Substandard engineering included disposal operations that did not incorporate basic safeguards in keeping with contemporary knowledge and understanding of waste containment principles. Industry and government guidelines, although sometimes vague, advocated a level of care for hazardous substances that would minimize damage to public water, both surface and subsurface. Environmental problems typically resulted when waste disposers ignored direct advice or standards. Finally, by transferring responsibility, waste generators released hazardous materials, in many cases, to unqualified parties or abandoned the wastes altogether and opened the door to inadequate maintenance of a site's integrity even if adequate engineering had been incorporated in its original design. Commonly, it has been a combination of these three conditions that produced hazardous outcomes. This section will present prominent examples of waste management failures and offer conclusions about the outcome of the decision-making process.

FAILURES

Inadequate Engineering

Rocky Mountain Arsenal, Colorado. Rocky Mountain Arsenal (RMA) came into being during World War II as the U.S. military expanded its chemical warfare capabilities, and it produced a variety of highly toxic chemical agents and residues. Following the war private companies began using the facilities to manufacture pesticides. Soon thereafter, groundwater contamination became a problem and today the popular press has portrayed RMA as containing the most contaminated square mile on the face of the earth. As a place for toxic products manufacture, early design and engineering plans incorporated numerous safety features—and many related to waste management and control. Yet contamination problems emerged because of highly inconsistent application of basic engineering knowledge and safeguards.

RMA's initial design included features to minimize the escape of dangerous products and by-products from the site's chemical warfare production facility. One fundamental component of the site's safety features was its placement within a nearly two-mile buffer, which was intended to provide military security, absorb explosive concussions, allow dilution of chemical gas leaks, and provide adequate space for training exercises.[1]

For liquid waste disposal, the army relied on traditional basins and ponds, although they took several special precautions. Planners took steps to segregate toxic, nontoxic, caustic, and uncontaminated wastes. Several of the production lines had their own settling basins, although the Lewisite, arsenic trichloride, acetylene, and thionyl chloride wastes initially flowed into a single unlined settling basin. Sludges and the waste liquor from this settling basin and those from other production lines, along with other toxic wastes, eventually flowed into a series of natural basins "for disposal by evaporation and seepage."[2] There was a spillway in the low earthen dam that enclosed the main pond and a culvert that directed any overflow to a nearby irrigation canal. Although toxic wastes could escape into the local irrigation system, the waste management plan sought to exclude toxic effluent from entering the sanitary sewer lines. A channel connecting two of the toxic waste ponds was lined with scrap lumber coated with asphalt paint "to avoid contamination of the sanitary sewage system from the toxic waste system and possible leakage into the sewer main."[3] Among the process wastes drained into the ponds were thionyl chloride, sludges from the arsenic trichloride plant, nontoxic surface drainage, and salt-contaminated wastes from the chlorine plant.[4] Presumably the army diverted the toxic wastes from the sanitary sewer to avoid knocking out their sewage treatment plant, which relied on a biological decomposition process.

RMA staff expended much greater care to control chlorine plant caustic wastes. The Chemical Warfare Service personnel sought advice from private companies on the best means for handling caustic wastes. The consistent response from consultants was that caustic ponds could contribute to groundwater contamination several miles distant from the point of disposal. In fact, an evaporation equipment manufacturer mentioned a situation in which caustic compounds migrated over fifteen miles and stated, "We are afraid this might occur again and in the case of caustic soda results might be disastrous."[5] Furthermore, a geology professor from the University of Colorado directed an "extensive study" to determine the best means for handling a 50 percent solution of caustic wastes. On the basis of the investigation, the army constructed a lined basin on the arsenal grounds to prevent seepage. After scarifying the ground surface, construction crews deposited "selected" clay soils to a depth of twelve to eighteen inches and compacted them "to make an effective blend of the layers."[6]

The disparity between the use of unlined basins for toxic wastes and basins with clay liners for caustic wastes represents unequal application of waste containment technologies. By the early 1950s, the consequences of inconsistent engineering had become apparent. Area farmers noticed the effects of contamination down-gradient from RMA in the early 1950s as they began to supplement surface irrigation sources with groundwater during dry years. The first reported incident occurred some three miles from the arsenal's main disposal pond in 1951,[7] and it caused serious yield declines in corn and barley crops on a neighboring farm. Other farmers reported in 1954 that their crops yellowed when irrigated with well water.[8]

Following the Great Western Sugar Company's formal request for an investigation, the arsenal called upon the Corps of Engineers and the U.S. Geological Survey to investigate "the potentially serious condition" in 1954.[9] Water samples indicated that elevated sodium chloride concentrations were spreading down-gradient from the arsenal. The USGS reported that "evidence for the disposal area [the arsenal liquid waste basin] being the source of these high salinities must be considered very strong, even if circumstantial."[10] The Geological Survey also analyzed the samples for suspected pollutants such as arsenic, organic acid radicals, and fluoride. At the time of the study, samples collected from the arsenal grounds yielded only sodium chloride in harmful concentrations. The investigation concluded that salt contaminants were to be found in the groundwater-damaged crops, but it also assigned partial responsibility to the farmers, who it claimed used too little irrigation water to leach the salt accumulation from the surface. The USGS called for periodic sampling to monitor the extent of off-base contamination.[11]

The following year the USGS produced a second, more detailed report. This investigation found high salt concentrations in the shallow aquifer used for irrigation, rendering it unsuitable for agricultural uses. It also noted that arsenal wells yielded water containing arsenic levels that exceeded U.S. Public Health Service limits for domestic use. It found no arsenic in wells outside the arsenal. Nonetheless, it indicated that the contaminants were moving into an area that supplied irrigation water and that the disposal reservoirs on the arsenal grounds were the source of contaminants.[12] The army, however, concluded that the report did not "conclusively point to the Arsenal as the primary source of contamination," recommended that the USGS continue monitoring the contamination, and restricted public access to the results.[13] The army also determined that even if they ceased to use the disposal ponds, contamination would continue moving through the local aquifer.[14] To blunt congressional inquiries in light of impending lawsuits against the government, the army constructed a lined basin in 1956 and diverted all liquid wastes to this receptacle.[15]

Subsequent investigations conducted by the U.S. Public Health Service found that "except for the Rocky Mountain Arsenal wastes, there are no known sources from which chlorates could have originated."[16] The Public Health Service also indicated that there were some 150 domestic wells in the contaminated area and that a public water supply further down-gradient was in danger. They called for more monitoring of domestic wells, cessation of practices that would contribute to further contamination at the arsenal, and consideration of ways to alleviate existing contamination.[17] Specific recommendations for preventing additional movement of contaminants from the disposal areas included transfer of the sludge or sealing it beneath an impermeable cap. The Public Health Service also suggested the installation of pumping wells in heavily contaminated areas to remove the undesirable substances from the groundwater.[18]

The army continued to support investigations that determined that a phytotoxic compound (resembling 2,4-dichlorophenoxyacetic acid) had migrated off the arsenal property. Researchers reported that although chlorates and the 2,4-D type of compounds were never direct waste products of the arsenal operations, a chemical reaction within the waste basin created them. Furthermore they acknowledged that the problem would not be readily resolved. The researchers concluded, however, that use of infiltration basins, while common, was inadvisable above shallow aquifers and that the army should have anticipated the situation.[19]

In response to waste generation rates that exceeded the capacity of the lined lagoon, the army designed, installed, and operated a deep-well injection system. They sought a geological stratum that provided adequate capacity to receive the toxic wastes, but that also had "natural barriers . . . to ensure confinement of waste water." They adapted well-known oil field techniques to explore for a suitable geological formation and to determine its suitability. Once operational, in the early 1960s and a decade after chemical companies had begun using the technology, the well's engineers concluded that it successfully provided long-term containment of the wastes.[20]

In sum, inconsistent application of engineering safeguards led to obvious groundwater problems, while a disjointed and protracted response allowed the situation to worsen. In retrospect, the extensive precautions taken for caustic wastes, contrasted with the lack of care exercised with highly toxic substances, make the latter appear reckless.

Love Canal, New York. According to industry trade publications and waste management specialists, the most rudimentary waste disposal choices included basic engineering safeguards such as fencing and evaluation of a site's characteristics. This was the context in which, with guidance from a recent local legal decision, Hooker Chemical established its Love Canal disposal grounds near Niagara Falls, New York. During the 1920s and 1930s industries of that area had found numerous areas on which to dump waste solids and establish lagoons. In 1924, for instance, Union Carbide Corporation bought a piece of property in Niagara Falls and began dumping "slag and dry waste" on it. In 1929 the company also constructed settling basins on that property for "liquid sludge." In 1934 one of the dikes failed, inundating a Mr. Belden's property, allowing the fluid to flow over some thirty-three lots.[21]

While the State Supreme Court ruled against Union Carbide and held them responsible for $2,310 in damages to Belden, the judge dismissed all the other nuisance claims associated with the dump operation. He concluded, "No sludge or liquid waste has reached plaintiff's lands by permeation, and none can reach the plaintiff's lands by permeation."[22] The judge also noted that the company had erected a fence between the properties and installed a ditch adequate to carry away any runoff from the dump.

The Belden case served as one guideline for subsequent operators to follow; that is, fences were appropriate and "permeation" of wastes into neighboring properties was a concern to keep in mind when siting and operating a dump for industrial wastes. The court reached this decision as Hooker Electrochemical Corporation of Niagara Falls was seeking a dump site for its chemical wastes. Reflecting on that decision and guidance from "city hall," a Hooker employee concluded, as recorded in an internal company memo, that a dumping area "should be adequately protected so as to prevent the possibility of persons or animals coming in contact with the dumped materials."[23] A hand-written note attached to the memo several days later described a conversation on the subject between the writer and a Union Carbide employee. The Union Carbide employee elaborated by saying that (1) rainwater should not be allowed to overflow on a neighbor's land, (2) dusting should not become a nuisance, (3) vegetation should not be killed, and (4) smells should not disturb neighbors.

In establishing their dump, Hooker staff considered some of these elements, but fell far short in adhering to them. As early as the fall of 1942, the company's insurance agent, Cary Insurance, wrote to Hooker's counsel, discussing changes to Hooker's liability insurance from the Hartford Company based on the recognized need for fencing.[24] Isolation of wastes from public contact appeared to be a critical element from the start. While Hooker apparently undertook no detailed geological assessments to check for the possibility of "permeation" at Love Canal prior to dumping, they did initiate a substantial topographical survey of the site, including several cross sections through the canal and its adjacent spoil berms.[25] To manage the water on site, they built dams. As far as minimizing vegetation damage and other nuisances, however, the record is fairly clear. They did very little.

In spite of the importance of fences around dump sites, at least to insurance people, Hooker's adherence to this principle fell short, in the Love Canal area. First, the separate dump adjacent to the Niagara River (now known as the 102nd Street dump) had no fence in 1942.[26] In addition, when Ansley Wilcox, Hooker's counsel, visited Love Canal itself in 1946, he appeared distressed to find that the water in the unfilled sections of the canal was contaminated and served as the local swimming hole for children. He concluded:

I feel very strongly that if this water is contaminated as a result of our dumping chemical residues, we are running a real hazard in not taking steps to prevent possible injuries to persons who may swim in the canal.[27]

Clearly, the Love Canal neighbors "overflowed" into the wastes instead of the other way around, at least at that time.

One neighbor complained about wastes overflowing the property lines through the air, causing the potential for risks to health from the dumping operations at the site. After complaining about Hooker's dumping "all year early in the morning," she lamented:

> My husband was home sick and the smell was so bad that we could hardly breathe and we had to put wet towels over my husband's mouth and nose. It came over toward the houses like a white cloud and killed the grass and trees and burnt the paint off the back of the houses and made the other houses all black. I know for sure they did it all in '43 because my husband . . . died October 28, 1943 with lung trouble and I think the gases that came this way helped shorten his life.[28]

Only a few months after dumping began, Hooker's operations had violated most of the practices that had been identified by the State Supreme Court and that Union Carbide had recommended to Hooker in 1941.

Many years later Hooker sold the property containing Love Canal to the Niagara Falls Board of Education and again exhibited inadequate attention to engineering practice. The site Hooker sold for the new school was less than perfect, to say the least. When a soils engineering firm evaluated the site in 1953, they discovered the following:

> Ground water stood a few feet from the surface . . . and appears [sic] to be at the same level as the water in the canal. Ample evidence of high water throughout the area exists in reports of difficulties in adjacent housing developments.
>
> Unless the proposed back-filling operation [Hooker's plan to continue dumping while the school was being built] is carefully planned and controlled an objectionable situation may be created. End dumping or bulldozing the fill into the water filled section of the canal will produce a soft, unstable area where gradual settlement will occur for many years necessitating frequent regrading and other forms of maintenance.
>
> Construction of the proposed building . . . appears to be feasible. . . . However, it appears at this time to involve somewhat more than ordinary expense. Consequently some further consideration of alternate sites might be in order.[29]

Mr. Hough, the report's author, also noted that among the three borings that he made at the site he found that "the overburden consists of silty sand to soils containing as much as 80% of clay sizes." Two of the three borings showed silt or sand to a depth of about five feet.

Somewhat similar soil conditions existed at another Hooker dump site that the company itself felt was inappropriate for dumping chemicals. A 1955 memorandum stated:

> The sandy soil at the Montague [Michigan] plant is not suitable for burial of organic residues.[30]

Excavation around the proposed school location adjacent to Love Canal in early 1954 encountered "soft spots in the ground resulting from chemicals having been dumped in the area."[31] As a result, the board of education voted to move the school eighty-five feet to the north. Soft spots like these, however, continued to appear. In 1955 an area twenty-five feet square "crumbled," revealing drums once dumped there. This area became a puddle where children splashed about, which led to their exposure to chemicals.[32] Hooker responded to this incident by ordering ten truckloads of dirt to cover the chemical puddles and thereby prevent further exposure.[33] Although they showed community concern in this incident, their actions also indicate that they knew the chemical residue had ongoing hazardous properties.

Deviance from Contemporary Guidelines

Stringfellow, California. Allen Hatheway and Glenn Brown characterize the Stringfellow Acid Pits of southern California as the "first legally constituted hazardous waste disposal site." It opened for operation as an industrial waste dump in 1956 and continued in active use until 1972. Over the course of its sixteen-year history, the owners relied on evaporation and subsurface seepage to reduce the volume of 34 million gallons of liquid wastes. Seepage eventually became apparent off site and led to regulatory and legal actions against the operators.[34]

As the "first" regulated hazardous waste disposal site, the Stringfellow site underwent a geological review and permitting process in 1954. A team of engineers and a geologist visited the site and found the dense granitic bedrock to be a suitable site for liquid waste disposal. They concluded, however, that the owners needed to construct a barrier "to hold the waste above the dense bedrock, the greater the volume, the higher the barrier."[35]

Following the advice of the county engineers and geologists, the owners began construction of a concrete "dam" to prevent wastes from leaching from the pits. Only about a quarter of the dam was ever completed, however.[36] Seepage became apparent in 1969 and the operator took steps to collect the leachate and pump it back into the pits. Without an adequate barrier, the leachate collection effort was futile. Consequently water wells in the vicinity began to show elevated levels of chromium in the early 1970s, and regulators notified the owners that they were in violation of requirements.[37]

The initial problem associated with Stringfellow stemmed from direct violation of requirements for operating the site. The partial construction of a leachate protection system defied advice offered by local authorities and ultimately contributed to the site failure.

Sauget, Illinois. The small village of Sauget, Illinois, situated across the Mississippi River from St. Louis and known until recently as Monsanto, contains several hazardous waste sites. The community is home to several waste generators that discarded hazardous wastes in sites throughout the town but to only a few hundred residents. Monsanto Chemical Company, for example, buried toxic wastes, whereas the Moss Tie Company used an impoundment for its creosote wastes.[38] In 1966 the State of Illinois issued land disposal site regulations that stipulated that hazardous waste disposal required prior written approval by the Illinois Department of Public Health.[39]

After the guidelines went into effect, public health inspectors began visiting waste disposal sites and documenting existing practices. An initial inspection of a site owned by the Sauget Company (a local landfill operation) that was located within the Mississippi River floodplain found active dumping of undetermined chemical wastes. According to the site inspection, "Liquid hauled to the site by tank trucks is pooled on the site and allowed to dry before it is finally covered. The 55-gallon drums are emptied into these pools." The inspector commented that the operator did not know the contents of the chemical wastes and indicated he was unaware of the health hazards created by the practice.[40] Two months later, the Sauget Company had applied for a permit but was operating without state approval as the state deliberated which division held authority over the site.[41] By year's end (1967), a second inspection reported two glaring deficiencies: inadequate fencing and receipt of hazardous substances.[42] The following year, the public health officers, with assistance from state police, attempted to shut down the site for receiving out-of-state wastes.[43] Subsequently, the Director of the Illinois Department of Public Health requested the local state's attorney to seek an injunction against the operation. The complaint cited the owner's violation of Rule 5.08, which prohibited acceptance of hazardous wastes without prior written approval.[44] Despite the state's efforts, disposal continued at the site until floodwaters inundated the site in March 1973. Several months later, the secretary of state revoked the authority of Sauget and Company to transact business in the state.[45]

This former dump has been identified as a state Superfund site,[46] and its failure is evidence of disregard for state regulations. Open pooling of toxic wastes in a floodplain, inadequate fencing, and illegal receipt of hazardous wastes were obvious transgressions of state regulations and were done in defiance of enforcement efforts.

Velsicol Chemical Site, Tennessee. The Velsicol chemical waste disposal site in Hardeman County, Tennessee, did not violate existing state law at its inception in 1964, but it stands as an example of an operator's failure to conform to contemporary industry standards of care for hazardous substances, at least according to the ruling of a federal district court.[47] After a series of chemical waste releases caused fish kills (pp. 344–345), Velsicol Chemical Company sought a rural land disposal site for waste from its Memphis production facility (pp. 344–345). They purchased over 240 acres of land in an area well known for its sandy soils and abundant groundwater supplies used by rural residents (pp. 353–354). Despite the obvious permeability of local soils and nearby residents' reliance on groundwater, Velsicol did not conduct any hydrogeological studies (p. 354). Nonetheless, from 1964 to 1973 Velsicol deposited approximately "16.5 million gallons of concentrated chemical waste" into pits excavated to receive the wastes (p. 359).

Velsicol reported to local public health authorities in 1964 that it had placed "semi-solid non-combustible residue" encased in "corrosion-resistant 55-gallon drums" at the site (p. 364). It further claimed to state authorities that only wastes that it could not incinerate went to Hardeman County, that it operated the disposal facility according to the "trench" method, and that "the soil on the dump site is extremely tight" (p. 365). Later evidence indicated that many of the drums were leaking upon arrival at the site or were punctured in the process of unloading or burial. The wastes were not all solids or semisolids and the soils were far from being "tight." Furthermore, Velsicol's 1965 assertion that it had instituted a monitoring program proved false as well (p. 366–367).

Testimony at the trial indicated the Velsicol operation fell far short of accepted waste disposal standards for the 1960s. Judged according to the American Public Works Association's (APWA) 1961 landfill guidelines, the Hardeman County site was wholly inadequate. Expert testimony revealed that there had been no geological review of the site, as the APWA recommended. Furthermore, the operators placed hazardous chemicals above usable groundwater supplies. The judge concluded that "Velsicol's dump did not even meet requirements for an ordinary landfill" (p. 389). Consequently, there was extensive contamination of private wells, which led to a multimillion-dollar judgment against Velsicol.

Transfer of Trusteeship

Love Canal, New York. The history of the Love Canal property and waste disposal facility exemplifies the transfer of responsibility for hazardous chemical byproducts. Although there were incidents of chemical exposure during Hooker Electrochemical Company's management of the property, the wholesale failure of control occurred only after they released the property to the Niagara Falls Board of Education, which was unprepared and unqualified to manage a repository of toxic chemicals. After the sale, residential development around the dump exacerbated the problem.

During its initial planning for use of the Love Canal property, Hooker staff noted that

> the property should be adequately protected so as to prevent the possibility of persons or animals coming in contact with the dumped materials. Although the matter of protection was not specifically defined, it would seem that a light gauge wire fence of reasonable height should prove adequate for this purpose.[48]

A subsequent memo indicated that Hooker constructed a fence around the portion of the canal south of Buffalo Avenue and kept it locked except when dumping was in progress. When that section was filled, they began using an unfenced section north of the railroad tracks. Company officials also witnessed children swimming in portions of the canal containing contaminated water and commented on this as a potential liability.[49]

Hooker personnel faced a critical decision by the early 1950s. Residential land uses had encroached on the Love Canal dump during the postwar years, and complaints about chemical odors required attention.[50] In addition, the local school district sought a new building site to serve the burgeoning population and the superintendent inquired with Hooker about the possibility of purchasing the Love Canal property in March 1952. In response to this initial inquiry Hooker's executive vice president wrote:

> It is rather clear that the territory on each side of the Love Canal will be used rapidly to provide buildings or a school and it may be advisable for us to discontinue using the Love Canal property for a dumping ground. It is also rather clear to me that we should not sell the property *in order to avoid any risks* [emphasis ours].[51]

Only a month later, the same vice president expressed a far different view. Klaussen wrote to the company president:

> The more we thought about it, the more interested Wilcox [Hooker's counsel] and I became in the proposition and finally came to the conclusion that the Love Canal property is rapidly becoming a liability because of housing projects in the near vicinity. . . . We became convinced that it would be a wise move to turn the property over to the school provided we would not be held responsible for future claims or damages resulting from underground storage of chemicals.[52]

In offering to donate the property to the board of education, a Hooker official wrote:

> In view of the nature of the property and the purposes for which it has been used, it will be necessary for us to have special provisions incorporated into the deed with respect to the use of the property and other pertinent matters.[53]

The property transfer document indicated that the parcel had been "filled, in whole or in part, to the present grade level thereof with waste products resulting from the manufacturing of chemicals."[54]

Only Hooker was thoroughly aware of the nature of the chemicals buried in the Love Canal. They had explored the toxic nature of their products and by-products and assigned a chemical engineer to oversee waste disposal.[55] During their own operation of the site, they recognized the risks associated with disposal of chemical residue and carried liability insurance.[56] The board of education did not share this level of expertise or recognition. In fact, whenever children came in contact with exposed chemical wastes in subsequent years, public health officials called upon Hooker as the toxicology experts. Hooker assisted when the Niagara County Department of Health inquired about the contents of the site, but they also repeated that they were not responsible.[57] Relinquishing title to the Love Canal to an unqualified trustee was not in keeping with knowledge of the waste's toxicity, the potential for subsidence, the proximity of schoolchildren and homeowners, and the lack of containment at the site.

This became all too obvious as the site's viability as a waste repository was threatened by public works and private projects in the area. Road construction in 1958 exposed "thionyl [chloride] residue" and "benzene hexachloride spent cake." When notified, Hooker staff advised recovering the exposed material but indicated that the company should not take any action unless requested to by the board of education.[58] Hooker apparently saw the board of education as the trustee and sought to distance itself from the long-term management of its chemical wastes. Despite the board's obvious inability to anticipate the consequences of construction work around the canal, the company lamented that it was "still being plagued with problems associated with the fill at the Love Canal area in spite of their best efforts to shed themselves of any responsibility."[59]

Hooker's intent to insulate itself from liabilities associated with Love Canal became more pronounced as years passed. In 1957 Arthur Chambers, of Hooker's Legal Department, appeared at a board of education meeting that was considering plans for parts of the undeveloped lands that Hooker had deeded to the board of education.[60] Chambers reminded the board that the land was not suitable for construction where excavation would be needed. While he opined that Hooker could not stop the board from selling the land or doing anything they wanted with it, the company intended that the board use the site just for the school building and parking, and not residential construction.

Most importantly, Chambers distanced the company further from liability by referring "to a moral obligation on the part of the Board of Education in the event the property was sold." It is ironic that Hooker assigned the board with a continuing duty to protect property buyers from chemicals when the company itself accepted no such "moral obligation." A press account of the meeting quotes Chambers as saying that subdivision could lead to problems. He warned, "You're apt to hit something we buried there,"[61] in part because the chemicals were buried "willy-nilly."[62]

It is not surprising that a press account of the meeting quotes one of the board members, Wesley Kester, as saying, "It's a liability to us. . . . There's something fishy someplace. Now they tell us it [the land] shouldn't be used."[63]

Mr. Chambers followed up on the meeting with a letter to William Salacuse, an attorney for the city. Citing Hooker's civic duties to warn the board of the canal's dangers, he offered the company's assistance in undertaking test borings to "reveal actual conditions beneath the surface" and to "locate possible danger areas." He then pledged the company's help in apprising the board of "potentially dangerous conditions which we believe exist and which we believe some of the members of the Board might not have known."[64]

The same day, Hooker's vice president, Ansley Wilcox, wrote to Dr. Brent, the board president, to clarify the history of the transfer to the board of the canal property.[65] He also mentioned that a reverter clause had been proposed for the deed but was removed because the board "had no facilities for maintaining a park," which, along with use as a school site, was the stated purpose for the transfer of the site to the board. Its omission, Wilcox claimed, "in no sense indicated that we felt it would be safe or proper to use the property for any other purpose." It is instructive to note, however, that Hooker did not make any attempt to stop the board in 1954 from removing three thousand cubic yards of earth from the canal area for fill around the 93rd Street School.[66] This fill may well have been part of the cover over the wastes buried in the landfill. In fact, that fill was later found to be so contaminated that the second school had to be closed.

In short, while Hooker was comfortable with transferring the liabilities associated with its dump to another party, it balked when that party was clearly tending toward managing the site in such a way that others were very likely to be injured.

Once filled and transferred, wastes from the Love Canal continued to haunt the neighbors. Exposure incidents persisted, at least one explosion occurred, and people complained about chemicals percolating into basement sumps. Eventually, during a period of elevated precipitation during the late 1970s, the problems with the site took on proportions that forced the state's health commissioner to issue an emergency health order that recommended evacuating homes in the area[67] and made the site world-famous.

The great irony of the Love Canal situation, the virtual birthplace of the Superfund legislation and public mistrust of hazardous waste disposal sites, was Hooker Electrochemical's objective in donating the property to the board of education. Hooker sought a means of avoiding liability by relinquishing control of the site and ceasing to provide security and maintenance, and in doing so, it placed responsibility in unqualified hands. This ultimately came back to haunt not only Hooker but all other chemical producers in the United States through the strict liability provisions of Superfund legislation.

Syracuse, New York. Another deed that illustrates the pattern of liability transfer involves another upstate New York property. A huge local industry owned by Allied Chemical and Dye Company attempted to pass liability associated with a prodigious quantity of waste products to the State of New York. The property near Syracuse contained sludges generated by the company and its predecessors since the late 1800s. Allied used the Solvay process to produce soda ash, and this created a slippery waste product that is very insusceptible to consolidation. Infused within the inorganic sludge were wastes from other chemical processes. This waste mixture covered hundreds of acres of Lake Onondaga shoreline.

The unconsolidated wastes became a larger problem for Allied's subsidiary when in 1943 a containment berm failed and a massive sludge wave inundated a portion of Solvay, a Syracuse suburb. The state became party to the ensuing lawsuits, and in 1946 the governor referred to the waste heaps as a "man-made desert." Nevertheless, by the 1950s the state needed land for an interstate highway and also parking for the state fair. The sludge piles were ideally situated and the property required no demolition or urban renewal costs. Transferring the title to the state provided an ideal solution to the problems faced by the chemical producer.

With ample press coverage, Governor Dewey, on December 29, 1953, took title to the industrial waste pile by calling the transaction a "marvelous demonstration of co-operation" that would "do much toward converting what has been a community liability into a tremendous asset."[68] The deed absolved Allied of future liabilities and also relieved it from pending litigation. In addition to taking title to what the state recognized at the time as an unstable mound of contaminated sludge, the governor agreed that the state would not try to recover damages if it decided the constituents were objectionable. The deed read:

> this conveyance is given and accepted upon the express condition
> that the party of the first part [Allied], its successors and assigns,
> shall be without liability to the People of the State of New York or
> its assigns for any present or future injury to, decrease in value of, or

loss of enjoyment of the above described caused by or in any way attributable to depositing or maintaining industrial waste on other lands now owned or hereafter acquired by said party of the first part, other than actual physical injury, or the immediate threat or actual physical injury, to said above described premises, or to any person or persons lawfully thereon, and except that the depositing or maintaining of industrial waste on other land now owned by or hereafter acquired by the party of the first part, the successors or assigns.[69]

The deed also contained a reverter clause that limited use by the state to a "park" or other "public purposes" and it called for reversion of the land to Allied if the land were put to other uses.

One can only speculate why corporate counsel required the reverter clause. Allied may have been uncomfortable with the possibility that subsequent owners might build on an unstable foundation or that excavations might create exposures to the wastes beneath the crust atop the mound. Regardless, the reverter clause indicates corporate management's exercise of hazard control while divesting liability.

CONCLUSIONS

That this country is plagued with insecure hazardous waste sites is indisputable, although the severity of the problems and ways to remediate them will remain a political, public health, and legal debate for years to come. The national Superfund legislation responded to the situation that emerged with the discovery of Love Canal and sought to address the problem of an undetermined number of serious public-health-threatening sites. With over twelve hundred sites currently on the National Priorities List (Superfund sites) and approximately fifteen thousand in the potential Superfund inventory, the landscape is still littered with serious contamination problems. We attempted to analyze how industry, government, and society allowed this condition to develop over the first two-thirds of this century. What we discovered was a complex decision-making process that appeared to permit engineering shortcuts and cost-cutting behavior at many junctures. Likewise, and equally important, a practice existed that encouraged industrial waste managers to assure long-term stewardship over hazardous substances even though it was often ignored. Our analysis indicates that decision makers, in many cases, chose to defer adequate technical review of waste management options and thereby consciously selected low-control techniques.

In regard to recognizing the endangerment potential, chemical waste manufacturers were in the best position to fathom and appreciate the toxic effects, both acute and chronic, of their products and by-products. Many major chemical producers employed toxicologists who participated in efforts to limit public exposure to toxic products and to prevent workers' exposure to hazardous chemicals. They also carried out research and guided programs to prevent dispersal of toxic chemicals to workers' families. Production chemists worked diligently to engineer environmentally persistent chemicals and were familiar with the literature on the short- and long-term effects of chlorinated organic chemicals. By the 1950s, company toxicologists were working hand-in-hand with government agencies to define the toxic effects of their effluent in waterways and identify appropriate limits for them. Within this milieu there resided the most advanced expertise on the chemical products of the day. Obviously, the right people were in positions to be aware of the endangerment potential.

Furthermore, there was sufficient knowledge that chemical waste could cause environmental damage to foster cautious practices. Producers and public health officials always regarded toxic chemical waste as a problem that was distinct from general urban waste. Although similar means of containment often were used on both, public health and industry policy did not endorse unconfined disposal of toxic wastes. As early as the 1920s, oil refinery experts called for complete engineering review of proposed waste disposal sites. By the 1940s appropriate specialists recognized that hazardous chemicals could migrate from land disposal sites. Industrial trade organizations and public health groups issued guidelines and published reports noting the imminent threat of groundwater contamination associated with disposal of chemicals in improper land repositories. As industry began to experiment with deep-well injection in the early 1950s, they routinely analyzed the related topics of underground hydrology and public exposure to toxics and were alert to the potential escape of hazardous wastes from poorly chosen and inadequately managed disposal locations. The very reason that public health agencies acted with exceptional caution in permitting deep-well disposal was their recognition that improper use of this technology could cause serious and long-term groundwater contamination. This conclusion sharply contrasts with the assertion that there was no knowledge of dangers or environmental processes that would create dangerous situations during the 1940s through the 1960s. It also undermines the claim that there were no technological options for high control of hazardous wastes.

Although no federal statute defined hazardous wastes until the late 1970s, there was a corpus of legal precedent and even enforcement capabilities to restrict reckless or even casual disposal of toxic chemical residue. This is not to say that enforcement and compliance were consistent or effective. Nuisance law provided a means for individuals and public agencies to address undesirable or hazardous conditions created by industrial activity. Despite common-law decisions during the twentieth century that increasingly accommodated industrial activity, chemical manufacturers received regular warnings to guard against creating offensive conditions—to say nothing of dangerous situations. Statutory law undermined traditional common-law efforts; nevertheless it gradually provided authority for government bodies to monitor and protect public waters and the air. These organizations worked to reduce the levels of water and atmospheric pollution. In some instances they found cooperation with industry satisfactory, while in other situations they used more direct enforcement tools to make headway. By the 1950s most states had pollution statutes that applied to surface-water and groundwater on the books, and industry was well aware of the legal liabilities for polluting behavior. Nonetheless, regulators complained that their efforts were futile against the rising tide of industrial effluent. Regardless of government's inability to facilitate implementation of satisfactory hazardous material disposal policies, there were some environmental regulations and procedures in place by the early 1950s. Finally, at the most basic level, there was a fundamental societal expectation that manufacturers were responsible for the proper and safe disposal of their residue and a trust that they were doing so. Government never assumed that responsibility as it did for general urban garbage; rather it allowed industry to retain nearly exclusive control of its waste management practices.

The level of knowledge and means for disseminating knowledge played an extremely important role in industrial-waste decision making. Many corporate officials in the chemical industry were trained chemists. This gave them insight into the toxicology and persistence of modern organic chemicals and their by-products. Their staffs had access to numerous professional trade organizations and their publications that provided advice on chemical waste management techniques. While much of the advice was rudimentary—neutralization or land disposal—by the early 1950s trade groups and professional organizations helped distribute information warning against groundwater contamination resulting from improperly managed chemical wastes. Furthermore, these professionals operated within intellectual subcultures and communications networks that had long-standing mechanisms for responding to new discoveries, especially hazardous ones. Technical publications and professional organizations considered how to respond to hazardous outcomes of their work, such as bridge failures. It may be argued, however, that in the absence of obvious linked and immediate fatalities, and given the tendency of companies to assign their least qualified to handle waste disposal problems, the escape of toxics was an inevitable development. Nevertheless, this outcome is ultimately attributable to conscious decisions by managers to follow a path of low-control waste management policy.

There were, in our conceptualization of the decision-making process, both sensitizers and desensitizers that further steered the actions of waste-managing entities. Sensitizers made managers more aware of their responsibilities to provide long-term control for hazardous substances, while desensitizers offered a rationale for deferring control. Common law presented a legal deterrent to polluting behavior during the early twentieth century, but the Restatement of Torts and wartime priorities weakened the effectiveness of nuisance law by the mid-1940s. Statutory law, while creating numerous public health agencies and enforcement mechanisms, was a minimal deterrent through the 1950s and marginally effective in the 1960s. Good-neighbor concerns and an industry concern with legal liability provided a greater sensitizing influence through the 1950s and into the 1960s. Meanwhile, corporate security and government training offered justification for a higher degree of control of hazardous wastes. Economic cycles affected pollution control by providing a boost to treatment efforts during production upswings other than during wartime, when pollution control succumbed to other priorities. Thus, during the first two-thirds of this century, sensitizers operated within the corporate decision-making apparatus and impelled experimentation with and installation of better waste treatment and waste confinement equipment. Desensitizers, however, offered justification for the installation of minimal treatment equipment and low-control options at critical junctures during the past half century.

The outcome of the decision-making process was a half century of waste isolation followed by a score of years characterized by rudimentary treatment practice. Although isolation prevailed before 1950, treatment technologies did provide partial solutions to numerous waste management problems. Isolation included several variations: Among them were buffer zones around hazardous activity, dilution, and simple burial or impoundment. Nonetheless, throughout the first half of the twentieth century, these practices were recognized as inadequate in many situations and certainly when toxic wastes were involved. Contamination of water supplies and repeated failures of impoundments and burial sites alerted waste producers and their trade organizations to the perils of unprotected disposal sites. Preliminary treatment provided one means for ameliorating the impact of toxic discharges to waterways or leachate from land disposal sites. Using even rudimentary treatment technologies in tandem was an improvement and became common during the 1950s. Installation of treatment equipment provided manufacturers with a public relations event and also a weapon to ward off intrusive legislation. Nevertheless, inadequate engineering of waste disposal sites and wide gaps between the availability and the implementation of treatment technologies permitted toxic litter to accumulate throughout industrialized areas. Failure to effectively sequester these wastes allowed industrial residue to escape its burial grounds. These steps each contributed to the toxic landscape that exists in this country today.

Notes

I. INTRODUCTION

1. Lois M. Gibbs, *Love Canal: My Story* (New York: Grove Press, 1982).

2. Terry L. Anderson and Donald R. Leal, *Free Market Environmentalism* (Boulder: Westview, 1991), and Eric Zuesse, "Love Canal: The Truth Seeps Out," *Reason* (February 1981): 16–33.

3. John Deegan, "Looking Back at Love Canal: Results and Conclusions of EPA's Investigations," *Environment Science and Technology* 21 (1987): 421–426, and Daniel Mazmanian and David Morell, *Beyond Superfund: America's Toxics Policy for the 1990s* (Boulder: Westview, 1992).

4. *United States et al. v. Hooker Chemicals and Plastics Corporation et al.*, U.S. District Court, Western District of New York, Final Decision, Civ. 79-990C, 1994, 181.

5. Prominent discussions include Joel A. Tarr, "Historical Perspectives on Hazardous Wastes in the United States," *Waste Management and Research* 3 (1985): 95–102; Martin Melosi, "Hazardous Wastes and Environmental Liability: An Historical Perspective," *Houston Law Review* 25 (1988): 741–779; and C. E. Colten, "Historical Hazards: The Geography of Relict Industrial Wastes," *Professional Geographer* 42 (1990): 143–156.

6. Contrasting views can be found in abundance in the Love Canal trial depositions and testimony. Industry supporters include Dwight Metzler and Richard Eldredge, while critics include Robert Cohen and Clarence Klassen. *United States et al. v. Hooker Chemicals and Plastics Corporation et al.*, U.S. District Court, Western District of New York, Civ. 79-990, 1990–1991.

7. Prior to 1976 and the enactment of the Resource Conservation and Recovery Act there was no national hazardous waste legislation.

8. Tarr, "Historical Perspectives on Hazardous Wastes"; Joel A. Tarr, "Industrial Wastes and Public Health," *American Journal of Public Health* 75 (1985): 1059–1067; and Joel A. Tarr and Charles Jacobson, "Environmental Risk in Historical Perspective," in *The Social and Cultural Construction of Risk*, ed. B. B. Johnson and V. T. Covello (Boston: Reidel,

1988), 317–344. See also Samuel P. Hays, "Three Decades of Environmental Politics: The Historical Context," in *Government and Environmental Politics*, ed. Michael J. Lacey (Baltimore: Johns Hopkins University Press, 1989), 19–80. Christopher Sellers, "Factory as Environment: Industrial Hygiene, Professional Collaboration and the Modern Sciences of Pollution," *Environmental History Review* 18 (1994): 55–84. See also Joseph A. Pratt, "Letting the Grandchildren Do It: Environmental Planning during the Ascent of Oil as a Major Energy Source," *Public Historian* 2 (1980): 28–61.

9. Melosi, "Hazardous Waste and Environmental Liability," 777–779.

10. Christine Rosen, "Differing Perceptions of the Value of Pollution Abatement across Time and Place: Balancing Doctrine in Pollution Nuisance Law, 1840–1906," *Law and Labor History* 11 (1993): 303–381.

11. Those decision makers who felt a personal moral duty to protect others and/or those who were aware of public policy principles (like the "good neighbor" policy) or laws which existed.

12. The degree of control for land disposal of long-lived industrial wastes is largely determined by the nature of the site, the method of dumping, and the waste's final form. This degree of control can be breached or undermined by people unaware of the hazard or unwilling to consider intrusion risks.

2. RECOGNIZING DANGERS

1. See Gerald F. Pyle, "The Diffusion of Cholera in the United States in the Nineteenth Century," in *Man, Space, and Environment*, ed. P. W. English and R. C. Mayfield (New York: Oxford University Press, 1972), 417–418.

2. See Joel A. Tarr, "Disputes over Water Quality Policy: Professional Cultures in Conflict," *American Journal of Public Health* 70 (1980): 527–535; and Christopher Sellers, "Factory as Environment: Industrial Hygiene, Professional Collaboration and the Modern Sciences of Pollution," *Environmental History Review* 18 (1994): 55–84.

3. George M. Price, *The Modern Factory: Safety, Sanitation and Welfare* (New York: John Wiley, 1914), 284.

4. George T. Mazuzan and J. Samuel Walker, *Controlling the Atom* (Berkeley: University of California Press, 1984), 214–245, 345–372.

5. See David Rosner and Gerald Markowitz, eds., *Dying for Work: Workers' Safety and Health in Twentieth Century America* (Bloomington: University of Indiana Press, 1989).

6. Sellers, "Factory as Environment," 74–75.

7. Thomas Oliver, *Dangerous Trades* (London: John Murray, 1902), 569.

8. Henry Carr, *Our Domestic Poisons: Poisonous Effects of Certain Dyes and Colours* (London: Ridgway, 1883).

9. W. H. Rand, "Composite Industrial Poisons: A Review," *Monthly Labor Review* 10 (February 1920): 482.

10. Oliver, *Dangerous Trades*, 17.

11. See Martin Cherniack, *Hawk's Nest Incident: America's Worst Industrial Disaster* (New Haven: Yale University Press, 1987).

12. When the U.S. Department of Labor published its initial inventory, it drew heavily on its European predecessors. It sought to collect and disseminate information "concerning those industrial poisons that are inimical to the health of the worker, with a view to the establishment of a scientific basis for international legislation to prohibit or regulate their

use" (Thomas Sommerfeld, Thomas Oliver, and Felix Putzeys, "List of Industrial Poisons," *Bulletin of the U.S. Bureau of Labor* 86 (January 1910): 147–168).

13. "Occupation Hazards and Diagnostic Signs," *Bulletin of the U.S. Bureau of Labor Statistics* 306 (1922): 1–31; and "Occupation Hazards and Diagnostic Signs," *Bulletin of the U.S. Bureau of Labor Statistics* 582 (1933): 1–49.

14. Ludwig Teleky, *History of Factory and Mine Hygiene* (New York: Columbia University Press, 1948), 55.

15. The government agency title even distinguished between hygiene and sanitation, that is, infectious disease. George M. Kober and Emery Hayhurst, *Industrial Health* (Philadelphia: Blakiston's Sons, 1924), xlii–xlvii.

16. Bernhard J. Stern, *Medicine in Industry* (New York: Commonwealth Fund, 1946), 35.

17. Sommerfeld et al., "List of Industrial Poisons," 151.

18. R. H. Britten and L. R. Thompson, "A Health Study of Ten Thousand Male Industrial Workers," *Public Health Bulletin* 162 (1926): 106.

19. Alice Hamilton, *Industrial Poisons in the United States* (New York: MacMillan, 1925), 1.

20. Britten and Thompson, "A Health Study," 106.

21. M. Bowditch, C. K. Drinker, Philip Drinker, H. H. Haggard, and Alice Hamilton, "Code for Safe Concentrations of Certain Common Toxic Substances Used in Industry," *Journal of Industrial Hygiene and Toxicology* 22 (1940): 251; and W. M. Gafafer, ed., *Manual of Industrial Hygiene* (Philadelphia: W. B. Saunders, 1943), 264.

22. R. A. Jewett, "Health Hazards in the Oil Industry," *American Journal of Public Health* 24 (1934): 1126.

23. G. M. Kober and W. C. Hanson, *Diseases of Occupation and Vocational Hygiene* (Philadelphia: Balkiston's, 1916) and G. M. Kober and E. R. Hayhurst, *Industrial Health* (Philadelphia: Balkiston's Sons and Co., 1924).

24. S. J. Williams, *Manual of Industrial Safety* (Chicago: A. W. Shaw, 1927), 159; H. E. Collier, *Outlines of Industrial Medical Practice* (Baltimore: Williams and Wilkins, 1941), 75; J. H. Foulger and A. J. Fleming, "Industrial Exposure to Toxic Chemicals," *Journal of the American Medical Association* 117 (1941): 832; W. J. McConnell, R. H. Flinn, and A. D. Brandt, "Occupational Diseases in Government-Owned Ordnance Explosive Plants," *Occupational Medicine* 1 (1946): 558.

25. Oliver, *Dangerous Trades*, 576–577.

26. C. P. McCord, *Industrial Hygiene for Engineers and Managers* (New York: Harper and Brothers, 1931), 167–170; F. J. Curtis, "New Products Bring New Hazards," *National Safety News* 24 (September 1931): 44; National Conservation Bureau, *Handbook of Industrial Safety Standards* (New York: National Conservation Bureau, 1938), 24–28.

27. Carman T. Fish, "Good Housekeeping in a Chemical Plant," *National Safety News* 33 (April 1936): 16.

28. National Conservation Bureau, *Industrial Safety Standards*, 31.

29. L. B. Clinton, "Periodic Examination of Workers in Toxic Chemicals," *Industrial Medicine* 13 (1944): 125. Also, Fish, "Good Housekeeping," 16.

30. D. A. Hounshell and J. K. Smith, Jr., *Science and Corporate Strategy: Du Pont R&D, 1902–1980* (Cambridge: Cambridge University Press, 1988), 555–563.

31. W. F. von Oettingen and W. Deichmann-Gruebler, "The Toxicity and Potential Dangers of Crude 'Duprene,'" *Journal of Industrial Hygiene and Toxicology* 18 (1936): 271–

272; W. F. von Oettingen, W. Deichmann-Gruebler, and W. C. Hueper, "Toxicity and Potential Dangers of Phenyl-Hydrazine Zinc Chloride," *Journal of Industrial Hygiene and Toxicology* 18 (1936): 301–309; W. F. von Oettingen, W. C. Hueper, W. Deichmann-Gruebler and F. H. Wiley, "2 Chloro-Butadiene: Its Toxicity and Pathology and the Mechanism of Its Action," *Journal of Industrial Hygiene and Toxicology* 18 (1936): 240–270; F. H. Wiley, W. C. Hueper, and W. F. von Oettingen, "On the Effects of Low Concentrations of Carbon Disulfide," *Journal of Industrial Hygiene and Toxicology* 18 (1936): 733–740; and H. H. Schrenk and Y. P. Yant, "Toxicity of Dioxan," *Journal of Industrial Hygiene and Toxicology* 18 (1936): 448–460.

32. J. S. Sconce (Hooker Electrochemical Company), "Toxicity of Our New Chlorinated Hydrocarbons," internal memo, August 21, 1944, Toxicity folder, New York State Department of Law, Love Canal Archives, Albany, NY (hereafter Love Canal Archives).

33. New York State Department of Labor, "From the Salt of the Earth," *Industrial Bulletin* (May 1948): 37.

34. W. F. von Oettingen et al., "The Toxicity and Potential Dangers of Toluene, with Special Reference to Its Maximal Permissible Concentration," *Public Health Service Bulletin* 279 (1942).

35. Gafafer, *Manual of Industrial Hygiene*, 264.

36. Hamilton, *Industrial Poisons*, 449–450.

37. Ethel Browning, *Toxicity and Metabolism of Industrial Solvents* (Amsterdam: Elsevier Publishing, 1965), 196.

38. F. D. Schaumburg, "Banning Trichloroethylene: Responsible Reaction or Overkill?" *Environmental Science and Technology* 24 (1990): 17–22.

39. Gafafer, *Manual of Industrial Hygiene*, 264; Allen D. Brandt, *Industrial Health Engineering* (New York: John Wiley, 1947), 5–8.

40. Browning, *Toxicity and Metabolism*, 196.

41. Frank A. Patty, "Industrial Hygiene: Retrospect and Prospect," in *Patty's Industrial Hygiene and Toxicology*, vol. 1, ed. G. D. Clayton and F. E. Clayton, 3rd ed. (New York: John Wiley, 1978), 7.

42. William J. Burke, "Combating Health Hazards in the Chemical Industry—Part 1," *Chemical Industries* 55 (September 1944): 370; Stern, *Medicine in Industry*, 28.

43. J. W. Thornberg (Hooker Electrochemical), notes of interview with John Burton (Diamond Alkalie, New Jersey) regarding dermatitis among TCP production workers, October 18, 1955, Love Canal Archives, New York City.

44. Curtis, "New Products Bring New Hazards," 84.

45. McCord, *Industrial Hygiene for Engineers*, 4.

46. Leonard Greenburg and Samuel Moskowitz, "Occupational Disease Hazards in the Chemical and Rubber Industries," *New York State Department of Labor Monthly Review* 25 (November 1, 1946): 63. See also William J. Burke, "Combatting Health Hazards in the Chemical Industry—Part 2," *Chemical Industries* 55 (October 1944): 565.

47. Oliver, *Dangerous Trades*, 576.

48. Price, *Modern Factory*, 283.

49. D. S. Beyer, *Industrial Accident Prevention* (Boston: Houghton Mifflin, 1916), 353.

50. F. C. Vilbrandt, *Chemical Engineering Plant Design* (New York: McGraw-Hill, 1934), 31; J. H. Perry, ed., *Chemical Engineer's Handbook* (New York, McGraw-Hill, 1941), 2863; J. H. Perry, ed., *Chemical Industry Handbook* (New York: McGraw-Hill, 1954), 18–43; Manufacturing Chemists' Association, *Organization and Method for Investigating Wastes*

in Relation to Water Pollution, Manual Sheet W-1 (Washington, DC: Manufacturing Chemists' Association, 1948), 4.

51. Patty, *Patty's Industrial Hygiene*, 12–13.

52. L. T. Fairhall, "Toxic Contaminants of Drinking Water," *Journal of the New England Water Works* 55 (1941): 400–401.

53. The estimated amount of TCE that caused adverse health effects after moving through the ground to contaminate a private well was only 18 ppm. See F. A. Lyne and T. McLachlan, "Contamination of Water by Trichlorethylene," *Analyst* 74 (September 1949): 513.

54. National Safety Council, *Industrial Explosion Hazards: Gases, Vapors, and Flammable Liquids* (Chicago: National Safety Council, 1941), 10.

55. Gafafer, *Manual of Industrial Hygiene*, 338; R. S. Smith and W. W. Walker, "Surveys of Liquid Wastes from Munitions Manufacturing," *Public Health Reports* 58 (September 10, 1943): 1365–1379; (September 17, 1943): 1393–1414.

56. National Safety Council, *Industrial Waste Disposal and Bibliography on Chemical Wastes* (Chicago: National Safety Council, 1948), 1.

57. There was also concern with atmospheric dispersal of toxic substances, particularly following the deadly incident at Donora, Pennsylvania, where seventeen people died in 1948. See Lynne P. Snyder, "'The Death-Dealing Smog over Donora, Pennsylvania': Industrial Air Pollution, Public Health Policy, and the Politics of Expertise," *Environmental History Review* 18 (1994): 117–1139.

58. F. M. Daugherty, "A Proposed Toxicity Test for Industrial Waste to Be Discharged to Marine Waters," *Sewage and Industrial Wastes* 23 (1951): 1029–1031; A. W. Anderson, "Proposed Toxicity Test for Industrial Wastes," *Sewage and Industrial Wastes* 25 (1953): 1450–1451.

59. E. J. Cleary, "Determining Risks of Toxic Substances in Water," *Sewage and Industrial Wastes* 26 (1954): 203.

60. Cleary, "Determining Risks," 204–210; and Kettering Laboratory, Interim Summary Report No. 5 of Tabulated Toxicity Data, unpublished paper, Kettering Laboratory, Cincinnati, Ohio, September 1955.

61. Jules S. Cass, "The Potential Toxicity of Chemicals in Water for Man and Domestic Animals," *Proceedings of the Tenth Industrial Waste Conference* (Lafayette, IN: Purdue University, 1955), 470.

62. Donald Pisani, "Fish Culture and the Dawn of Concern over Water Pollution in the United States," *Environmental Review* 8 (1984): 117–131.

63. H. S. Davis, "Effects of Oil Pollution on Fisheries," in U.S. Congress, House, *Hearings on the Subject of the Pollution of Navigable Waters*, 68th Cong., 1st sess., Washington, 1924, 25–26.

64. David M. Neuberger (president, National Coast Antipollution League), testimony before Congress, U.S. Congress, *Hearings on the Subject of the Pollution of Navigable Waters*, 60 and 81.

65. Illinois State Board of Fish Commissioners, *Commissioners' Report, 1899–1900* (Springfield, IL: George T. Williams, 1900), 11.

66. In the case of the Illinois River, a thriving commercial fishery was subjected to massive quantities of urban pollution. Although initially seen as beneficial, owing to the increased food supply offered to aquatic life, the sewage and industrial wastes eventually overwhelmed and destroyed the commercial species. C. E. Colten, "Illinois River Pollu-

tion Control, 1900–1970," in *The American Environment: Interpretations of Past Geographies*, ed. Lary M. Dilsaver and C. E. Colten (Lanham, MD: Rowman and Littlefield, 1992), 193–216.

67. M. O. Leighton, "Industrial Wastes and Their Sanitary Significance," *Public Health Papers and Reports* 31 (1905): 29–40; and Joel A. Tarr, "Industrial Wastes and Public Health: Some Historical Notes, Part 1, 1876–1932," *American Journal of Public Health* 75 (1985): 1059–1067. Also see Tarr, "Disputes over Water Quality Policy."

68. "Progress Report of Committee on Industrial Wastes in Relation to Water Supply," *Journal, American Water Works Association* 10 (1923): 415–430.

69. Tarr, "Disputes Over Water Quality."

70. See Philip V. Scarpino, *Great River: An Environmental History of the Upper Mississippi, 1890–1950* (Columbia: University of Missouri Press, 1985), esp. pp. 80–113. Also, M. M. Ellis offered testimony to Congress implicating chemical wastes as highly toxic to aquatic life in the Mississippi River. See "Statement," in U.S. Congress, Senate, *Stream Pollution and Stream Purification*, 74th Cong., 1st sess., S. Doc. 16, Washington, 1935, 42.

71. L. V. Carpenter and E. W. Klinger, "Effects of Road Oils and Tars on Public Water Supplies," *Journal, American Water Works Association* 27 (1934): 235–247.

72. C. K. Calvert, "Contamination of Ground Water by Impounded Garbage Waste," *Journal, American Water Works Association* 24 (1932): 266–270.

73. Burt Harmon, "Contamination of Ground-Water Resources," *Civil Engineering* 11 (1941): 345–347.

74. Arthur Pickett, "Protection of Underground Water from Sewage and Industrial Wastes," *Sewage Works Journal* 19 (1947): 469–470.

75. L. T. Fairhall, "Toxic Contaminants," 403.

76. Vilbrandt, *Chemical Engineering Plant Design*, 31; and T. R. Walker, "Ground-Water Contamination in the Rocky Mountain Arsenal Area, Denver, Colorado," *Bulletin of the Geological Society of America* 72 (1961): 489–494.

77. "Effect of Benechlor-3 on Potable Water Supplies," *Water Works and Sewage* 87 (1940): 231–236.

78. Howard Potter, "The Effects of War Gases on Water Supplies: Decontamination," *Journal of the New England Water Works Association* 57 (1943): 152–153; C. C. Ruchoft, O. R. Placak, and S. Schott, "The Detection and Analysis of Arsenic in Water Contaminated with Chemical Warfare Agents," *Public Health Reports* 58 (1943): 1761–1771.

79. H. C. McLean and A. L. Weber, "Influence of Spray Practices on Arsenical Residues," *Journal of Economic Entomology* 21 (1928): 921–928.

80. "Spray Residue on Food," *Journal, American Medical Association* 106 (April 3, 1937): 1178. For an extended discussion of the residue issue see Thomas R. Dunlap, *DDT: Scientists, Citizens, and Public Policy* (Princeton, NJ: Princeton University Press, 1981), esp. 39–58.

81. J. S. Jones and M. B. Hatch, "Spray Residues and Crop Assimilation of Arsenic and Lead," *Soil Science* 60 (1945): 287.

82. J. H. Draize et al., "Summary of Toxicological Studies of the Insecticide DDT," *Chemical and Engineering News* 22 (September 10, 1944) 1503–1504.

83. G. C. Decker, "Agricultural Applications of DDT, with Special Reference to the Importance of Residues," *Journal of Economic Entomology* 39 (1946): 561.

84. F. M. Pottenger and B. Krohn, "Poisoning from DDT and Other Chlorinated

Hydrocarbon Pesticides: Pathogenesis, Diagnosis and Treatment," in U.S. Congress, House, *Chemicals in Foods and Cosmetics: Hearings*, 82nd Cong., 1st sess., Washington, 1952, 956.

85. J. J. Lehman, "Some Toxicological Reasons Why Certain Chemical May or May Not Be Permitted as Food Additives," in U.S. Congress, House, *Chemicals in Food Products: Hearings*, 82nd Cong., 1st sess., Washington, 1951, 275.

86. Jones and Hatch, "Spray Residues and Crop Assimilation," 287.

87. J. R. Callaham, "DDT Fights Insects in War and Peace," *Chemical and Metallurgical Engineering* 51 (October 1944): 110.

88. F. L. Knowles and C. S. Smith, "Duration of Toxicity of Several DDT Residual Spray under Conditions of Malaria Control Operations," *Public Health Reports* 61 (December 13, 1946): 1806.

89. E. E. Fleck and H. L. Haller, "Compatibility of DDT with Insecticides, Fungicides, and Fertilizers," *Industrial and Engineering Chemistry* 37 (1945): 403. L. Hopkins, G. G. Gyrisco, and L. B. Norton, "Effects of Sun, Wind, and Rain on DDT Dust Residues on Forage Crops," *Journal of Economic Entomology* 45 (1952): 629–633.

90. E. E. Fleck, "Residual Action of Organic Insecticides," *Industrial and Engineering Chemistry* 40 (1948): 708.

91. J. M. Ginsburg, R. S. Filmer, and J. P. Reed, "Longevity of Parathion, DDT and Dichlorodiphenyl Dichloroethane Residues on Field and Vegetable Crops," *Journal of Economic Entomology* 43 (1950): 90–94; Paul A. Dahm, "Effects of Weathering and Commercial Dehydration upon Residues of Aldrin, Chlordane, and Toxaphene Applied to Alfalfa," *Journal of Economic Entomology* 45 (1952): 763–766.

92. Peter Doudroff and Max Katz, "Critical Review of Literature on the Toxicity of Industrial Wastes and Their Components to Fish," *Sewage and Industrial Wastes* 22 (November 1950): 1432–1458.

93. Peter Doudroff and Max Katz, "Critical Review of Literature on the Toxicity of Industrial Wastes and Their Components," *Sewage and Industrial Wastes* 25 (1953): 802–839.

94. J. A. Carollo, "The Removal of DDT from Water Supplies," *Journal, American Water Works Association* 37 (1945): 1316.

95. Peter Doudroff, Max Katz, C. M. Tarrwell, "Toxicity of Some Organic Insecticides to Fish," *Sewage and Industrial Wastes* 25 (1953): 840.

96. M. S. Shane, "Effect of DDT Spray on Reservoir Biological Balance," *Journal, American Water Works Association* 40 (1948): 333–336.

97. Sellers, "Factory as Environment."

98. Cleary, "Determining Risks," 203.

99. A brief review of the Kettering scientists' work appears in J. S. Cass, "Potential Toxicity of Chemicals in Water," 466–472. Their investigations centered on determining the toxic effects of industrial chemicals to humans, wildlife, and livestock and considered both chronic and acute effects.

100. Rolf Eliassen, "Why You Should Avoid Housing Construction on Refuse Landfills," *Engineering News Record* 138 (1947): 756–760. A good review of the adoption of sanitary landfills appears in J. A. Tarr, "The Search for the Ultimate Sink: Urban Air, Land, and Water Pollution in Historical Perspective," *Records of the Columbia Historical Society* 51 (1984): esp. 16–27.

101. Gerald N. McDermott, "Pollutional Characteristics of Land-fill Drainage,"

Activity Report No. 3 (Cincinnati, OH: Public Health Service, Environmental Health Center, 1950).

102. Clarence W. Klassen, "Sanitary Fill Standards," *American City* 66 (February 1951): 104; Klassen, "Locating, Designing, and Operating Sanitary Landfills," *Public Works* 81 (November 1950): 42–43.

103. R. F. Goudey, "The Industrial Waste Problem," *Sewage Works Journal* 16 (1944): 1180.

104. The groundwater problems in Long Island and Michigan will be discussed in greater detail in the groundwater section. See Morris Deutsch, *Groundwater Contamination and Legal Controls in Michigan*, Water-Supply Paper 1691 (Washington, DC: U.S. Geological Survey, 1963).

105. Task Group E4-C, "Findings and Recommendations on Underground Waste Disposal," *Journal, American Water Works Association* 45 (1953): 1296–1297.

106. R. G. Butler, G. T. Orlob, and P. H. McGauhey, "Underground Movement of Bacterial and Chemical Pollutants," *Journal, American Water Works Association* 46 (1954): 110.

107. Richard W. Eldredge, report of Richard W. Eldredge, for the defense, *United States et al. v. Occidental Chemical Corporation et al.*, U.S. District Court, Western District of New York, Civ. 79 990, 1989, 2.

108. James E. Etzel, Land Disposal of Industrial Wastes in the 1940's and 1950's, report for the defense, *United States et al. v. Occidental Chemical Corporation et al.*, U.S. District Court, Western District of New York, Civ. 79-990, 1989, 2.

109. D. H. Sharp, "The Disposal of Waste Materials in the Pesticides Industry," in *Proceedings, Disposal of Industrial Waste Materials* (Sheffield, England: Sheffield University, 1957), 10.

110. As early as 1901, public health officials reported that "experiments show that putrefaction is still strong twenty feet beneath the surface in land which has been garbage filled for ten years" (Joseph M. Patterson, *Report to the Mayor and City Council on the Collection, Removal, and Final Disposition of Garbage* [Chicago: Department of Public Works, 1906], 3). Rolf Eliassen ("Housing Construction on Refuse Landfills," *Engineering News-Record* 138 (May 1, 1947): 90–94) recognized that organic decomposition continued for more than five years.

111. James E. Etzel, Deposition, *United States v. Occidental Chemical Corporation et al.*, U.S. District Court, Western District of New York, Civ. 79-990, 1989, 231–232.

112. W. R. Gould and T. C. Dorris, "Toxicity Changes of Stored Oil Refinery Wastes," *Journal, Water Pollution Control Federation* 33 (1961): 1107–1111.

113. O. J. Sproul and D. W. Ryckman, "Significant Physiological Characteristics of Organic Pollutants," *Journal, Water Pollution Control Federation* 35 (1963): 1136–1145.

114. We would like to thank Joel Tarr, Michael McMahon, Douglas McManis, and Richard Bergstrom for helpful comments on an earlier draft. A more extensive version of this section appeared as C. E. Colten, "A Historical Perspective on Industrial Wastes and Groundwater Contamination," *Geographical Review* 81 (1991): 215–228. It is reprinted here with permission.

115. Joel A. Tarr, "Historical Perspectives on Hazardous Wastes in the United States," *Waste Management and Research* 3 (1985): 100–101.

116. Harry E. LeGrand, "Historical Review of Knowledge of the Effect on Ground Water as Related to Buried Wastes," report for the defense, *United States v. Occidental*

Chemical Corporation et al., U.S. District Court, Western District of New York, Civ. 79-990, n.d., 2.

117. Colten, "A Historical Perspective."

118. For a general overview see Asit K. Biswas, *History of Hydrology* (New York: Elsevier, 1970).

119. C. S. Slichter, *The Motion of Underground Waters*, Water Supply and Irrigation Paper 67 (Washington, DC: U.S. Geological Survey, 1902), 18.

120. A thorough discussion of knowledge of groundwater at the turn of the century is found in Franklin H. King, "Principles and Conditions of the Movement of Ground Water," U.S. Congress, House, *Nineteenth Annual Report of the U.S. Geological Survey*, 59-294, 55th Cong., 3rd sess., H. Doc. 5, 1899.

121. Slichter, *Motion of Underground Waters*, 23–33, 63–65.

122. William P. Mason, *Water-supply* (New York: John Wiley, 1896), 291; Slichter, *Motion of Underground Waters*, 54. See also Daniel W. Mead, *Notes on Hydrology* (Chicago: Shea Smith, 1904); and A. F. Meyer, *Elements of Hydrology* (New York: John Wiley, 1917).

123. W. J. Jewell and B. L. Seabrook, *A History of Land Application as a Treatment Alternative*, Technical Report 43019-79-012 (Washington, DC: U.S. Environmental Protection Agency, 1979).

124. Frank Leverett, *Flowing Wells and Municipal Water Supplies*, Water Supply and Irrigation Paper 182 (Washington, DC; U.S. Geological Survey, 1906), 180; and D. W. Mead, *Hydrology* (New York: McGraw-Hill, 1919), 411–412.

125. S. W. McCallie, "Experiment Relating to Problems of Well Contamination at Quitman, Georgia," in *Contributions to the Hydrology of the Eastern United States*, Water-supply and Irrigation Paper 110, ed. M. L. Fuller (Washington, DC: U.S. Geological Survey, 1905), 45–54.

126. Mason, *Water-supply*, 297.

127. O. E. Meinzer, *Outline of Ground-water Hydrology*, Water Supply Paper 494 (Washington, DC: U.S. Geological Survey, 1923); M. Muskat, *The Flow of Homogeneous Fluids through Porous Media* (New York: McGraw-Hill, 1937). Meinzer noted that groundwater hydrology was offered at some universities and urged it as a standard part of an undergraduate geology education in 1931. See O. E. Meinzer, "Hydrology: The History and Development of Ground-water Hydrology," *Journal of the Washington Academy of Sciences* 24 (January 1934): 32.

128. C. F. Tolman, *Ground Water* (New York: McGraw-Hill, 1937), 194.

129. Tolman (*Ground Water*) discusses artificial recharge (pp. 240–245) and mounding of subsurface waters (174–177 and 252).

130. Tolman, *Ground Water*, 383–384.

131. L. K. Wenzel, *Methods for Determining Permeability of Water-Bearing Materials*, Water Supply Paper 887 (Washington, DC: U.S. Geological Survey, 1942). An extensive discussion of developments in groundwater science appears in Peter N. Skinner, "Avoiding the Environmental Timebomb: The Historical Scientific Foundations for Responsible Industrial Waste Disposal" (master's thesis, Rensselaer Polytechnic Institute, 1994).

132. Pyle, "Diffusion of Cholera," 417–418.

133. Austin Flint, "The Relations of Water to the Propagation of Fever," *Reports and Papers of the American Public Health Association* 1 (1873): 164–172; Edward Orton, "Certain Relations of Geology to the Water Supplies of the Country," *Reports and Papers of the American Public Health Association* 2 (1874): 296.

134. Meinzer, "Hydrology," 25.

135. Mason, *Water-supply*, 314. North Dakota, North Carolina, and Connecticut had statutes that recognized cemeteries as sources of water contamination; see Edwin B. Goodell, *A Review of Laws Forbidding Pollution of Inland Waters in the United States*, Water-Supply and Irrigation Paper 152 (Washington, DC: U.S. Geological Survey, 1905).

136. Slichter, *Motion of Underground Waters*, 68.

137. Leverett, *Flowing Wells*, 180.

138. George M. Price, *Handbook on Sanitation* (New York: John Wiley, 1913), 49.

139. "Abstracts," *Journal, American Water Works Association* 23 (October 1929): 918.

140. McCallie, "Experiment Relating to Problems."

141. Mason, *Water-supply*, 296–297; Isaiah Bowman, "Problems of Underground Water Contamination," in *Underground Water Papers*, Water Supply Paper 160, ed. M. L. Fuller (Washington, DC: U.S. Geological Survey, 1906), 92–95.

142. C. W. Stiles and H. R. Crouhurst, "The Principles Underlying the Movement of *Bacillus coli* in Ground-water, with Resulting Pollution of Wells," *Public Health Reports* 38 (1923): 1350–1353.

143. C. W. Stiles, H. R. Crouhurst, and G. E. Thompson, *Experimental Bacterial and Chemical Pollution of Wells via Groundwater, and the Factors Involved*, Bulletin 147 (Washington, DC: U.S. Public Health Service Hygienic Laboratory, 1927), 11–12.

144. E. L. Caldwell, "Pollution Flow from Pit Latrine, *Journal of Infectious Diseases* 61 (1937): 229; E. L. Caldwell and L. W. Parr, "Direct Measurement of the Rate of Ground Water Flow in Pollution Studies," *Journal of Infectious Diseases* 62 (1938): 259.

145. Tolman, *Ground Water*, 393.

146. H. W. Whittaker et al., "Ground-Water Supplies: Progress Report of the Committee on Ground-Water Supplies," *Public Health Reports*, Supplement 124 (1937): 1, 4, and 23.

147. A. G. Fiedler, "The Occurrence of Ground Water with Reference to Contamination," *Journal, American Water Works Association* 28 (1936): 1958.

148. Robert F. Leggett, *Geology and Engineering* (New York: McGraw-Hill, 1939), 441.

149. Charles H. Lee, "Sealing the Lagoon Lining at Treasure Island with Salt," *Transactions of the American Society of Civil Engineers* 106 (1941): 577–593.

150. Dr. Scheelhaase and G. M. Fair, "Producing Artificial Ground Water at Frankfort Germany," *Engineering News-Record* 93 (1924): 174–176.

151. R. F. Goudey, "Reclamation of Treated Sewage," *Journal, American Water Works Association* 23 (1931): 230–240.

152. Arthur Pickett, "Disposal of Industrial Wastes in Los Angeles County," *Water and Sewage Works* 95 (1948): 33–36; Warren A. Schneider, "Industrial Waste Disposal in Los Angeles City," *Water and Sewage Works* 94 (1948): 37–39.

153. C. E. Arnold, H. E. Hedger, and A. M. Rawn, "Report on the Reclamation of Water from Sewage and Industrial Waste in Los Angeles County," California (Los Angeles, CA: Los Angeles County Board of Engineers, 1949).

154. See A. Lang, "Pollution of Water Supplies, Especially of Underground Streams, by Chemical Wastes and by Garbage (abstract)," *Journal, American Water Works Association* 25 (1933): 1181; Fritz Egger, "Ground Water Affected by Industrial Plants (abstract)," *Journal, American Water Works Association* 36 (1944): 229–230.

155. Burt Harmon, "Contamination of Ground-water Resources," 345–347.

156. R. F. Goudey, "Symposium: Disposal of Liquid Industrial Wastes," *Sewage Works Journal* 16 (1944): 1180.

157. Arthur Pickett, "Protection of Underground Water," 469. Transport of these contaminants was likely facilitated by intermittent flow in dry stream channels.

158. Sheryl Luzzadder-Beach, "Geographic Sampling Strategies for Groundwater Quality Evaluation" (Ph.D. dissertation, University of Minnesota, 1990), 155–156.

159. N. V. Olds, "Legal Aspects of Ground Water Contamination," *Proceedings of the Seventh Industrial Waste Conference* (Lafayette, IN: Purdue University, 1952), 244–268; H. W. Davids, and M. Lieber, "Underground Water Contamination by Chromium Wastes," *Sewage and Water Works* 98 (1951): 528–534; Walker, "Ground-water Contamination in the Rocky Mountain Arsenal Area," 489–494.

160. D. J. Cederstrom, "The Arlington Gasoline Contamination Problem," unpublished report (Washington, DC: U.S. Geological Survey, 1947).

161. Mason, *Water-supply*, 413.

162. Butler, Orlob, and McGauhey, "Underground Movement of Bacterial and Chemical Pollutants," 105–106.

163. Sheppard T. Powell, "Industrial Wastes," *Industrial and Engineering Chemistry* 46 (September 1954): 98A.

164. Whittaker et al., *Ground-Water Supplies*, 1.

165. U.S. Public Health Service, "Sanitation Manual for Public Ground Water Supplies," *Public Health Reports* 59 (1944): 138–143.

166. Rolf Eliassen, "Housing Construction on Refuse Landfills," 756–760.

167. C. C. Spencer, "Recommended Wartime Refuse Disposal Practice," *Public Health Reports*, Suppl. 173 (1943): esp. p. 10; Klassen, "Sanitary Fill Standards," 104–105.

168. "Dr. George E. Ekblaw has been answering requests for information on effects of sanitary landfill on underground pollution where specific water supplies are not involved. This procedure, stated by Dr. Ekblaw to have been standard procedure for about 20 years." See Frank C. Foley (Illinois State Geological Survey, Groundwater Division), file memo, June 10, 1952, Illinois State Geological Survey, Historical Groundwater Files, Champaign, IL.

169. Max Bookman (California Department of Public Works) to Linne C. Larson (Regional Water Pollution Control Board No. 4), correspondence, February 27, 1951, Love Canal Archives.

170. R. F. Goudey, "Developing Standards for the Protection of Groundwater," *Journal, American Water Works Association* 39 (1947): 1018.

171. National Safety Council, *Industrial Waste Disposal*, 3–4.

172. Thomas H. Edgar, *Conservation of Groundwater: A Survey of the Present Groundwater Situation in the U.S.A* (New York: McGraw-Hill, 1951), 203.

173. Henry Anderson, "Insurance and Loss Prevention," in *Chemical Industry Handbook*, ed. John H. Perry (New York: McGraw-Hill, 1954), 18–42.

174. Task Group E4-C, "Control of Underground Waste Disposal," *Journal, American Water Works Association* 44 (1952): 685–689.

175. Task Group E4-C, "Findings and Recommendations on Underground Waste Disposal," 1295–1297.

176. N. J. Lusczynski, quoted in R. W. Hess, "1952 Industrial Waste Forum," *Sewage and Industrial Wastes* 25 (1953): 79.

177. California State Water Pollution Control Board, *Investigation of Leaching of a Sanitary Landfill*, Publication No. 3 (Sacramento, CA: California State Water Pollution Control Board, 1954).

178. American Public Works Association, *Municipal Refuse Disposal* (Chicago: American Public Works Association, 1960); American Society of Civil Engineers, *Ground Water Basin Management*, Manual of Engineering Practice No. 40 (New York: American Society of Civil Engineers, 1961).

179. A more extensive discussion of this point appears in Peter N. Skinner, "Avoiding the Environmental Time Bomb."

180. American Petroleum Institute, *Manual on Disposal of Refinery Wastes*, vol. 3, *Chemical Wastes* (New York: American Petroleum Institute, 1951), 31.

181. Manufacturing Chemists' Association, *Water Pollution Abatement Manual: Oils and Tars* (Washington, DC: Manufacturing Chemists' Association, 1955), 8.

182. James Lee, "Throw Your Wastes Down a Well," *Chemical Engineering* 57 (September 1950): 137–139; William Black, "Underground Waste Disposal," *Sewerage and Industrial Wastes* 30 (May 1958): 660–672.

183. Butler, Orlob, and McGauhey, "Underground Movement of Bacterial and Chemical Pollutants," 97–113.

184. A. E. Williamson, "Land Disposal of Refinery Wastes," *Proceedings of the Thirteenth Industrial Waste Conference* (Lafayette, IN: Purdue University, 1958), 337–340.

185. Task Group 2450 R, "Underground Waste Disposal and Control," *Journal, American Water Works Association* 49 (1958): 1336.

186. Task Group 2450 R, "Underground Waste Disposal and Ground Water Contamination," *Journal, American Water Works Association* 52 (1960): 621–622.

187. W. E. Stanley and R. Eliassen, *Status of Knowledge of Ground Water Contaminants* (Washington: U.S. Federal Housing Administration, Technical Studies Program, 1960).

188. U.S. Department of Health, Education and Welfare, Public Health Service, *Ground Water Contamination: Proceedings of the 1961 Symposium* (Cincinnati: Robert Taft Sanitary Engineering Center, 1961), 1. Papers covered a variety of topics including organic chemical contamination.

189. American Society of Civil Engineers, *Ground Water Basin Management* (New York: American Society of Civil Engineers, 1961), 107.

190. Morris Deutsch, *Groundwater Contamination and Legal Controls in Michigan.*

191. Tarr, "The Search for the Ultimate Sink," 1–29.

192. Federal Water Pollution Control Administration, *The Cost of Clean Water*, vol. 2, *Detailed Analyses* (Washington: U.S. Department of the Interior, 1968), 69.

3. ACCOMMODATING HAZARDS

1. There may be over 100,000 undetected sites according to U.S. General Accounting Office, *Superfund: Extent of Nation's Potential Hazardous Waste Problem Still Unknown*, GAO/RCED-88-44 (Washington, DC: GAO, 1987).

2. Portions of this section appeared as "Creating a Toxic Landscape," *Environmental History Review* 18 (1994): 85–116. We would like to thank Christine Rosen, Jeffrey Stine, and Joel Tarr for valuable comments on a previous draft.

3. The principle of isolation is being employed again. Dow Chemical Company has purchased a buffer zone around a Louisiana plant and has relocated residents. See Susan

L. Cutter and John Tiefenbacher, "Chemical Hazards in Urban America," *Urban Geography* 12 (1991): 428.

4. Harrison P. Eddy, "Industrial Waste Disposal," *Metallurgical and Chemical Engineering* 25 (1917): 32–36.

5. Victor V. Kelsey, "Location as a Factor in Eliminating Industrial Waste," *Chemical and Metallurgical Engineering* 25 (1921): 401–402.

6. *Birmingham Age Herald*, June 5, 1892, in Hazard Powder Company, miscellaneous papers, series II, part 1, accession 472, box 698, Hagley Museum and Library Archives, Wilmington, DE.

7. The Du Pont Powder Yards was developed on the banks of the Brandywine River near Wilmington, Delaware; the Illinois Powder Company occupied a narrow hollow in the steep limestone bluffs along the Mississippi River near the town of Grafton, Illinois. See Arthur P. Van Gelder and Hugo Schlatter, *History of the Explosives Industry in America* (New York: Columbia University Press, 1927), 630–631. Susan Cutter has surveyed accidents in the chemical industry and concluded that explosions were the most common form of calamity in the early twentieth century. See Susan L. Cutter, *Living with Risk* (London: Edward Arnold, 1993), 106.

8. A. D. Smith, "Refining," in *A Handbook of the Petroleum Industry*, vol. 2, ed. David T. Day (New York: John Wiley, 1922), 1–3.

9. Richard Hartshorne, "The Economic Geography of Plant Location," *Industrial Property,* Proceedings and Reports of the Industrial Property Division of the National Association of Real Estate Boards, 6 (1926): 56–57. The engineering literature of the early 1930s perpetuated this concept, commonly advising that a chemical factory beyond the city limits was free of restrictions that would hamper operations. See Fred D. Hartford, "Deciding on Chemical Plant Location," *Chemical and Metallurgical Engineering* 38 (1931): 72.

10. U.S. Department of Commerce, Bureau of Census, *Location of Manufacturers, 1899–1929* (Washington, DC: 1933), 47.

11. W. K. Hasfurther and C. W. Klassen, "Industrial Waste Discharges from Industries at Monsanto [Illinois]," unpublished Illinois Sanitary Water Board Report, March 6, 1942, microfilm files, reel 0958, Illinois Environmental Protection Agency, Land Pollution Control Division, Springfield, IL.

12. G. R. Taylor, *Satellite Cities: A Study of Industrial Suburbs* (New York: Appleton and Company, 1915); see also C. E. Colten, "Environmental Development in the East St. Louis Region, 1890–1970," *Environmental History Review* 14 (1990): 93–116.

13. *O'Connor v. Aluminum Ore Company*, 224 Ill. App. 613 (1922). As was common, the circuit court found in favor of the plaintiff. The appeals court concluded "that if appellant operated its plant in such a manner that dangerous acids, gases, smoke, dust, etc., were thrown into the air and were carried by the wind into, over and upon plaintiff's residence, and that she was deprived of the comfortable use and enjoyment of her property by reason thereof, appellant would be liable for maintaining a nuisance." The plaintiff, however, failed to prove that the nuisance arose from the defendant's property, and the appeals court reversed the earlier decision.

14. W. C. Platt, "Business Protected from Encroachment of Residences," *National Petroleum News* 20 (March 21, 1928): 30.

15. The contract between J. C. Charvat and E. I. du Pont Nemours and Company, September 14, 1915, released the latter from "any and all claims, demands, suits, actions,

at law or in equity, now existing or claimed, or that may hereafter be claimed" on Charvat's land. It also relieved the company from responsibility "for any injury by drainage or sewerage into the James River or Bailey's Creek." Legal Department records, series II, accession 1305, box 626, folder 21, Hagley Museum and Library Archives, Wilmington, DE.

16. DuPont chief engineer to H. F. Brown (Director of Legal Department), February 15, 1917, provided a $5,000 estimate for dredging Bailey's Creek and recommended that action await the court's decision. He also outlined steps to reduce pollution of the creek by constructing two settling basins on the plant site and thereby intercept cotton and other sediments escaping into the creek. Legal Department records, series II, part 2, accession 1305, box 626-30, folder 4, Hagley Museum and Library Archives, Wilmington, DE.

17. R. L. Kraft, "Locating the Chemical Plant," *Chemical and Metallurgical Engineering* 34 (1927): 678.

18. Clarence Klassen, Rebuttal Expert Report of Clarence Klassen, unpublished report for the plaintiffs, *U.S. et al. v. Occidental Chemical Corporation et al.*, U.S. District Court, Western District of New York, Civ. 79-990, June 1990, 6–7.

19. U.S. Congress, House, *Waste Disposal Site Survey*, Committee Print 96-IFC 33, 96th Cong, 1st sess., 1979, x.

20. H. McLean Wilson and H. T. Calvert, *A Text Book on Trade Waste Waters: Their Nature and Disposal* (Philadelphia: J. B. Lippincott, 1913), 24–49.

21. Eddy, "Industrial Waste Disposal."

22. Frank Bachman and E. B. Besselievre, "Treatment of Industrial Waste to Prevent Stream Pollution," *Transactions of the American Institute of Chemical Engineers* 16, pt. 1 (1924): 204.

23. E. B. Besselievre, "Industrial Waste Disposal as a Chemical Engineering Problem," *Chemical and Metallurgical Engineering* 38 (1931):501–503. A discussion of waste treatment options appeared in the same edition; see Editorial Staff, "Equipping Plants for Trade Waste Disposal," *Chemical and Metallurgical Engineering* 38 (1931): 524–530. See also Anthony Anable, "Refinements in Design for Mechanical Separation," *Chemical and Metallurgical Engineering* 38 (1931): 220–223.

24. Testimony of E. E. Butterfield, in U.S. Congress, Senate, Committee on Commerce, *Stream Pollution: Hearings before a Subcommittee*, 74th Cong., 2d sess., 1936, 291.

25. J. B. Hill, "Waste Problems in the Petroleum Industry," *Industrial and Engineering Chemistry* 31 (1939): 1363.

26. National Resources Committee, *Water Pollution in the United States* (Washington, DC: Government Printing Office, 1939), 48–49.

27. Joel A. Tarr, "Searching for a 'Sink' for an Industrial Waste: Iron-Making Fuels and the Environment," *Environmental History Review* 18 (1994): 9–34; Joseph A. Pratt, "Letting the Grandchildren Do It: Environmental Planning During the Ascent of Oil as a Major Energy Source," *Public Historian* 2 (1980): 28–61.

28. American Petroleum Institute, *Disposal of Refinery Wastes: Section III, Waste Water Containing Solutes* (New York: American Petroleum Institute, 1935); Willem Rudolfs, "Stream Pollution in the State of New Jersey," *Transactions, American Institute of Chemical Engineers* 27 (1931): 42.

29. Dow Chemical Company began installation of these systems in the mid-1930s. See I. F. Harlow, "Waste Problems of a Chemical Company," *Industrial and Engineering Chemistry* 31 (1939): 1347–1349.

30. C. E. Mensing, R. L. Cassell, C. H. Bean, H. C. Spencer, and V. L. King, "Calco's New Waste Treatment Plant," *Chemical and Metallurgical Engineering* 48 (March 1941): 85.

31. Testimony by Dr. Max Trumper, in U.S. Congress, Senate, *Stream Pollution: Hearings*, 402. See also L. T. Fairhall, "Toxic Contaminants in Drinking Water Supplies," *Journal of the New England Water Works Association* 55 (1941): 400–410.

32. R. D. Hoak, "Industrial Stream Pollution Problems and their Solution," *Chemical Industries* 49 (August 1941): 173; M. M. Ellis, "A Study of the Mississippi River from Chain of Rocks, St. Louis, Missouri, to Cairo, Illinois, with Special Reference to the Proposed Introduction of Ground Garbage into the River by the City of St. Louis," Special Scientific Report Number 8, mimeographed (Washington, DC: U.S. Fish and Wildlife Service, 1940), esp. 17.

33. E. F. Eldridge, *Industrial Waste Treatment Practice* (New York: McGraw-Hill, 1942), 348–349 and 289–290.

34. E. B. Besselievre, "Safe Disposal of Industrial Chemical Wastes," *Chemical Markets* 29 (1931): 494–496.

35. F. B. Langreck (Monsanto vice president) to H. F. Ferguson (Illinois Sanitary Water Board), January 23, 1933, microform records, Illinois Sanitary Water Board, Village of Monsanto, housed in Water Pollution Control Division, Illinois Environmental Protection Agency, Springfield, IL. For a general discussion see C. E. Colten and T. B. Samsel, "Historical Assessment of Hazardous Waste Management in Madison and St. Clair Counties, Illinois, 1890–1980," Research Report 30 (Champaign, IL: Hazardous Waste Research and Information Center, 1988).

36. New York State Department of Health, *Love Canal: A Special Report to the Governor and Legislature* (Albany, NY: Author, 1981), 4.

37. Mensing et al., "Calco's New Waste Treatment," 84.

38. There were numerous important works on industrial hygiene that provided guidance on how to limit worker exposure to harmful chemicals. See Carey P. McCord, *Industrial Hygiene for Engineers and Managers* (New York: Harper & Brothers, 1931); and William M. Gafafer, ed., *Manual of Industrial Hygiene* (Philadelphia: W. B. Saunders, 1943), chap. 2.

39. Eldridge, *Industrial Waste Treatment Practice*, 294.

40. Hooker Electrochemical Thionyl Chloride Plant 1942 Design, prepared under contract No. W-285-CWS-4848, January 25, 1943 (design date), April 20, 1943 (document date), New York State Department of Law, Love Canal Archives, Albany, NY (hereafter Love Canal Archives).

41. Richard Bailie and Burton Crocker, "Incinerators," *Kirk/Othmer Chemical Encyclopedia*, 3d ed., vol. 13 (New York: Wiley, 1978) 182; Dan Walsh, "Solid Wastes in New York City: A History," *Waste Age Magazine* 20 (April 1989): 114.

42. Besselievre, "Industrial Waste Disposal," 499. See also Harlow, "Waste Problems," 1348.

43. T. R. Olive, "Incineration Solves Waste Disposal Problem," *Chemical Engineering* 55 (March 1948): 110.

44. John Edwards (Hooker Electrochemical), "Operation Request for Engineering Assistance, #79—Disposal of Thionyl Chloride (Niagara Falls Plant)," July 12, 1943, Love Canal Archives. Hooker Electrochemical, "Report—Operation Department Annual Report: Fiscal Year 1944," April 1945, Love Canal Archives.

45. Bailie and Crocker, "Incinerators," 183; R. H. Van Horne and D. E. Springer

(Hooker Electrochemical), file memo regarding Manufacturing Chemists' Association Stream Pollution Abatement Conference, December 16–17, 1948, Love Canal Archives; L. H. Schurstein and D. E. Springer (Hooker Electrochemical), Trip report regarding visit to Dow Chemical Company's Plant in Midland, Michigan, July 30, 1948, Love Canal Archives.

46. "Stream Pollution Becomes a Problem for Chemical Engineers," *Chemical and Metallurgical Engineering* 45 (1938): 139.

47. Willem Rudolfs and L. R. Setter, "Industrial Wastes in New Jersey," *New Jersey Agricultural Experiment Station Bulletin* 610 (New Brunswick, NJ: 1936).

48. Natural Resources Committee, *Water Pollution in the United States*, 7.

49. H. W. De Ropp, "Chemical Waste Disposal at Victoria, Texas, Plant of the DuPont Company," *Sewage and Industrial Wastes* 23 (1951): 194–197. Monsanto advocated a similar position in H. E. Morris, "How Monsanto Controls Air and Water Pollution," *Oil and Gas Journal* 53 (1954): 114–116.

50. C. K. Nagy, "The Construction and Operation of an Incinerator for Chemical Plant Wastes," in *Proceedings of the Twelfth Industrial Waste Conference* (Lafayette, IN: Purdue University, 1957), 177–185.

51. A. F. Martin and R. E. Rostenbach, "Industrial Waste Treatment and Disposal," *Industrial and Engineering Chemistry* 45 (1953): 2683.

52. "Superior Refractories," *Chemical and Metallurgical Engineering* 21 (October 8, 1919), 462–464; "Carborundum Refractories to Be Made at Perth Amboy," *Chemical and Metallurgical Engineering* 22 (May 12, 1920): 907.

53. W. S. Dickie, "Designing Heavy Rotary Equipment," *Chemical and Metallurgical Engineering* 41 (May 1939): 326; W. S. Dickie, "Trouble Free Operation of Rotary Kilns, Coolers, Dryers, etc.," unpublished report from Vulcan Iron Works, Wilkes Barre, PA, ca. 1940s, Love Canal Archives.

54. Manufacturing Chemists' Association, *Water Pollution Abatement Manual: Oils and Tars*, Manual W-4 (Washington, DC: Manufacturing Chemists' Association, 1955), 7–8; Manufacturing Chemists' Association, *Disposal of Hazardous Wastes: Safety Guide* (Washington: Manufacturing Chemists' Association, 1961).

55. Earl C. Mirus, "National Aniline's Incinerator Plant," *Proceedings, 1957 MCA Air and Water Abatement Conference* (Washington, DC: MCA, 1957, 77.)

56. Richard Woodland, M. C. Hall, and R. R. Russell, "Process for Disposal of Organic Residues," unpublished internal report (Niagara Falls, NY: Hooker Electrochemical, n.d., post-1961). Engineers estimated that incineration with this equipment would offer a 50 percent saving over conventional drum burial.

57. James A. Lee, "Throw Your Wastes Down a Well," *Chemical Engineering* 57 (September 1950): 137–139; William B. Black, "Underground Waste Disposal," *Sewage and Industrial Wastes* 30 (May 1958): 669–672; Robert Bergstrom, *Feasibility of Subsurface Disposal of Industrial Wastes in Illinois*, Circular 426 (Champaign: Illinois State Geological Survey, 1968); De Ropp, "Chemical Waste Disposal at Victoria, Texas."

58. O. E. Mechem and J. H. Garrett, "Deep Injection Disposal for Liquid Toxic Wastes," *Journal of the Construction Division: Proceedings of the American Society of Civil Engineers* 89 (1963): 111–121.

59. Manufacturing Chemists' Association, *Organization and Method for Investigating Wastes in Relation to Water Pollution*, Manual W-1 (Washington, DC: Manufacturing Chemists' Association, 1948), 4.

60. Manufacturing Chemists' Association, *Water Pollution Abatement Manual: Oils and Tars*, 7–8.

61. Manufacturing Chemists' Association, *Water Pollution Abatement Manual: Neutralization of Acidic and Alkaline Plant Effluents*, Manual W-3 (Washington, DC: Manufacturing Chemists' Association, ca. 1954), 6.

62. Ralph Stone, "Land Disposal of Sewage and Industrial Wastes," *Sewage and Industrial Wastes* 25 (1953): 406.

63. C. E. Colten, "A Historical Perspective on Industrial Wastes and Groundwater Contamination," *Geographical Review* 81 (1991): 215–228.

64. Sheppard T. Powell, "Industrial Wastes," *Industrial and Engineering Chemistry* 49 (1954): 95A–98A.

65. Task Group E4-C, "Findings and Recommendations of Underground Waste Disposal," *Journal, American Water Works Association* 45 (1953): 1295–1297.

66. Manufacturing Chemists' Association, *Water Pollution Abatement Manual: Oils and Tars*, 8.

67. H. L. Jacobs, "Waste Treatment Methods: Recovery and Disposal," *Chemical Engineering* 62 (April 1955): 186.

68. G. R. Amery (design engineer), Disposal of Solid Industrial Wastes, from Electrochemicals Department, E. I. du Pont de Nemours Company, West Batavia, New York, Waste Management Proposal to the New York Bureau of Environmental Sanitation, May 10, 1956, Albany, NY.

69. Powell, "Industrial Wastes," 95A–98A.

70. Ralph Porges, "Industrial Waste Stabilization Lagoons in the United States," *Journal, Water Pollution Control Federation* 35 (April 1963): 456–468.

71. The issue of isolation versus engineered security is discussed by George T. Mazuzan and J. S. Walker, *Controlling the Atom* (Berkeley: University of California Press, 1984), 214–245. An excellent history of the Hanford site is Michele S. Gerber, *On the Homefront: The Cold War Legacy of the Hanford Nuclear Site* (Lincoln: University of Nebraska Press, 1992), 42–43, 143–48.

72. Mazuzan and Walker, *Controlling the Atom*, 345, 347; Arthur E. Gorman, "Disposal of Atomic Energy Industry Wastes," *Industrial and Engineering Chemistry* 45 (1953): 2672.

73. Gorman, "Disposal of Atomic Energy Wastes," 2674.

74. Harlow et al., "Phenolic Waste Treatment of the Dow Chemical Company"; Harlow, "Waste Problems"; T. J. Powers, "The Treatment of Some Chemical Industry Wastes," *Sewage Works Journal* 17 (1947): 330–337.

75. I. F. Harlow and T. J. Powers, "Pollution Control at a Large Chemical Works," *Industrial and Engineering Chemistry* 39 (1947): 574–576.

76. Ibid., 573.

77. There were some plants that reported both industrial and municipal treatment facilities. This accounts for the sum of 450 chemical plant treatment systems. See U.S. Department of Health Education and Welfare, Public Health Service, *Municipal and Industrial Waste Facilities: 1957 Inventory, Regions 1, 2, 3, 4, 5, and 6* (Washington, DC: DHEW, 1958); definitions appear on pp. 8–10. These regions included the entire eastern seaboard, the Southeast, the lower Midwest, along with Kansas and Iowa (from region 6). This summary does not include all 48 states inventoried, but covers the states with consistent data supplied by local authorities.

78. Federal Water Pollution Control Administration, *The Cost of Clean Water*, vol. 2, *Detailed Analysis* (Washington: U.S. Department of the Interior, 1968), 69.

79. U.S. Congress, House, Committee on Interstate and Foreign Commerce, Sub-committee on Oversight and Investigations, *Hazardous Waste Disposal Report*, 96th Cong. 1st sess., 1979.

80. Illinois Environmental Protection Agency, *Cleaning Illinois: Status of the State's Hazardous Waste Cleanup Programs* (Springfield, IL: IEPA, Summer 1989).

81. H. L. Jacobs, "A 1955 Survey: Waste Treatment Methods—Recovery and Disposal," *Chemical Engineering* 62 (1955): 184–188.

82. H. E. Babbitt and E. R. Baumann, *Sewerage and Sewage Treatment*, 8th ed. (New York: John Wiley, 1958), 637–638.

83. Paul Hodges, "Industry, Municipality Join Forces," *Oil and Gas Journal* 64 (March 28, 1966): 143–150. Hailed as an innovative and cooperative venture, the treatment system sustained repeated failures after it commenced operation.

84. Brian J. L. Berry, ed., *Land Use, Urban Form and Environmental Quality*, Research Paper 155 (Chicago: University of Chicago Department of Geography, 1974), 105; U.S. Department of Health, Education, and Welfare, *Statistical Summary of Sewage Works in the United States*, Publication No. 609 (Washington, DC: Public Health Service, 1958), 5.

85. Willem Rudolfs, ed., *Industrial Wastes: Their Disposal and Treatment* (New York: Reinhold, 1953); E. B. Besselievre, *Industrial Waste Treatment* (New York: McGraw-Hill, 1952).

86. William McGucken, *Biodegradable: Detergents and the Environment* (College Station, TX: Texas A&M University Press, 1991).

87. "Federal Waste Law," *Chemical Engineering* 56 (March 1949): 112; "U.S. Pollution Research Goes on Ice," *Chemical Week* 79 (August 11, 1956): 56.

88. The Illinois Sanitary Water Board undertook extensive efforts to eliminate cyanide wastes from metal plating operations during the early 1950s. See C. E. Colten and G. E. Breen, *Historical Industrial Waste Disposal Practices in Winnebago County, IL 1870–1980*, Research Report 11 (Savoy, IL: Hazardous Waste Research and Information Center, 1986).

89. "Pollution Control Wins Corporate Level Status," *Chemical and Engineering News* 44 (May 2, 1966): 34–35; Davis Dyer and David B. Sicilia, *Labors of a Modern Hercules* (Boston: Harvard Business School Press, 1990), 377.

90. "MCA Protests Pollution Stand," *Chemical and Engineering News* 32 (August 23, 1954): 3361; "Pollution Bill Hit by Chemical Industry," *Oil, Paint and Drug Reporter* 169 (March 19, 1956): 1, 45. Harold Jacobs (for the MCA), testimony before Congress, Senate, *Water and Air Pollution Control Hearings*, 147–152.

91. G. Edward Pendray, "PR Aspects of Industrial Wastes," *Modern Industry* 19 (1950): 134–135; Lloyd Stackhouse, "Public Relations and Industrial Wastes," *Journal, Water Pollution Control Federation* 32 (1959): 960–963.

92. Walter A. Lyon makes the explicit point that installation of treatment equipment was not a significant factor in business failure. Lyon, "Industry and Pollution Abatement," *Journal, Water Pollution Control Federation* 33 (1961): 1112.

93. U.S. Environmental Protection Agency, *Assessment of Industrial Hazardous Waste Practices: Organic Chemical, Pesticides and Explosives Industry*, SW-118c (Washington: U.S. Environmental Protection Agency, 1975), 6–9.

94. *Urban wastes* here refers to garbage, ash, building debris, and other nonindustrial forms of waste. Hazardous waste is a subset of industrial waste that includes toxic, reactive, corrosive, or ignitable substances.

95. This point was a cornerstone of Occidental Chemical's position in the Love Canal trial, in which they presented the disposal site as a sanitary landfill. It also commonly appears in depositions in Superfund insurance litigation. A published exposition of this viewpoint is R. D. Mutch and W. W. Eckenfelder, Jr., "Out of the Dusty Archives," *Hazmat World* 6 (October 1993): 59–68.

96. The most extensive discussion of urban garbage is Martin V. Melosi, *Garbage in the City: Refuse, Reform and the Environment* (College Station, TX: Texas A&M University Press, 1981), esp. 1–50.

97. Murray F. Tuley, comp., *Laws and Ordinances Governing the City of Chicago* (Chicago: Bulletin Printing Co., 1873), 83, 113–114.

98. *Revised Code of Chicago*, vol. 1 (Chicago: City of Chicago, 1897), 352. A subsequent ordinance required citizens to separate their garbage and ashes; see Chicago Department of Public Works, *Annual Report* (Chicago: Author, 1901), 200. This general distinction found expression in municipal ordinances elsewhere. See J. Waterman and W. Fowler, *Municipal Ordinances, Rules, and Regulations Pertaining to Public Health, 1917–1919* (Washington, DC: U.S. Public Health Service, 1921), 188.

99. *Revised Code of Chicago*, vol. 1, pp. 221–222.

100. M. O. Leighton, "Industrial Wastes and Their Sanitary Significance," *Public Health: Papers and Reports* 31 (1905): 209.

101. Eldridge, *Industrial Waste Treatment Practice*, 294, 366–367.

102. Harold E. Babbitt, *Sewerage and Sewage Treatment* (New York: John Wiley, 1952), 7th ed., esp. chap. 7; Nelson Nemerow, *Liquid Waste of Industry* (Reading, MA: Addison-Wesley, 1971), esp. chap. 1.

103. Lewis Carpenter and Lloyd Setter, "Some Notes on Sanitary Landfills," *American Journal of Public Health* 30 (April 1940): 386.

104. C. C. Spencer, "Recommended Wartime Refuse Disposal Practice," *Public Health Reports*, Suppl. 173 (1943): 8.

105. "Refuse Collection and Disposal," *American Society of Civil Engineers, Reports* (June 1949): 816–817.

106. Clarence Klassen, "Sanitary Fill Standards," *American City* 66 (February 1951): 104–105.

107. The Illinois State Geological Survey (ISGS) claimed twenty years of experience in landfill site evaluations in 1952. Frank C. Foley to ISGS Groundwater Division files, memo, June 10, 1952, Champaign, IL. The U.S. Public Health Service pointed out the need for adequate fill and also repeated general recommendations that landfills "should be planned as an engineering project." *The Chicago–Cook County Health Survey* (New York: Columbia University Press, 1949), 193–194.

108. National Safety Council, *Industrial Waste Disposal*, Industrial Safety Series No. 7 (Chicago: National Safety Council, 1948), 3–4.

109. Department of the Army, "Explosives: Explosive Ordnance Disposal Policies and Responsibilities," Army Regulation 75-15 (Washington, DC: 1949).

110. Manufacturing Chemists' Association, *Water Pollution Abatement Manual: Oils and Tars*, 8.

68th Cong., 1st sess., 1924, 40. Reports on pollution included U.S. Department of the Interior, Bureau of Mines, *Pollution by Oil of the Coast Waters of the United States: Preliminary Report* (Washington, DC: 1923). The text of the bills appears in U.S. Congress, House, *Hearings on the Subject of Pollution of Navigable Waters*, 1–8. A discussion of the industry's involvement is found in J. A. Pratt, "Letting the Grandchildren Do It: Environmental Planning During the Ascent of Oil as a Major Energy Source," *Public Historian* 2 (1980): 28–61.

30. R. D. Leitch, "Stream Pollution by Wastes from By-product Coke Ovens," *Public Health Reports* 40 (1925): 2021–2026; E. S. Tisdale, "Cooperative State Control of Phenol Wastes on the Ohio River Watershed," *Journal, American Water Works Association* 18 (1927): 574–586; J. A. Tarr, "Searching for a 'Sink' for an Industrial Waste: Iron-Making Fuels and the Environment," *Environmental History Review* 18 (1994): 9–34.

31. U.S. Congress, House, *Pollution Affecting Navigation or Commerce on Navigable Waters*, 69th Cong., 1st sess., H. Doc. 417, 1926, 18.

32. Joel A. Tarr et al., "Water and Wastes: A Retrospective Assessment of Wastewater Technology in the U.S., 1800–1932," *Technology and Culture* 25 (1984): 226–263.

33. C. E. Colten and G. B. Breen, *Historical Industrial Waste Disposal Practices in Winnebago County, Illinois, 1870–1980*, Research Report 11 (Savoy, IL: Hazardous Waste Research and Information Center, 1986); C. E. Colten and T. B. Samsel, *Historical Assessment of Hazardous Waste Management in Madison and St. Clair Counties, Illinois, 1890–1980*, Research Report 30 (Savoy, IL: Hazardous Waste Research and Information Center, 1988).

34. R. Bachmann and E. B. Besselievre, "Treatment of Industrial Wastes to Prevent Stream Pollution," *Transactions of the American Institute of Chemical Engineers* 16 (1924): 203.

35. Statement of Kenneth A. Reid (member, Pennsylvania Board of Fish Commissioners) in U.S. Congress, House, *Stream Pollution and Stream Pollution Purification*, 74th Cong., 1st sess., 1935, H. Doc. 16, 74–75.

36. *Rose v. Socony Vacuum*, 173 Atl. 627 (1934).

37. *Rose v. Socony-Vacuum*, 173 Atl. 631–632 (1934).

38. Tamburello, "Torts—Pollution of Water," 886–887.

39. C. F. Tolman and A. C. Stipp, "Analysis of Legal Concepts of Subflow and Percolating Waters," *American Society of Civil Engineers, Proceedings* 65 (1939): 1687–1706; E. F. Treadwell, O. E. Meinzer, M. R. Lewis, and B. F. Snow, "Analysis of Concepts of Subflow and Percolating Waters: Discussion," *American Society of Civil Engineers, Proceedings* 66 (1940): 1020–1030.

40. U.S. Congress, *Stream Pollution*, H. Doc. 16, v.

41. U.S. Congress, *Stream Pollution*, H. Doc. 16; see testimony by Grover Ladner (Philadelphia Izaak Walton League), pp. 17–20 and 22–27; and by M. M. Ellis (U.S. Bureau of Fisheries), pp. 42–43.

42. U.S. Congress, Senate, *Stream Pollution: Hearings before a Subcommittee of the Committee on Commerce*, 74th Cong., 2nd sess., 1936. Text of the bills is presented on pp. 2–3 and 409–410.

43. Passage and veto notices appear in *Congressional Record–Senate*, June 6, 1936, 9182; June 8, 1936, 9192; *Congressional Record–House*, June 16, 1938, 9710. A more extensive discussion of failed legislative efforts appears in U.S. Congress, Senate, *Stream Pollution Control: Hearings*, 80th Cong., 1st sess., 1947, 114–117.

44. E. W. Bennison, *Ground Water: Its Development, Uses and Conservation* (St. Paul, MN: Edward Johnson, 1947), 5–6.

45. Leal, "Legal Aspects."

46. Goodell, *A Review of Laws*, 89.

47. Lewis Miller, comp., *The Compiled Laws of the State of Michigan*, vol. 1 (Lansing, MI: Robert Smith, 1899), sec. 27, 3427; M. Starr and R. H. Curtis, eds., *Annotated Statutes of the State of Illinois*, vol. 1 (Chicago: Callaghan and Co., 1896), chap. 38, para. 369, p. 1333.

48. Goodell, *Review of Laws*. North Dakota restricted the location of cemeteries within 80 feet of lakes or streams (p. 39); North Carolina law prohibited cemeteries within 500 yards of a source of water supply (p. 58); Connecticut forbade cemeteries within one-half mile of reservoirs (p. 74).

49. *Thompson v. Board of Education*, 209 N.Y.S. 362 (1925).

50. *Masten v. Texas Co.*, 140 S.E. 89 (1927).

51. *Rose v. Socony-Vacuum*, 173 Atl. 627 (1934).

52. "An Act to Establish a Sanitary Water Board," *Illinois Revised Statutes* (Chicago: Burdette and Smith, 1929), chap. 19, 239.

53. Nicholas V. Olds, "Legal Aspects of Ground Water Contamination," *Proceedings of the Seventh Industrial Waste Conference* (Lafayette, IN: Purdue University, 1952), 256.

54. See Byron E. Doll, "Formulating Legislation to Protect Ground Water from Pollution," *Journal, American Water Works Association* 39 (1947): 1003–1009; Arthur Pickett, "Protection of Underground Water from Sewage and Industrial Wastes," *Sewage Works Journal* 19 (1947): 464–472; and Sheryl Luzzadder-Beach, "Geographic Sampling Strategies for Groundwater Evaluation," (Ph.D. dissertation, University of Minnesota, 1990), esp. 154–165.

55. Percival E. Jackson, *Law of Cadavers and of Burial and Burial Places*, 2d ed. (New York: Prentice-Hall, 1950), 208.

56. Illinois Sanitary Water Board, "Status of Sewerage and Industrial Wastes, Sanitary Water Board Policies and Projected 1946 Program," unpublished report, microform files, January 1946, Illinois Environmental Protection Agency, Water Pollution Control Division, Springfield, IL, p. 6.

57. International Joint Commission, *Report of the International Joint Commission: United States and Canada, on the Pollution of Boundary Waters* (Washington: 1951), 308.

58. The 1972 Federal Water Pollution Law initiated a new era of pollution regulation. Leonard Dworsky, "Analysis of Federal Water Pollution Control Legislation, 1948–1966," *Journal, American Water Works Association* 59 (1967): 651–668; Joseph M. Petulla, *Environmental Protection in the United States* (San Francisco: San Francisco Study Center, 1987); Samuel P. Hays, "Three Decades of Environmental Politics: The Historical Context," in *Government and Environmental Politics*, ed. Michael J. Lacey (Baltimore: Johns Hopkins University Press, 1989), 19–80; A. Myrick Freeman, III, "Water Pollution Policy," in *Public Policies for Environmental Protection*, ed. Paul R. Portney (Washington, DC: Resources for the Future, 1991), 97–149.

59. Regulation was highly fragmented and unsystematic. See Schroeder, "Evolution of Federal Regulation," 263–313. Also Rachel Carson, *Silent Spring* (Boston: Houghton Mifflin, 1962); and Linda J. Lear, "Rachel Carson's *Silent Spring*," *Environmental History Review* 17 (1993): 23–47.

60. James Whorton, *Before "Silent Spring": Pesticides and Public Health in Pre-DDT America* (Princeton, NJ: Princeton University Press, 1974), 97–115.

61. Whorton, *Before "Silent Spring*," 178–186.

62. Robert L. Rudd, *Pesticides in the Living Landscape* (Madison: University of Wisconsin Press, 1964), 71; Thomas R. Dunlap, *DDT: Scientists, Citizens, and Public Policy* (Princeton, NJ: Princeton University Press, 1981), 46–55.

63. J. A. Zapp, "Industrial Toxicology: Retrospect and Prospect," in *Patty's Industrial Hygiene and Toxicology*, 3d ed., ed. G. D. Clayton and F. E. Clayton (New York: John Wiley, 1981), 1475.

64. Thomas W. Nale, "The Federal Hazardous Substances Labeling Act," *Archives of Environmental Health* 4 (1962): 239–240.

65. Quoted in John H. Foulger, "Industrial Toxicology," in *Chemical Business Handbook*, ed. J. H. Perry (New York: McGraw-Hill, 1954), 17-3.

66. Nale, "Federal Hazardous Substances Labeling Act," 241.

67. David S. Beyer, *Industrial Accident Prevention* (Boston: Houghton Mifflin, 1916), 1–3.

68. Carey P. McCord, *Industrial Hygiene for Engineers and Managers* (New York: Harper and Brothers, 1931), 240.

69. Bernhard J. Stern, *Medicine in Industry* (New York: Commonwealth Fund, 1946), 31; also Ludwig Teleky, *History of Factory and Mine Hygiene* (New York: Columbia University Press, 1948).

70. See Allen D. Brandt, *Industrial Health Engineering* (New York: John Wiley, 1947); and Zapp, "Industrial Toxicology," 1467–1491.

71. David F. Zoll, "Product Liability and Labels," in *Handbook of Chemical Industry Labeling*, ed. C. J. O'Connor and S. I. Lirtzman (Park Ridge, NJ: Noyes, 1984), 220.

72. Foulger, "Industrial Toxicology," 17-2.

73. W. J. McConnell, R. H. Flinn, and A. D. Brandt, "Occupational Diseases in Government-Owned Ordnance Explosive Plants," *Occupational Medicine* 1 (1946): 551–555.

74. William Gafafer, *Manual of Industrial Hygiene and Medical Service in War Industries* (Philadelphia: W. B. Saunders, 1943), 125–126.

75. Gafafer, *Manual of Industrial Hygiene*, 264.

76. Gafafer, *Manual of Industrial Hygiene*, 338.

77. Russell S. Smith, "Surveys of Liquid Wastes from Munitions Manufacturing," *Public Health Reports* 58 (1943): 1365–1379 and 1393–1414.

78. War Department, *Operation of Sewerage and Sewage Treatment Facilities at Fixed Army Installations*, Technical Manual TM5-665 (Washington, DC: War Department, 1945), 2.

79. Lazarus Rubin, "Chemical Contamination of Water Supplies," *Journal of the New England Water Works Association* 56 (1942): 276–287; Howard Potter, "The Effects of War Gases on Water Supplies: Decontamination," *Journal of the New England Water Works Association* 57 (1943): 137–162; C. C. Ruchhoft, O. R. Placak, and Stuart Schott, "The Detection and Analysis of Arsenic in Water Contaminated with Chemical Warfare Agents," *Public Health Reports* 58, no. 49 (1943): 1761–1771.

80. C. C. Spencer, "Recommended Wartime Refuse Disposal Practice," *Public Health Reports*, Suppl. 173 (1943): 7–8.

81. Chemical Warfare Service, *Storage and Shipment of Dangerous Chemicals*, Technical Manual 3-250 (Washington: War Department, 1940).

82. L. W. Munchmeyer (Lt. Colonel in Chemical Warfare Service) to commanding

officers of CWS arsenals and depots, March 10, 1945, New York State Department of Law, Love Canal Archives, Albany, NY (hereafter Love Canal Archives).

83. "History of Work Done by the Hooker Electrochemical Company for the Chemical Warfare Service," unpublished manuscript, October 1944, Love Canal Archives, 12–13.

84. Memorandum from Mr. Gilcrease (Division of Sanitation) to Division of Sanitation files, April 24, 1942, regarding meeting with Metcalf and Eddy Consulting Engineers about disposal of TNT plant wastes, Love Canal Archives, 3–4; and M. E. Barker (Col. CWS), "Report of Inspection Trip to Niagara Falls, New York, Midland, Michigan, and Monsanto, Illinois," unpublished report, January 31, 1942, Love Canal Archives.

85. For general discussions of this topic see Melosi, "Hazardous Waste and Environmental Liability"; and Joel A. Tarr, "Industrial Wastes and Public Health: Some Historical Notes, Part I, 1876–1932," *American Journal of Public Health* 75 (1985): 1059–1067.

86. A summary of the testimony is found in Leighton, *Pollution of Illinois and Mississippi Rivers by Chicago Sewage*.

87. Citizens filed complaints when livestock were harmed in Madison County, Illinois. See Colten and Samsel, *Historical Assessment of Hazardous Waste Management*, 35.

88. U.S. Congress, H. Doc. 417, 18.

89. Illinois State Board of Fish Commissioners, *Report, 1899–1900* (Springfield, IL: George T. Williams, 1900), 11.

90. See Philip Scarpino, *The Great River: An Environmental History of the Upper Mississippi, 1890–1950* (Columbia, MO: University of Missouri Press, 1985); Donald J. Pisani, "The Polluted Truckee: A Study in Interstate Water Quality," *Nevada Historical Quarterly* 20 (1970): 151–166; and Colten, "Illinois River Pollution Control, 1900–1970."

91. Sherman, *Stream Pollution*, 15.

92. A review of the hearings and judgment for the year is found in Illinois Rivers and Lakes Commission, *Annual Report for 1916* (Chicago: 1916), 6–16.

93. Leitch, *Stream Pollution*; Tisdale, "Cooperative State Control"; Tarr, "Searching for a 'Sink.'"

94. "Abatement of Industrial Waste Pollution in Illinois," *Public Works* 67 (1936): 18.

95. M. Wheeler, "Commercial Solvents Corporation Waste Disposal Plan, Peoria, Illinois Plant," in *Proceedings of the Fifth Industrial Waste Conference* (Lafayette, IN: Purdue University, 1949), 175–180.

96. R. W. Parker, "Summary of Events and Status: Industrial Wastes, City of Bronson [Michigan]," unpublished report, NR RG 86-77, lot 150, folder 37, November 26, 1962, Michigan Department of Natural Resources, Michigan State Archives, Lansing, Michigan.

97. Herbert W. Davids and Maxim Lieber, "Underground Water Contamination by Chromium Wastes," *Water and Sewage Works* 98 (1951): 528–534.

98. Illinois Sanitary Water Board, "Status of Sewerage and Industrial Wastes," 6.

99. V. H. Manning (American Petroleum Institute), testimony to U.S. Congress, House, Committee on Rivers and Harbors, *Hearings on the Subject of the Pollution of Navigable Waters*, 68th Cong., 1st sess., 1924, 40.

100. For an example of the manuals see American Petroleum Institute, *A.P.I. Manual on Disposal of Refinery Wastes* (New York: American Petroleum Institute, 1930). The position that the API sought internal domination of waste management is argued by Pratt, "Letting the Grandchildren Do It."

101. Lyman Cox, statement on the Manufacturing Chemists' Association Water Pollution Abatement Committee, in *Proceedings of the National Technical Task Committee on Industrial Waste, May 9–10, 1950* (Washington, DC: 1950), 1–4.

102. "Stream Pollution Becomes a Problem for Chemical Engineers," *Chemical and Metallurgical Engineering* 45 (1938): 139.

103. U.S. Department of Health, Education and Welfare, Public Health Service, *Municipal and Industrial Waste Facilities: 1957 Inventory, Regions 1, 2, and 5* (Washington, DC: 1958).

104. *Lansing State Journal*, February 16, 1943, p. 3 and February 19, p. 6.

105. Texas Game, Fish, and Oyster Commission, *Annual Report, 1939–1940* (Austin, TX: 1940), 18.

106. Texas Game, Fish and Oyster Commission, *Annual Report 1946–47* (Austin, TX: 1947), 8.

107. Olds, "Legal Aspects of Ground Water Contamination," 256–259.

108. Pickett, "Protection of Underground Water from Sewage and Industrial Wastes," 469–471.

109. Luzzadder-Beach, "Geographic Sampling Strategies for Groundwater Quality Evaluation," 156–158.

110. Marvin D. Weiss, *Industrial Water Pollution: Survey of Legislation and Regulations* (New York: Chemonics, 1951); Don E. Bloodgood, "Effect on Stream Pollution Legislation and Control," *ASCE Proceedings* 74 (1948): 1048–1057; "Federal Waste Law," *Chemical Engineering* 56 (1949): 112; "U.S. Pollution Research Goes on Ice," *Chemical Week* 79 (August 11, 1956): 56; Carl E. Schowb, "The 1948 Federal Stream-Pollution-Control Law," in *Proceedings of the Second Industrial Waste Conference* (Lafayette, IN: Purdue University, 1948), 15–19.

111. "States Step Up Pollution War," *Chemical Week* 80 (May 11, 1957): 22; "MCA Protests Pollution Stand," *Chemical and Engineering News* 32 (August 23, 1954): 3361.

112. *United States v. Republic Steel et al.*, 362 U.S. 482 (1959); Albert Cowdrey, "Pioneering Environmental Law: The Army Corps of Engineers and the Refuse Act," *Pacific Historical Review* 44 (1975): 331–344.

113. Warren H. Resh, "Court Decisions and Statutory Provisions in Water Pollution Control Law," *Sewage and Industrial Wastes* 28 (1956): 212.

114. *Illinois Attorney General's Report, 1969–70* (Springfield: 1970), xx. See also Allen Lavin, "Energetic Enforcement of Industrial Waste Ordinances," in *Proceedings of the 23rd Industrial Waste Conference*, pt. 1 (Lafayette, IN: Purdue University, 1968), 550–553.

115. Rudd, *Pesticides and the Living Landscape*, 78.

116. See Dunlap, *DDT*, 251–256; and F. M. Pottenger and B. Krohn, "Poisoning from DDT and Other Chlorinated Hydrocarbon Pesticides," reprinted in U.S. Congress, House, *Chemicals in Foods and Cosmetics: Hearings*, pt. 2, 82nd Cong., 1st sess., 1952, 954–963.

117. See Brandt, *Industrial Health Engineering*. Also, Foulger, "Industrial Toxicology," 17-1–17-16.

118. Stern, *Medicine in Industry*, 28; Teleky, *Factory and Mine Hygiene*, 74.

119. "Report of Advisory Committee on Official Water Standards," *Public Health Reports* 49 (April 10, 1925): 693–721; "Public Health Service Drinking Water Standards," *Public Health Reports* 58 (January 1943): 72–111.

120. M. E. Barker (Col., CWS), "Report of Inspection Trip to Niagara Falls, New York, Midland, Michigan, and Monsanto, Illinois," unpublished report, January 31, 1942, Love Canal Archives.

121. C. E. Colten, "Historical Hazards: The Geography of Relict Industrial Wastes," *Professional Geographer* 42 (1990): 143–156.

122. Joel A. Tarr, "The Search for the Ultimate Sink: Urban Air, Land, and Water Pollution in Historical Perspective," *Records of the Columbia Historical Society of Washington* 51 (1984): 1–29.

123. I. F. Harlow, T. J. Powers, and R. B. Ehlers, "The Phenolic Waste Treatment Plant of the Dow Chemical Company," *Sewage Works Journal* 10 (1938): 1043–1059.

124. H. W. De Ropp, "Chemical Waste Disposal at Victoria, Texas, Plant of the Du Pont Company," *Sewage and Industrial Wastes* 23 (1951): 194–197.

125. "MCA Protests Pollution Stand," 3361.

126. Sheppard Powell, "Creation and Correction of Industrial Wastes," *Industrial and Engineering Chemistry* 39 (1947): 566.

127. G. E. Pendray, "PR Aspects of Industrial Wastes," *Modern Industry* 19 (April 1950): 134–135; Lloyd Stackhouse, "Public Relations and Industrial Wastes," *Journal, Water Pollution Control Federation* 32 (1959): 960–963.

128. Harold E. Babbitt, "The Administration of Stream Pollution Prevention in Some States," in *Proceedings of the Sixth Industrial Waste Conference* (Lafayette, IN: Purdue University, 1951), 248.

129. "Pollution Control Wins Corporate-Level Status," *Chemical and Engineering News* 44 (May 2, 1966): 34–35.

130. U.S. Congress, House, *Waste Disposal Survey: Report*, 96th Cong., 1st sess., Committee Print 96-IFC 33, 1979, x, and Appendix E.

131. American Petroleum Institute, *Manual on Disposal of Refinery Wastes*, vol. 6, *Solid Wastes* (New York: American Petroleum Institute, 1963), 36.

5. WORKING WITH EXISTING KNOWLEDGE

1. David F. Noble, *America by Design: Science, Technology and the Rise of Corporate Capitalism* (New York: Knopf, 1977), 5–6. Also, Terry S. Reynolds, "Defining Professional Boundaries: Chemical Engineering in the Early 20th Century," *Technology and Culture* 27 (1986): 699–700.

2. Frank S. Taylor, *A History of Industrial Chemistry* (London: Heinemann, 1957), 258.

3. Newton Copp and Andrew Zanella, *Discovery, Innovation, and Risk: Case Studies in Science and Technology* (Cambridge: MIT Press, 1993), 177–180.

4. William Haynes, *American Chemical Industry*, vol. 3, *The World War I Period, 1912–1922* (New York: Nostrand, 1945), 214–220.

5. Haynes, *American Chemical Industry*, vol. 4, *The Merger Era*, 431.

6. C. R. Hall, *History of American Industrial Science* (New York: Library Publishers, 1954), 134.

7. Taylor, *History of Industrial Chemistry*, 233–234. The publication of basic reference books on the subject underscores the rising demand for chemical engineers. See J. H. Perry, ed., *Chemical Engineers' Handbook* (New York: McGraw-Hill, 1934). Also, see Noble, *America by Design*, 12–19; and John K. Smith, "The Ten-Year Invention: Neo-

prene and Du Pont Research, 1930–1939," *Technology and Culture* 26 (1985): 34–55.

8. David Hounshell and J. K. Smith, *Science and Corporate Strategy: Du Pont R&D, 1902–1980* (New York: Cambridge University Press, 1988), 556–558.

9. G. H. Gehrmann (Medical Division, DuPont) to E. G. Robinson (general manager, Organic Chemicals Department) [copy to W. F. Harrington], October 11, 1935, W. F. Harrington Papers, accession 1813, box 20, file 4, Hagley Museum and Library Archives, Wilmington, DE (hereafter Hagley).

10. In response to concerns about the safety of Freon, DuPont staff filed a lengthy rebuttal memorandum that considered the various tests conducted to establish its consumer safety. "Rebuttal Memorandum in Support of Freon," Hearing before the Board of Hazardous Trades of the Fire Department of the City of New York, (1932), W. F. Harrington Papers, accession 1813, box 3, folder 12, Hagley. Also in the Harrington files were reports on the toxicity of hazardous chemicals. They included the following: W. P. Yant, W. W Shoaf, and J. Chornyak, "Observations on the Possibility of Methyl Chloride Poisoning by Ingestion with Food and Water," *Public Health Reports* 45 (1930); and Manufacturing Chemists' Association Bulletin No. 284, December 15 (Washington: Manufacturing Chemists' Association, 1930), 5 (which includes a discussion of the toxicity of methanol).

11. F. A. Wardenburg (president, Lazote) to H. E. Howe (editor, *Industrial and Engineering Chemistry*), June 10, 1930, W. F. Harrington Papers, accession 1813, box 6, folder 12, Hagley.

12. Lammot du Pont (president of DuPont) to C. R. Mudge, March 30, 1936, Administrative Papers, accession 1662, box 45, CMA January–December 1936 folder, Hagley.

13. Lammot du Pont to Warren N. Watson (secretary, Manufacturing Chemists' Association), February 24, 1936, Administrative Papers, accession 1662, box 45, MCA January–December 1936 folder, Hagley.

14. G. H. Gehrmann (director of DuPont Medical Division), Proposal for Scientific Medical Research, November 28, 1933, Harrington Papers, accession 1813, box 16, Medical Division 1933 folder, Hagley.

15. G. H. Gehrmann (director of DuPont Medical Division), "Haskell Laboratory of Industrial Toxicology," presentation at dedication of laboratory, January 14, 1935, 3–4, Public Relations Papers, accession 1410, box 39, Hagley.

16. American Petroleum Institute, *API Manual on Disposal of Refinery Wastes* (New York: American Petroleum Institute, 1930), 3.

17. F. B. Langreck (Monsanto assistant vice president) to Harry Ferguson (Illinois Sanitary Water Board), January 23, 1933, Sanitary Water Board Historical files, 1932–1952, Illinois Environmental Protection Agency, Water Pollution Control Division, Springfield, IL (hereafter IEPA records).

18. Stephen Witkowski (Hooker Electrochemical yard crew member), affidavit for *United States et al. v. Occidental Chemical Corporation et al.*, U.S. District Court, Western District of New York, Civ. 79-990, May 1, 1985, exhibit 1985, State of New York Department of Law, Love Canal Archives, Albany, NY (hereafter Love Canal Archives).

19. For example, see Manufacturing Chemists' Association, *Chemical Safety Data Sheet SD-24: Perchloroethylene* (Washington: Manufacturing Chemists' Association, 1948); and Manufacturing Chemists' Association, *Chemical Safety Data Sheet SD-14: Trichloroethylene* (Washington: Manufacturing Chemists' Association, 1948).

20. E. Ewalt (Hooker Electrochemical) to D. W. Gurip (Givaudan Corporation of New Jersey), correspondence, February 2, 1955, Love Canal Archives.

21. J. Wilkenfeld (Hooker Electrochemical), confidential internal memo, regarding chloracne caused by impurities in trichlorophenol, May 15, 1957, Love Canal Archives.

22. Manufacturing Chemists' Association, *Manual Sheet W-1: Organization and Method for Investigating Wastes in Relation to Water Pollution* (Washington: Manufacturing Chemists' Association, 1948), 4.

23. H. L. Jacobs, "Waste Disposal," in *Chemical Business Handbook*, ed. J. H. Perry (New York: McGraw-Hill, 1954), 8-49–8-50.

24. Dwight Metzler, trial testimony, *United States et al. v. Hooker Chemicals and Plastics Corporation et al.*, U.S. District Court, Western District of New York, Civ. 79-990, 6814–6815.

25. "Pollution Control Wins Corporate-Level Status," *Chemical and Engineering News* 44 (May 2, 1966): 34–35.

26. Until plant managers became convinced that pollution control devices actually reduced operating costs, they balked at the idea according to Davis Dyer and David Sicilia, *Labors of a Modern Hercules: The Evolution of a Chemical Company* (Boston: Harvard Business School Press, 1990), 377.

27. Albert H. Mowbray, *Insurance: Its Theory and Practice in the United States* (New York: McGraw-Hill, 1937), 201.

28. Richard Cary (Cary Insurance, Niagara Falls, NY) to Ansley Wilcox (second secretary, Hooker Electrochemical), September 22, 1942, Love Canal Archives.

29. Lawrence S. Myers, *The Manufacturer and Insurance* (Cincinnati: National Underwriter Company, 1948), 47.

30. Richard Y. Levine, "Insurance Aspects of Industrial Waste Disposal," *Proceedings of the Seventh Industrial Waste Conference* (Lafayette, IN: Purdue University, 1952), 322.

31. The Manufacturing Chemists' Association obliquely encouraged manufacturers to conform to pollution regulations. Manufacturing Chemists' Association, *Manual Sheet W-1: Organization and Method for Investigating Wastes* (Washington, DC: Manufacturing Chemists' Association, 1948), 4. Also, Henry Anderson, "Insurance and Loss Prevention," in Perry, *Chemical Business Handbook*, 18-4.

32. This argument found repeated expression throughout the 1950s. A representative example is F. W. Mohlman, "Are Industrial Wastes Always Liabilities?" *Chemical and Metallurgical Engineering* 45 (April 1938): 200.

33. National Safety Council, *Industrial Waste Disposal and Bibliography on Chemical Wastes* (Chicago: National Safety Council, 1948); American Petroleum Institute, *Manual on Disposal of Refinery Wastes*, vol. 3, *Chemical Wastes* (New York: American Petroleum Institute, 1951); Manufacturing Chemists' Association, *Water Pollution Abatement Manual: Oils and Tars* (Washington, DC: Manufacturing Chemists' Association, 1955).

34. G. E. Pendray, "PR Aspects of Industrial Wastes," *Modern Industry* 19 (April 1950): 134–135.

35. W. F. Bixby, "Industrial Public Relations in Pollution Abatement," *Sewage and Industrial Wastes* 30 (July 1958): 923; Lloyd Stackhouse, "Public Relations and Industrial Wastes," *Journal, Water Pollution Control Federation* 32 (1959): 960–963; J. D. Frame, "How Pollution Control Builds Good Public Relations," *Petroleum Refiner* 39 (May 1960): 169–171.

36. Sheppard T. Powell (spokesman for Manufacturing Chemists' Association), con-

gressional testimony, *Stream Pollution: Hearings*, U.S. Senate, 74th Cong., 2nd sess., 1936, 230–231; Harold Jacobs (spokesman for the Manufacturing Chemists' Association), congressional testimony, *Water and Air Pollution Hearings*, U.S. Senate, 84th Cong., 1st sess., 1955, 147–152.

37. Experts from the period made this point in reports as part of the Love Canal litigation. See Clarence W. Klassen, "Rebuttal Expert Report of Clarence Klassen," *United States et al. v. Occidental Chemical Corporation et al.*, United States District Court, Western District of New York, Civ. 79-990, June 1990, 5; and Richard W. Eldredge, "Report of Richard W. Eldredge, *United States et al. v. Occidental Chemical Corporation et al.*, United States District Court, Western District of New York, Civ. 79-990, 1989, 3.

38. Hounshell and Smith, *Science and Corporate Strategy*, 560–563. Hooker Chemical actively engaged in research on the toxicology of various chlorinated hydrocarbons; see W. J. Marsh (Hooker Electrochemical), memorandum to R. L. Murray, February 17, 1942, Love Canal Archives; and J. S. Sconce (Hooker Electrochemical) to R. L. Murray and others, memo, August 21, 1944, Love Canal Archives.

39. Harold Jacobs (Manufacturing Chemists' Association), congressional testimony, *Water and Air Pollution Hearings*, 84th Cong., 1st sess., 1955, 151, expressed himself in favor of additional federal funding for research into pollution control technology.

40. Industry supported toxicity research at the Kettering Laboratory in Cincinnati. See Edward J. Cleary, "Determining Risks of Toxic Substances in Water, *Sewage and Industrial Wastes* 26 (1954): 203–211; and Jules Cass, "The Potential Toxicity of Chemicals in Water for Man and Domestic Animals," *Proceedings of the Tenth Industrial Waste Conference* (Lafayette, IN: Purdue University, 1955), 466–472.

41. Citations in reports published by industry waste management personnel demonstrate that they were aware of reports published by independent labs. See Jack T. Garrett, "Toxicity Considerations in Pollution Control," *Industrial Wastes* 2 (January/February 1957): 17–19.

42. E. B. Besselievre (with Dorr Company), "The Disposal of Industrial Chemical Waste," *Chemical Age* 25 (December 12, 1931): 516–518; Robert S. Weston (with Weston and Sampson), "Water Pollution," *Industrial and Engineering Chemistry* 31 (1939): 1311–1315; Willem Rudolfs and Willem Rudolfs, Jr., "Effect of Dilution on Sludge Formed by Neutralizing Acid Wastes with Lime," *Public Works* 75 (1944): 24–28; and J. E. Tarman (with W. H. and L. D. Betz), "The Chemical Engineer's Approach to Industrial Waste Problems," *Journal, American Water Works Association* 38 (1946): 333–341.

43. Harry H. Gehm, "Coordinated Industrial Waste Research," *Sewage Works Journal* 17 (1945): 782–785.

44. W. B. Hart, "The Waste Control Laboratory of Atlantic Refining Company," *Water and Sewage Works* 88 (January 1941): 30–31.

45. I. F. Harlow, T. J. Powers, and R. B. Ehlers, "The Phenolic Waste Treatment Plant of the Dow Chemical Company," *Sewage Works Journal* 10 (1938): 1043–1059; I. F. Harlow, "Waste Problems of a Chemical Company," *Industrial and Engineering Chemistry* 31 (1939): 1346–1349; and Thomas Power, "The Treatment of Some Chemical Industry Wastes," *Sewage Works* 17 (1945): 330–337.

46. Sheppard T. Powell, "Creation and Correction of Industrial Wastes," *Industrial and Engineering Chemistry* 39 (1947): 566.

47. Raymond Hess, "Wastes from Chemical Manufacturing," *Sewage Works Journal* 21 (1949): 674–684; V. L. King, R. F. Bann, R. C. Conn, R. E. Lester, J. E. Stanley, and D.

Tarvin, "Relation of Stream Characteristics to Disposal of Chemical Manufacturing Effluents," *Sewage Works Journal* 21 (1949): 534–552; and H. W. de Ropp, "Chemical Waste Disposal at Victoria, Texas, Plant of the Du Pont Company," *Sewage and Industrial Wastes* 23 (1951): 194–197.

48. MCA, *Manual Sheet W-1*, 4.

49. H. C. Haskell (assistant director, Legal Department, DuPont) to Lammot du Pont (president, DuPont), April 3, 1936, Administrative Papers, accession 1662, box 45, CMA 1936 folder, Hagley.

50. Fred Zeisberg (DuPont Chemical Company), file memorandum, re: MCA Water Pollution Committee, May 18, 1936, accession 1662, box 45, MCA 1936 folder, Hagley. The Chemical Manufacturers' Association reports that it cannot locate the results of the survey and that such information is privileged.

51. Fred C. Zeisberg (DuPont Development Department) to Lammot du Pont (company president), September 24, 1936, Administrative Papers, accession 1662, box 45, MCA 1936 folder, Hagley.

52. W. H. Wisely, "Stream Pollution Control Activities of Industrial Associations," *Sewage Works Journal* 21 (1949): 54.

53. R. H. VanHorne and D. E. Springer (Hooker Electrochemical), trip report, December 27, 1948, Love Canal Archives.

54. Lyman Cox (chairman, MCA Water Pollution Abatement Committee), statement, *Proceedings of the National Technical Task Committee on Industrial Waste, 1950*, vol. 1 (Washington, DC: 1950), 1–2.

55. "M.C.A.'s 5th Conference on Pollution Abatement," *Water and Sewage Works* 98 (1951): 308.

56. "MCA Protests Pollution Stand," *Chemical and Engineering News* 32 (August 23, 1954): 3361; and Ruth Patrick, "Biological Measure of Stream Conditions," *Sewage and Industrial Wastes* 22 (1950): 927–938.

57. James Etzel, a professor of sanitary engineering at Purdue University, served as a consultant for numerous private companies. James E. Etzel, deposition, U.S. District Court, Western New York District, *U.S. et al. v. Occidental Chemical Corporation et al.*, Civ. 79-990, vol. 1, 1989, 79–85.

58. American Petroleum Institute, *API Manual on Disposal of Refinery Wastes*, 3; and MCA, *Manual Sheet W-1*, 4–6.

59. R. L. Wright, "Treatment of Petrochemical Wastes at Port Lavaca, Texas," *Sewage and Industrial Wastes* 29 (September 1957): 1033–1037.

60. Eldredge, "Report of Richard W. Eldredge," 2, argues that there was little interdisciplinary discourse on solid waste topics and that industry personnel were not attentive to "academic concerns." See also Joel A. Tarr, "Environmental Risks in Historical Perspective," in *Social and Cultural Construction of Risk*, ed. B. B. Johnson and V. T. Covello (Boston: D. Reidel, 1988), 328.

61. The significance of the technical press to chemical company engineers is discussed in Smith, "Ten-Year Invention," 50–51.

62. S. D. Kirkpatrick, "Waste—Byproduct—Staple," *Chemical and Metallurgical Engineering* 38 (September 1931): 497.

63. A. R. Powell, "Disappearance of the 'Gas-House District,'" *Chemical and Metallurgical Engineering* 38 (1931): 541–542; L. A. Mekler, "Useful Conversion of Refinery Byproducts," *Chemical and Metallurgical Engineering* 38 (1931): 538–540; and E. B.

Besselievre, "Industrial Waste Disposal as a Chemical Engineering Problem," *Chemical and Metallurgical Engineering* 38 (1931): 498–503.

64. Besselievre, "Industrial Waste Disposal," 501.

65. The following articles all appeared in *Industrial and Engineering Chemistry* 31 (1939): R. S. Weston, "Water Pollution," 1311–1315; I. F. Harlow, "Waste Problems of a Chemical Company," 1346–1348; and J. B. Hill, "Waste Problems in the Petroleum Industry," 1361–1363.

66. H. Maclean Wilson and H. T. Calvert, *Trade Waste Waters: Their Nature and Disposal* (Philadelphia: Lippincott, 1913), 24–49.

67. E. F. Eldridge, *Industrial Waste Practice* (New York: McGraw-Hill, 1942), 300–317 and 333–350).

68. Norris Shreve, *The Chemical Process Industries* (New York: McGraw-Hill, 1945), 39–41 and 59–62; and E. R. Riegel, *Industrial Chemistry* (New York: Reinhold, 1949), 267–276.

69. Willem Rudolfs, ed., *Industrial Wastes: Their Disposal and Treatment* (New York: Reinhold, 1953), 419–449.

70. E. B. Besselievre, *Industrial Waste Treatment* (New York: McGraw-Hill, 1952), 176, 200–205.

71. Kirkpatrick, "Waste—Byproduct –Staple," 497.

72. E. B. Besselievre, "The Disposal of Industrial Chemical Wastes," *Chemical Age* 25 (December 12, 1931): 516–518.

73. Sheppard T. Powell, "Industrial Wastes," *Industrial and Engineering Chemistry* 39 (1947): 558.

74. From 1944 through 1949 the *Proceedings of the Annual Industrial Waste Conference* (Lafayette, IN: Purdue University) listed the number of attendees by employment affiliation.

75. Bruce W. Dickerson, "Treatment of Powder Plant Wastes," *Proceedings of the Sixth Industrial Waste Conference* (Lafayette, IN: Purdue University, 1951), 30–42; C. O. Huntress, "Treatment of Petro-Chemical Wastes," *Proceedings of the Eighth Industrial Waste Conference* (Lafayette, IN: Purdue University, 1953), 105–111; F. Majewski, "The Treatment of Wastes at the Rohm & Hass Company," *Proceedings of the Eighth Industrial Waste Conference* (Lafayette, IN: Purdue University, 1953), 328–345.

76. R. W. Hess, "Wastes from Chemical Manufacturing," *Sewage Works Journal* 21 (July 1949): 680.

77. The role of the MCA's committee is discussed in Wisely, "Stream Pollution Control Activities," 53–54. See also "M.C.A.'s 5th Conference on Pollution Abatement," *Water and Sewage Works* 98 (July 1951): 308–310.

78. Manufacturing Chemists' Association, *Organization and Method; Water Pollution Abatement Manual: Insoluble and Undissolved Substances* (Washington, DC: MCA, 1949), *Water Pollution Abatement Manual: Neutralization of Acidic and Alkaline Plant Effluents* (Washington, DC: MCA, n.d.), and *Water Pollution Abatement Manual: Oils and Tars* (Washington, DC: MCA, 1955). The Chemical Safety Data Sheets also included brief discussions on proper waste disposal practices for harmful chemicals.

79. F. W. Gilcrease (Hooker Electrochemical) file memorandum, April 14, 1942, Hooker Electrochemical files, Love Canal Archives.

80. F. W. Gilcrease (Hooker Electrochemical), file memorandum, April 24, 1942, Hooker Electrochemical Company files, Love Canal Archives.

81. W. J. Marsh to R. L. Murray (Hooker Electrochemical), internal memorandum, February 17, 1942, Hooker Chemical Company files, Love Canal Archives.

82. Bureau of Mines, U.S. Department of the Interior, *Pollution by Oil of the Coast Waters of the United States: Preliminary Report* (Washington, DC: 1923).

83. U.S. Public Health Service, "A Study of the Pollution and Natural Purification of the Ohio River," *Public Health Bulletin* 143 (1924); W. C. Purdy, "A Study of the Pollution and Natural Purification of the Illinois River," *Public Health Bulletin* 198 (1930).

84. U.S. Congress, House, *Ohio River Pollution Control: Report of the U.S. Public Health Service*, 78th Cong., 1st sess., 1944, H. Doc. 266, esp. Suppl. D: "Industrial Waste Guides."

85. E. J. Cleary, *The Orsanco Story: Water Quality Management in the Ohio Valley under an Interstate Compact* (Baltimore: Johns Hopkins Press, 1967), 128.

86. Cleary, *The Orsanco Story*, 129.

87. V. G. MacKenzie, "The United States Public Health Service Program in Industrial-Waste Research," *Proceedings of the Fifth Industrial Waste Conference* (Lafayette, IN: Purdue University, 1949), 10.

88. "U.S. Pollution Research Goes on Ice," *Chemical Week* 79 (August 11, 1956), 57.

89. Harold Jacobs (Manufacturing Chemists' Association) testimony to Congress, Senate, *Water and Air Pollution Control Hearings*, 84th Cong., 1st sess., 1955, 147; Hayse Black, "Federal Industrial Pollution Studies," *Sewage and Industrial Wastes* 22 (1950): 1052.

90. Tarr and Jacobson contend that knowledge about the risk of new chemical hazards was limited to a small group of "experts" in the 1940s and 1950s and only followed the great advances in analytical techniques during the 1950s. See J. A. Tarr and C. Jacobson, "Environmental Risk in Historical Perspective," in *The Social and Cultural Construction of Risk*, ed. B. B. Johnson and V. T. Covello (Boston: Reidel, 1988), 328–329.

91. L. K. Wenzel, *Methods for Determining the Permeability of Water Bearing Materials*, Water Supply Paper 887 (Washington, DC: U.S. Geological Survey, 1942), 11–13 and 71–76.

92. Standard texts on engineering geology provided extensive background about groundwater; see R. F. Leggett, *Geology and Engineering* (New York: McGraw-Hill, 1939), 428–473. The Illinois State Geological Survey and the State Water Survey were already battling over which agency should conduct landfill site analysis in 1952. The Geological Survey claimed that it had had a standardized procedure in place for twenty years. Frank C. Foley to Groundwater Division files, June 10, 1952, Illinois State Geological Survey, historical files, Champaign, IL. Among their earliest surviving reports, from the mid-1950s, they showed concern with groundwater contamination. See also C. W. Klassen, "Sanitary Fill Standards," *American City* 66 (February 1951): 104.

93. American Society of Civil Engineers, *Engineering and Contracting Procedure for Foundations* (New York: American Society of Civil Engineers, 1937), 5–7.

94. American Society for Testing Materials, *Procedures for Testing Soils* (Philadelphia: ASTM, 1944); American Standards Association, *American Standard Building Code Requirements for Excavations and Foundations* (New York: ASA, 1952); American Society of Civil Engineers, *Subsurface Exploration and Sampling of Soils for Civil Engineering Purposes* (Vicksburg, MS: Waterways Experiment Station, 1949).

95. American Standards Association, *Building Code Requirements*, 17.

96. R. B. Peck, W. E. Hanson, and T. H. Thornburn, *Foundation Engineering* (New York: John Wiley, 1953), 139.

97. ASCE, *Subsurface Exploration*, 15.

98. ASTM, *Procedures for Testing Soils*, 9–13.

99. ASCE, *Subsurface Exploration*, 16.

100. ASCE, "Rainfall, and Run-off in Storm-water Sewers," *Transactions, ASCE* 59 (1907): 458.

101. Ernest W. Steel, *Water Supply and Sewerage* (New York: McGraw-Hill, 1947), 343–357.

102. See C. C. Spencer, "Recommended Wartime Refuse Disposal Practice," *Public Health Reports*, Suppl. 173 (1943); American Public Works Association, *Municipal Refuse Disposal* (Chicago: American Public Works Association, 1960); and American Society of Civil Engineers, *Sanitary Landfill* (New York: American Society of Civil Engineers, 1959).

103. See Joel A. Tarr, "Industrial Wastes and Public Health: Some Historical Notes, Part 1, 1876–1932," *American Journal of Public Health* 75 (September 1985) 1059–1067.

104. "Report of Advisory Committee on Official Water Standards," *Public Health Reports* 49 (April 10, 1925): 717–718.

105. L. T. Fairhall, "Toxic Contaminants of Drinking Water," *Journal of the New England Water Works Association* 60 (1941): 404–407. Analytical methods are discussed in C. C. Ruchhoft, O. R. Placak, and Stuart Schott, "The Detection and Analysis of Arsenic in Water Contaminated with Chemical Warfare Agents," *Public Health Reports* 58 (December 3, 1943): 1761–1771.

106. "Public Health Service Drinking Water Standards," *Public Health Reports* 58 (January 1943): 80–82.

107. See Herbert W. Davids and Maxim Lieber, "Underground Water Contamination by Chromium Wastes," *Water and Sewage Works* 98 (1951): 528.

108. P. Doudoroff and M. Katz, "Critical Review of Literature on the Toxicity of Industrial Wastes and Their Components to Fish: Part 1, Alkalies, Acids, and Inorganic Gases," *Sewage and Industrial Wastes* 22 (1950): 1432–1458; and "Part 2: The Metals, as Salts," *Sewage and Industrial Wastes* 25 (1953): 802–848.

109. Byron E. Doll, "Formulating Legislation to Protect Groundwater from Pollution," *Journal, American Water Works Association* 39 (1947): 1006; Arthur Pickett, "Protection of Underground Water from Sewage and Industrial Wastes," *Sewage Works Journal* 19 (1947): 469–470.

110. R. H. Van Horne (Hooker Electrochemical) to six other Hooker employees, memo, February 8, 1949, Love Canal Archives.

111. T. R. Walker, "Ground-water Contamination in the Rocky Mountain Arsenal Area, Denver, Colorado," *Geological Society of America Bulletin* 72 (1961): 492.

112. L. F. Warrick, "Blitz on Insects Creates Water Problems," *Proceedings of the Sixth Industrial Waste Conference* (Lafayette, IN: Purdue University, 1951), 458.

113. Morris B. Jacobs, *The Analytical Chemistry of Industrial Poisons, Hazards, and Solvents* (New York: Interscience, 1941), 404.

114. F. A. Lyne and T. McLachlan, "Contamination of Water by Trichloroethylene," *Analyst* 74 (September 1949): 513.

115. Davids and Lieber, "Underground Water Contamination," 530–531.

116. Norman Billings, "Ground-water Pollution in Michigan," *Sewage and Industrial Wastes* 22 (1950): 1596–1600.

117. U.S. Army Corps of Engineers, *Report on Ground Water Contamination: Rocky Mountain Arsenal, Denver, Colorado* (Omaha, NE: U.S. Army Corps of Engineers, 1955), 2.

118. See also Doudoroff and Katz, "Critical Review of Literature," Parts 1 and 2.

119. William A. Stanley and Rolf Eliassen, *Status of Knowledge of Ground Water Contaminants* (Cambridge, MA: Massachusetts Institute of Technology, Department of Civil and Sanitary Engineering, for the Federal Housing Administration, Contract HA fh–757, 1960).

120. Harry E. LeGrand, "Historical Review of Knowledge of the Effect on Ground Water as Related to Buried Wastes," unpublished report for the defense, *U.S. et al. v. Occidental Chemical Corporation et al.*, U.S. District Court, Western District of New York, Civ. 79-990, exhibit 2474, February 1990.

121. D. J. Cederstrom, "The Arlington Gasoline Contamination Problem" (U.S. Geological Survey, Washington, DC, 1947, unpublished paper).

122. Maxim Lieber, Nathaniel M. Permutter, and Henry L. Fraunethal, "Cadmium and Hexavalent Chromium in Nassau County Ground Water," *Journal, American Water Works Association* 56 (1964): esp. maps, p. 742.

123. Corps of Engineers, *Report on Ground Water Contamination*, 3.

124. L. R. Petri and R. O. Smith, "Investigation of Quality of Ground Water in the Vicinity of Denver, Colorado," U.S. Geological Survey, Open-File Report 56, 1956. Cited in Walker, "Ground-Water Contamination"; see map, p. 490.

125. Michele S. Gerber, *On the Home Front: The Cold War Legacy of the Hanford Nuclear Site* (Lincoln: University of Nebraska Press, 1992), 150.

126. Stanley and Eliassen, *Status of Knowledge of Ground Water Contaminants*, 79–80.

127. H. E. LeGrand, "Environmental Framework of Groundwater Contamination," *Ground Water* 3 (1965): 13.

128. A discussion of the historical schism between the fields of sanitary engineering and public health appears in Joel A. Tarr, "Disputes over Water Quality Policy: Professional Cultures in Conflict, 1900–1917," *American Journal of Public Health* 70 (April 1980): 427–435. The division between the fields of industrial toxicology and waste engineering is discussed by Christopher Sellers, "Factory as Environment: Industrial Hygiene, Professional Collaboration and the Modern Sciences of Pollution," *Environmental History Review* 18 (1994): 55–84.

129. U.S. Public Health Service, *Ohio River Pollution Control, Supplement D: Industrial Waste Guides, An Industrial Waste Guide to the Oil Industry* (Washington, DC: 78th Cong., 1st sess., H. Doc. 266, 1944), 1185.

130. Alfred D. Chandler, *The Visible Hand: The Managerial Revolution in American Business* (Cambridge, MA: Harvard University Press, 1977), 96–99. A further discussion of accident prevention appears in Mark Aldrich, "Combating the Collision Horror: The Interstate Commerce Commission and Automatic Train Control, 1900–1939," *Technology and Culture* 34 (1993): 49–78.

131. See Arthur M. Greene, "The ASME Boiler Code," *Mechanical Engineering* 74 (1952): 555–562; and J. H. Harlow, "The ASME Boiler," *Mechanical Engineering* 81 (1959): 56–59.

132. Henry Petroski, *To Engineer Is Human: The Role of Failure in Successful Design* (New York: St. Martin's Press, 1982), 69–70.

133. W. A. Bugge and W. B. Snow, "The Complete Highway," in *The Highway and the Landscape*, ed. W. B. Snow (New Brunswick: Rutgers University Press, 1959), 3–32.

134. Copp and Zanella, *Discovery, Innovation, and Risk*, 325.

135. Richard F. Hirsh, *Technology and Transformation in the American Electric Utility Industry* (Cambridge: Cambridge University Press, 1989), 75.

136. Copp and Zanella, *Discovery, Innovation, and Risk*, 325–326.

137. E. P. Wilson (H. K. Ferguson Company) to Clifford L. Sayre (Chemical Warfare Service), September 1942; and Stanley Hughes (Zaremba Company) to Clifford L. Sayre (Chemical Warfare Service), August 20, 1942, Love Canal Archives.

138. Lynne Page Snyder, "'The Death-Dealing Smog over Donora, Pennsylvania': Industrial Air Pollution, Public Health Policy, and the Politics of Expertise," *Environmental History Review* 18 (1994): 117–140.

139. Tarr, "Disputes over Water Quality Policy."

140. Edwin T. Layton, *The Revolt of the Engineers: Social Responsibility and the American Engineering Profession* (Cleveland: Case Western Reserve University, 1971), 210.

141. Hirsch, *Technology and Transformation*, 149–150.

142. California State Water Pollution Control Board, "Investigation of Leaching of a Sanitary Landfill," Publication No. 10 (Sacramento, CA: California State Water Pollution Control Board, 1954).

143. See American Public Works Association, *Municipal Refuse Disposal* (Chicago: American Public Works Association, 1960); and American Society of Civil Engineers, *Ground Water Basin Management*, ASCE Manual of Engineering Practice no. 40 (New York: ASCE, 1961).

144. D. A. Mazmanian and J. Nienabar, *Can Organizations Change? Environmental Protection, Citizen Participation, and the Corps of Engineers* (Washington, DC: Brookings Institution, 1979), 182–194.

6. INFLUENCING THE DECISION MAKERS

1. Morton J. Horwitz, *The Transformation of American Law, 1780–1860* (Cambridge: Harvard University Press, 1977), 33 and 97–99.

2. Christine Rosen, "Differing Perceptions of the Value of Pollution Abatement across Time and Place," *Law and History Review* 11 (1993): 303–381.

3. Stanley D. Montgomery and Earl B. Phelps, *Stream Pollution: A Digest of Judicial Decisions*, Public Health Bulletin 87 (Washington, DC: U.S. Public Health Service, 1918).

4. See R. L. Kraft, "Locating the Chemical Plant," *Chemical and Metallurgical Engineering* 34 (September 1937): 678–679.

5. A discussion of the issue of legislative authorization of harms to property is found in Louise A. Halper, "Nuisance, Courts and Markets in the New York Court of Appeals, 1850–1915." *Albany Law Review* 54 (1990): 309–319.

6. See R. Dale Grinder, "The Battle for Clean Air: The Smoke Problem in Post–Civil War America," in *Pollution and Reform in American Cities, 1870–1930*, ed. Martin V. Melosi (Austin: University of Texas Press, 1980), 83–103; Harold L. Platt, "Invisible Gases: Smoke, Science, and the Redefinition of Environmental Policy in Chicago, 1900–1920," unpublished paper presented to the meeting of the American Society for Environmental History, Pittsburgh, PA, March 1993; and Christine Rosen, "Defending the Urban Environment: Businessmen Against Pollution in Late Nineteenth Century Chicago," unpublished paper presented to the Annual Business History Meeting, Williamsburg, VA, March 1994.

7. *Ballantine and Sons v. Public Service Corporation of New Jersey*, 91 Atl. 95 (1914).

8. Several neighbors filed suit against DuPont in 1915. Correspondence and documents recounting this episode are found in *J. G. Charvat v. du Pont*, Hagley Museum and

Library Archives, Legal Department Papers, accession 1305, box 626-3, folder 2, Wilmington, DE.

9. W. A. Hasfurther and C. W. Klassen, "Report on Industrial Waste Discharges from Industries at Monsanto" (now Sauget), unpublished report issued by the Illinois Department of Public Health, Sanitary Water Board, 1942, 2. Microform collection of Sanitary Water Board historical files, Illinois Environmental Protection Agency, Division of Water Pollution Control, Springfield, IL.

10. *Shelby Loan and Trust Co. v. White Star Refining*, 271 Ill. App. 266 (1933).

11. A summary of the complaints heard each year by the Illinois Rivers and Lakes Commission is found in the *Annual Report of the Rivers and Lakes Commission* (Chicago: 1915 and 1916).

12. See National Resources Committee, *Water Pollution Control in the United States*, 76th Cong., 1st sess., H. Doc. 155, Appendix 1, 89–159; and E. S. Tisdale, "Cooperative State Control of Phenol Wastes on the Ohio River Watershed," *Journal, American Water Works Association* 18 (1927): 574–586.

13. Jeff L. Lewin, "Boomer and the American Law of Nuisance: Past, Present, and Future," *Albany Law Review* 54 (1989–1990): 210–211.

14. *Rose v. Sacony-Vacuum*, 173 Atl. 627 (1934).

15. S. B. Lincoln, "How to Turn a Cornfield into a Factory," *Chemical and Metallurgical Engineering* 48 (1941): 95–96.

16. William Haynes, *American Chemical Industry*, vol. 3 (New York: Van Nostrand, 1945), 113.

17. Lyman Cox, "Manufacturing Chemists' Association Pollution Abatement Committee," in *Proceedings of the National Technical Task Committee on Industrial Wastes* (Washington, DC: 1950), 1.

18. *Decennial Edition of the American Digest* (St. Paul, MN: West Publishing, 1906–1916, 1916–1926, 1926–1936, 1936–1946, and 1946–1956).

19. Illinois Sanitary Water Board, "Brief Summary of Illinois Stream Pollution Abatement Activities, with special reference to the period 1932–1936," unpublished report, Sanitary Water Board general file, 1932–1950, in the historical microform files of the Illinois Environmental Protection Agency, Water Pollution Control Division, Springfield, IL (hereafter IEPA files), 2. The only significant state legal action against a polluter during the span 1940–1950 involved a suit against the State of Indiana; see *Illinois v. Indiana*, 340 U.S. 869 (1950).

20. Roland Cross (chairman, Illinois Sanitary Water Board) to Latham Castle (Illinois attorney general), correspondence, March 18, 1954, National-Petro Chemical Corporation, IEPA files.

21. *Illinois v. National Petro-Chemicals*, injunction filed in Douglas County Circuit Court, May 27, 1954. Extensive documentation of this case appears in Douglas County, Tuscola, U.S. Industrial Chemical, roll 223, 1953–1970, IEPA files.

22. F. C. Vilbrandt, *Chemical Plant Engineering and Design*, 4th ed. (New York: McGraw-Hill, 1959), 284.

23. International Joint Commission, *Report of the International Joint Commission: United States and Canada on the Pollution of Boundary Waters* (Washington: 1951), 19 and 307.

24. Harold E. Babbitt, "The Administration of Stream Pollution Prevention in Some States," *Proceedings of the Sixth Industrial Waste Conference* (Lafayette, IN: Purdue University, 1951), 247.

25. Murray Stein, "Federal Water Pollution Control Enforcement Activities," *Proceedings of the Eighteenth Industrial Waste Conference* (Lafayette, IN: Purdue University, 1963), 264–272.

26. Allen S. Lavin, "Energetic Enforcement of Industrial Waste Ordinances," *Proceedings of the Twenty-third Industrial Waste Conference* (Lafayette, IN: Purdue University, 1968), 550–552.

27. *Illinois Attorney General's Report, 1969–1970* (Springfield: 1970), xx.

28. "California's Water Pollution Problem," *Stanford Law Review* 3 (1951): 649–650.

29. "Particular Problems of Water Pollution under New York Law and Federal Law," *Buffalo Law Review* 10 (1961): 496–499.

30. Warren H. Resh, "Court Decisions and Statutory Provisions in Water Pollution Control Law," *Sewage and Industrial Wastes* 28 (1956): 218.

31. Leland Burroughs, "Effect of Water Pollution on Industry," in *Proceedings: The National Conference on Water Pollution* (Washington, DC: U.S. Department of Health, Education and Welfare, Public Health Service, 1960), 103.

32. James Whorton, *Before "Silent Spring"* (Princeton, NJ: Princeton University Press, 1974), 100.

33. Thomas Nale, "The Federal Hazardous Substances Labeling Act," *Archives of Environmental Health* 4 (March 1962): 239–244.

34. James A. Tobey, "Legal Aspects of the Industrial Waste Problem," *Industrial and Engineering Chemistry* 31 (November 1939): 1320.

35. Harrison P. Eddy, "Industrial Waste Disposal," *Metallurgical and Chemical Engineering* 18 (1917): 34–35.

36. R. L. Kraft, "Locating the Chemical Plant," *Chemical and Metallurgical Engineering* 34 (1927): 679.

37. Fred D. Hartford, "Deciding on Chemical Plant Location," *Chemical and Metallurgical Engineering* 38 (February 1931): 74.

38. Edmund B. Besselievre, "Industrial Waste Disposal as a Chemical Engineering Problem," *Chemical and Metallurgical Engineering* 38 (September 1931): 503.

39. Frank C. Vilbrandt, *Chemical Engineering Plant Design* (New York: McGraw-Hill, 1934), 28.

40. James Emery (National Association of Manufacturers), testimony to Congress in *Pollution Hearings*, 74th Cong., 2nd sess., 1936, 199.

41. Sheppard Powell, testimony to Congress in *Pollution Hearings*, 74th Cong., 2nd sess., 1936, 229.

42. Harrison Howe, "Abhor Waste," *Industrial and Engineering Chemistry* 31 (November 10, 1939): 1310.

43. R. Briggs (Hooker Electrochemical), unpublished report on chlorine emissions, Hooker Electrochemical Company, 1939, New York State Department of Law, Love Canal Archives, Albany, NY (hereafter Love Canal Archives).

44. Walter J. Murphy, "Industrial Wastes: A Chemical Engineering Approach to a National Problem," *Industrial and Engineering Chemistry* 39 (1947): 557–558.

45. Manufacturing Chemists' Association, *Organization and Method for Investigating Wastes in Relation to Water Pollution* (Washington: Manufacturing Chemists' Association, 1948), 3.

46. R. H. VanHorne and D. E. Springer (Hooker Electrochemical Company person-

nel), "Trip Report, Manufacturing Chemists' Association Conference, December 16–17, 1948," December 27, 1948, Hooker Chemical Company files, vol. 1, Love Canal Archives.

47. Minutes of a meeting of the Board of Directors of Hooker Electrochemical Company, October 22, 1952, p. 3, Love Canal Archives.

48. J. S. Coey (vice president, Eastern Chemical Division, Hooker Electrochemical) to T. F. Willers (vice president, Hooker Chemical), memo, July 12, 1960, states that "the disposal of organic residues at Niagara Falls has been a difficult problem for many years. The attached report by R. F. Schultz enumerates these difficulties . . . most of which have to do with whether or not we are 'a good neighbor'"; see also R. F. Schultz (production manager, Eastern Chemical Division, Hooker Electrochemical) to J. S. Coey, memo, July 12, 1960, Love Canal Archives.

49. H. W. de Ropp, "Chemical Waste Disposal at Victoria, Texas, Plant of the du Pont Company," *Sewage and Industrial Wastes* 23 (1951): 194.

50. James E. Etzel, deposition, *United States et al. v. Occidental Chemical Corporation et al.*, U.S. District Court, Western District of New York, Civ. 79-990 (JTC), July 28, 1989, vol. 1, 37–41.

51. James E. Etzel, deposition, *United States et al. v. Occidental Chemical Corporation et al.*, U.S. District Court, Western District of New York, Civ. 79-990 (JTC), July 28, 1989, vol. 2, 252.

52. George R. Amery, trial testimony, *United States et al. v. Occidental Chemicals and Plastics Corporation et al.*, United States District Court, Western District of New York, Civ. 79-990, vol. 42-A, February 27, 1991, 87.

53. Willem Rudolfs, ed., *Industrial Wastes: Their Treatment and Disposal* (New York: Reinhold, 1953), 6.

54. H. L. Jacob, "Waste Disposal," in *Chemical Business Handbook*, ed. John H. Perry (New York: McGraw-Hill, 1954), 8–49. This position follows the guidance of the Manufacturing Chemists' Association. See MCA, *Manual Sheet W-1: Organization and Method for Investigation of Wastes in Relation to Water Pollution* (Washington: MCA, 1948), 4.

55. W. F. Bixby, "Industrial Public Relations in Pollution Abatement," *Sewage and Industrial Wastes* 30 (July 1958): 922. See also Lloyd Stackhouse, "Public Relations and Industrial Wastes," *Journal, Water Pollution Control Federation* 32 (1959): 960–963.

56. John D. Frame, "How Pollution Control Builds Good Public Relations," *Petroleum Refiner* 39 (May 1960): 169–171.

57. K. S. Watson, "Discussion," in *Proceedings: The National Conference on Water Pollution* (Washington, DC: U.S. Department of Public Health, Public Health Service, 1960), 110–111.

58. A discussion of the attempts to control oil pollution appears in Joseph A. Pratt, "Letting the Grandchildren Do It: Environmental Planning during the Ascent of Oil as a Major Energy Source," *Public Historian* 2 (Summer 1980): 28–61.

59. See Tisdale, "Cooperative State Control," and Joel A. Tarr, "Searching for a 'Sink' for an Industrial Waste: Iron-Making Fuels and the Environment," *Environmental History Review* 18 (1994): 9–34.

60. The most complete account of this period and the public response is found in William McGucken, *Biodegradable: Detergents and the Environment* (College Station: Texas A&M University Press, 1991).

61. See the discussion on endangerment in Chapter 2 and Peter Doudoroff and Max

Katz, "Critical Review of Literature on the Toxicity of Industrial Wastes and Their Components to Fish," *Sewage and Industrial Wastes* 22 (1950): 1432–1458 and 25 (1953): 802–848.

62. Initially the U.S. Public Health Service mounted investigations of integrated steel mills and beet sugar plants; see V. G. MacKenzie, "The United States Public Health Service Program in Industrial-Waste Research," *Proceedings of the Fifth Industrial Waste Conference* (Lafayette, IN: Purdue University, 1949), 10. By 1956 the industrial waste research program had stalled owing to inadequate funding, but it targeted petroleum refining as a priority industry when work resumed. "U.S. Pollution Research Goes on Ice," *Chemical Week* 79 (August 11, 1956): 58.

63. Richard W. Eldredge, "Report," unpublished expert report for the defense, *United States et al. v. Occidental Chemical Corporation et al.*, United States District Court, Western District of New York, Civ. 79-990, 1989, 3.

64. Clarence Klassen, "Rebuttal Expert Report of Clarence Klassen," unpublished expert report for the plaintiff, *United States et al. v. Occidental Chemical Corporation et al.*, United States District Court, Western District of New York, Civ. 79-990, June 22, 1990, 6–7.

65. W. B. Hart, "Waste Treatment Problems from the Viewpoint of Industry," *Sewage Works Journal* 20 (1948): 276.

66. Babbitt, "The Administration of Stream Pollution Prevention," 248.

67. *The Edgewood Arsenal* 5 (March 1919): 9 and 27.

68. Published under different titles, *Chemical Warfare* or *Chemical Warfare Bulletin* appeared regularly between 1919 and 1945.

69. G. L. Turner, "Special Equipment for Protection against Toxics in the Chemical Industry," *Chemical Warfare* 17 (January 1931): 883–888; "Detection of Toxic Gases," *Chemical Warfare Bulletin* 23 (July 1937): 95–100; Theodore F. Bradley, "Storage of Chemical Munitions," *Chemical Warfare* 30 (November–December 1944): 40–42.

70. William C. Kabrich, "Solving CWS Technical Problems," *Chemical Warfare Bulletin* 29 (October 1943): 8–12.

71. Walter C. Baker, *Proceedings of a Board Meeting of the Chemical Warfare Service* (Washington, DC: Government Printing Office, 1929), 9–18.

72. Amos A. Fries, "By-products of Chemical Warfare," *Industrial and Engineering Chemistry* 20 (October 1928): 1079–1084.

73. Chemical Warfare Service, *Instructions for Storing, Handling, Packing, Shipping and Surveillance of Class I, II, III, and IV Material*, Bulletin No. 1 (Washington: Chemical Warfare Service, 1931), 63–64; War Department, *Storage and Shipment of Dangerous Chemicals*, Technical Manual No. 3-250 (Washington: War Department, 1940), 75–76.

74. "Chemical Man-Power for National Defense," *Chemical and Metallurgical Engineering* 48 (January 1941): 96–98.

75. M. E. Baker (colonel, Chemical Warfare Service), "Report of Inspection Trip" (Niagara Falls, New York, Midland, Michigan, and Monsanto, Illinois), January 31, 1942, Love Canal Archives.

76. L. W. Munchmeyer (lieutenant colonel, Chemical Warfare Service) to Commanding Officers, Northeast District, Chemical Warfare Depots, memo regarding disposal of contaminated drums, March 10, 1945, Love Canal Archives.

77. War Department, *Operation of Sewerage and Sewage Treatment Facilities at Fixed Army Installations*, Technical Manual TM5-665 (Washington: War Department, 1945);

War Department, *Refuse Collection and Disposal*, Technical Manual TM 5-634 (Washington: War Department, 1946).

78. W. B. Hart, "Waste Treatment Problems from the Viewpoint of Industry," *Sewage Works Journal* 20 (March 1948): 273–274.

79. Kraft, "Locating the Chemical Plant."

80. "Chemical Man-Power," 96.

81. "Perspective: Stream Pollution Control," *Engineering News-Record* 138 (April 10, 1947), quoted in *Stream Pollution Control Hearings*, 80th Cong., 1st sess., 1947, 170.

82. Dwight F. Metzler, "Report," unpublished expert report for the defense, *U.S. et al. v. Occidental Chemical Corporation et al.*, United States District Court, Western District of New York, Civ. 79-990, 1989, 4–5.

83. Wesley E. Gilbertson, "Public Policy and the Third Pollution: A Report on the Evolution of Public Policy Regarding Environmental Pollution Control with Emphasis on Solid Waste Disposal," unpublished expert report for the defense, *U.S. et al. v. Occidental Chemical Corporation et al.*, United States District Court, Western District of New York, Civ. 79-990, 1989, 2.

84. Hayse H. Black, "Federal Industrial Pollution Studies," *Sewage and Industrial Wastes* 22 (August 1950): 1049.

85. See W. M. Gafafer, ed., *Manual of Industrial Hygiene* (Philadelphia: W. B. Saunders, 1943), 264.

86. M. H. Miller (counsel, DuPont) to G. P. Church, correspondence April 8, 1941, Hagley Museum and Library Archives, series III, Explosives Department, accession 1305, box 414, folder 1, Real Estate–Indiana Ordnance, Wilmington, DE.

87. J. S. Queeny (DuPont) to R. E. Hardy (Ordnance Department), memo, August 29, 1941, Hagley Museum and Library Archives, series III, Explosives Department, accession 1305, box 414, folder 1, Wilmington, DE.

88. Herbert W. Davids and Maxim Lieber, "Underground Water Contamination by Chromium Wastes," *Water and Sewage Works* 98 (1951): 530.

89. *Gardner et al. v. International Shoe*, 49 Northeast 2nd 335 and 54 Northeast 2nd 482.

90. *People v. Amecco Chemicals*, 43 New York Supplement 2nd 331–332; the judge also ruled that "in time of war, the construction of peacetime statutes, contractual relations, and individual liberties must be subjected to such modifications as are the natural offspring of national emergency and necessity" (p. 330).

91. David F. Noble, *Forces of Production: A Social History of Industrial Automation* (New York: Alfred A. Knopf, 1984), 3–15.

92. Noble, *Forces of Production*, 16.

93. Joel A. Tarr and Charles Jacobson, "Environmental Risk in Historical Perspective," in *The Social and Cultural Construction of Risk*, ed. M. B. Johnson and V. T. Covello (Boston: D. Reidel, 1988), 328.

94. See C. E. Colten, "Creating a Toxic Landscape: Chemical Waste Disposal Policy and Practice, 1900–1960," *Environmental History Review* 18 (1994): 85–116.

95. Thomas Parran, "The Public Health Service and Industrial Pollution," *Industrial and Engineering Chemistry* 39 (1947): 560; Sheppard T. Powell, "Some Aspects of the Requirements for the Quality of Water for Industrial Uses," *Journal, American Water Works Association* 40 (1948): 8–23.

96. National Resources Council, *Water Pollution in the United States*, 2.

97. Parran, testimony, in *Stream Pollution Control Hearings*, 31.

98. M. D. Hollis, "Water Pollution Abatement in the United States," *Sewage and Industrial Wastes* 23 (January 1951): 90.

99. "MCA Protests Pollution Stand," *Chemical and Engineering News* 32 (August 23, 1954): 3361.

100. Walter A. Lyon, "Industry and Pollution Abatement," *Journal, Water Pollution Control Federation* 33 (1961): 1112.

101. T. Koller, *The Utilization of Waste Products* (London: Scott, Greenwood and Son, 1915); A. Bruttini, *Uses of Waste Materials* (London: P. S. King, 1923). A general treatment of this subject is C. E. Colten, "Historical Development of Waste Minimization," *Environmental Professional* 11 (1989): 94–99.

102. Progress was pronounced in the field of petroleum refining but was less promising with pickle liquors. See J. B. Hill, "Waste Problems in the Petroleum Industry," *Industrial and Engineering Chemistry* 31 (1939): 1361–1363; and W. W. Hodge, "Waste Problems of the Iron and Steel Industry," *Industrial and Engineering Chemistry* 31 (1939): 1364–1380.

103. Harold E. Babbitt, *Sewerage and Sewage Treatment*, 7th ed. (New York: John Wiley, 1952), 555; I. Berkovitch, "Chemical Salvage: Profitable Applications in Many Industries," *Chemical Age* 63 (October 1950): 361–363; "Greater Utilization of Industrial Waste Urged as Conservation Step," *Chemical and Engineering News* 29 (September 1951): 3944–3945. The general sequence of economic cycles draws on Brian J. L. Berry, *Long-Wave Rhythms in Economic Development and Political Behavior* (Baltimore: Johns Hopkins University Press, 1991), esp. 123–125.

104. Richard Cary (Cary Insurance) to Ansley Wilcox (Hooker Electrochemical), correspondence, September 22, 1942, Love Canal Archives; and Henry Anderson, "Insurance and Loss Prevention," in *Chemical Business Handbook*, ed. John H. Perry (New York: McGraw-Hill, 1954), 18-5.

105. Almon L. Fales, "Progress in Control of Oil Pollution," *Journal, American Water Works Association* 18 (1927): 589–590.

106. Babbitt, "Administration of Stream Pollution," 248.

107. See *J. G. Charvat v. du Pont, J. F. Dvork v. du Pont*, and *E. G. Temple v. du Pont*, Hagley Library Archives, Legal Department files, accession 1305, box 626-3, folders 2, 4, 5, and 6. Outright damages awarded were over $9,000, while dredging and treatment were estimated to cost $38,000.

108. I. V. Harlow, T. J. Powers, and R. B. Ehlers, "The Phenolic Waste Treatment Plant of the Dow Chemical Company," *Sewage Works Journal* 10 (1938): 1043–1059.

109. Babbitt, *Sewerage and Sewage Treatment*, 555.

110. U.S. Department of Health, Education and Welfare, *1957 Inventory: Municipal and Industrial Waste Facilities*, 7 vols. (Washington: U.S. Department of Health, Education and Welfare, 1958).

111. National Safety Council, *Industrial Waste Disposal and Bibliography on Chemical Wastes* (Chicago: National Safety Council, 1948), 1 and 3. See also Henry Anderson, "Insurance and Loss Prevention," in *Chemical Business Handbook*, ed. John H. Perry (New York: McGraw-Hill, 1954), 18-3–18-46; and Richard Y. Levine, "Industrial Aspects of Industrial Waste Disposal," *Proceedings of the Seventh Industrial Waste Conference* (Lafayette, IN: Purdue University, 1952), 320–325.

112. Lawrence S. Myers, *The Manufacturer and Insurance* (Cincinnati: National Underwriter Company, 1948), 47.

7. OUTCOMES

1. U.S. Army, Chemical Warfare Service, *History of Rocky Mountain Arsenal*, vol. 1, pt. 1 (Denver, CO: 1945), 13–14.

2. U.S. Army, *History of Rocky Mountain Arsenal*, vol. 1, pt. 1, sec. 1D, 218; Casimir Kuznear, "History of Pollution Sources and Hazards at Rocky Mountain Arsenal," unpublished manuscript, September 1980, Rocky Mountain Arsenal Information Center, Commerce City, CO, 21.

3. U.S. Army, *History of Rocky Mountain Arsenal*, pt. 1, sec. 1D, 220.

4. Kuznear, "History of Pollution Sources," 21.

5. Stanley Hughes (Zaremba Company, Buffalo, New York) to Lt. Col. Clifford Sayre (Chemical Warfare Service), correspondence, August 20, 1942, New York State Department of Law, Love Canal Archives, Albany, NY (hereafter Love Canal Archives); E. P. Wilson (H. K. Ferguson Company, Cleveland, Ohio) to Lt. Col. Clifford Sayre (Chemical Warfare Service), correspondence, September 1942, Love Canal Archives.

6. U.S. Army, *History of Rocky Mountain Arsenal*, pt. 1, sec. 1D, 221–222. The 1980 summary of pollution sources makes no mention of the lined caustic basin; Kuznear, "History of Pollution Sources," 29–31.

7. Graham Walton, "Public Health Aspects of the Contamination of Ground Water in South Platte River Basin in Vicinity of Henderson, Colorado, August 1959" (Cincinnati, OH: U.S. Public Health Service, Robert A. Taft Sanitary Engineering Center, November 1959), 2.

8. Walton, "Public Health Aspects," 2; U.S. Army Corps of Engineers, "Report on Ground Water Contamination" (Omaha, NE: September 1955), Exhibit C.

9. U.S. Army Corps of Engineers, "Report on Ground Water Contamination," 1.

10. U.S. Army, "Report on Ground Water Contamination," 7.

11. U.S. Army, "Report on Ground Water Contamination," 15.

12. Lester R. Petri and Rex O. Smith, "Investigation of the Quality of Ground Water in the Vicinity of Derby, Colorado" (Lincoln, NE: U.S. Geological Survey, Water Resources Division, 1956), 58–60.

13. Office of the Chief of Engineers to Chief Chemical Officer, memo, December 20, 1956, attached to Petri and Smith, "Investigation of the Quality of Ground Water." The memo stated: "The contents of this report would be prejudicial to the interests of the United States if it becomes public information."

14. Omaha Division Engineer (U.S. Army Corps of Engineers) to Office Chief of Engineers, Washington, DC, memo, December 20, 1956, 2, attached to Petri and Smith, "Investigation of the Quality of Ground Water."

15. Ibid.

16. Walton, "Public Health Aspects," 16.

17. Walton, "Public Health Aspects," 16–17.

18. Walton, "Public Health Aspects," 22.

19. Theodore R. Walker, "Ground-water Contamination in the Rocky Mountain Arsenal Area, Denver, Colorado," *Geological Society of America Bulletin* 72 (March 1961): 489–494.

20. O. E. Mechem and J. H. Garrett, "Deep Injection Disposal for Liquid Toxic Wastes," *Journal of the Construction Division, Proceedings of the American Society of Civil*

Engineers 89 (September 1963): 111–121. The practice was eventually abandoned after it was linked to seismic disturbances.

21. *Belden v. Union Carbide*, Special Proceedings, no. 17931, State of New York Supreme Court (filed in Niagara County Clerk's Office, Niagara Falls, NY, October 13, 1938).

22. *Belden v. Union Carbide*, 6.

23. L. H. Moyer (Hooker Electrochemical) to T. L. B. Lyster (Hooker Electrochemical) correspondence, September 12, 1941, Love Canal Archives, New York City.

24. Richard Cary (Cary Insurance) to Ansley Wilcox (Hooker Electrochemical), correspondence, September 22, 1942, Love Canal Archives.

25. Hooker Electrochemical, Love Canal Site Survey, 1942, Trial Exhibit 2002, *U.S. et al. v. Hooker Electrochemical*, U.S. District Court, Western District of New York, Civ. 79-990, 1941.

26. Richard Cary, correspondence, September 22, 1942.

27. Ansley Wilcox, 2nd (Hooker counsel) to R. E. Bartlett (Hooker Electrochemical), memo regarding Love Canal, August, 16, 1946, Love Canal Archives.

28. A. Warner to *Niagara Gazette*, 1943, quoted in Adeline G. Levine, *Love Canal: Science, Politics and People* (Lexington, MA: Lexington Books, 1982), 11.

29. B. K. Hough (Hough Soils Engineering), "Report on Site Investigation—99th Street and Reed Avenue (Proposed) Grade School, Niagara Falls, NY," April 28, 1953, 2, Love Canal Archives, New York City.

30. L. P. Nutting, Hooker Conference Notes: Residue Disposal, July 26, 1955, Love Canal Archives, New York City.

31. Niagara Falls Board of Education, minutes of regular meeting, January 21, 1954, p. 21, Love Canal Archives, New York City.

32. Arnold Arch (Niagara Falls air pollution control director) to Mr. Curts (acting city manager, Niagara Falls), memorandum, May 23, 1955, Love Canal Archives.

33. Dwight Metzler, trial testimony, *United States et al. v. Hooker Electrochemical*, U.S. District Court, Western District of New York, Civ. 79-990, 1991, 6809.

34. Allen W. Hatheway and Glenn A. Brown, "Stringfellow Acid Pits: World's First Legally Constituted Hazardous Waste Disposal Site," in *Engineering Geology Practice in Southern California*, Special Publication 4, ed. B. W. Pipkin and R. J. Proctor (Los Angeles, CA: Association of Engineering Geologists, 1992), 81–117; see p. 93.

35. Hatheway and Brown, "Stringfellow Acid Pits," 87.

36. Hatheway and Brown, "Stringfellow Acid Pits," 90–91.

37. Hatheway and Brown, "Stringfellow Acid Pits," 94.

38. General descriptions of the Sauget hazardous waste sites are found in Illinois Environmental Protection Agency, *Cleaning Illinois* (Springfield, IL: Illinois Environmental Protection Agency, Division of Land Pollution Control, 1988), 32–33.

39. Illinois Department of Public Health, *Rules and Regulations for Refuse Disposal Sites and Facilities* (Springfield, IL: Illinois Department of Public Health, Division of Sanitary Engineering, 1966), 6.

40. Stephen Billingsley (Illinois Department of Public Health [IDPH], West Central Region) to O. S. Hallden (IDPH, Bureau of General Sanitation), memo, March 2, 1967, reel 0958, microfilm files, Illinois Environmental Protection Agency, Land Pollution Control Division, Springfield, IL (hereafter IEPA Land Files).

41. Ernest C. Bennet (IDPH) to D. B. Morton and Otto S. Hallden (IDPH), memo, May 26, 1967, reel 0958, IEPA Land Files.

42. Richard A. Esenkoff (IDPH), "Refuse Disposal Site Resurvey: Sauget/Monsanto, December 29, 1967," reel 0958, IEPA Land Files.

43. IDPH, E. St. Louis Regional Office to IDPH, Division of Sanitary Engineering, memo, July 11, 1968, reel 0958, IEPA Land Files.

44. Franklin Yoder (director, IDPH) to J. M. Kerns (St. Clair County state's attorney), correspondence, July 26, 1968, reel 0958, IEPA Land Files; *Illinois v. Sauget and Company*, complaint filed with Circuit Court of the Twentieth Judicial Court, Belleville, Illinois.

45. Ecology and Environment, *Expanded Site Investigation: Dead Creek Project Sites at Cahokia/Sauget, Illinois*, Final Report, vol. 1 (Springfield, IL: Illinois Environmental Protection Agency, 1988), 2–54.

46. IEPA, *Cleaning Illinois*, 33.

47. All comments on the Velsicol site draw on the lengthy decision offered by the U.S. District Court, Western District Tennessee, *Sterling v. Velsicol Chemical*, 647 F. Suppl. 303 (1986). Page numbers in the text refer to this document.

48. L. H. Moyer (Hooker Electrochemical) to T. L. B. Lyster, memo regarding dumping lot, September 12, 1941, Love Canal Archives.

49. Ansley Wilcox (Hooker) to E. R. Bartlett (Hooker), memo regarding Love Canal, August 16, 1946, Love Canal Archives.

50. J. Wilkenfeld (Hooker) to R. F. Schultz (Hooker), memo regarding inspection of Love Canal property, October 26, 1950, Love Canal Archives.

51. B. Klaussen (Hooker) to H. B. Young (works manager), memo, March 27, 1952, Love Canal Archives.

52. B. Klaussen (Hooker) to R. L. Murray (president, Hooker), memo regarding Love Canal, April 25, 1952, Love Canal Archives.

53. B. Klaussen (Hooker) to William J. Small (Niagara Falls Board of Education), correspondence, October 16, 1952, Love Canal Archives.

54. Contract between Hooker Electrochemical Company and Board of Education of the School District of the City of Niagara Falls, New York, April 28, 1953, Love Canal Archives.

55. J. S. Sconce (Hooker Electrochemical) to R. L. Murray, J. H. Babcock, F. W. Dennis, and L. A. McGee (Hooker Electrochemical), memo, "Toxicity of Our New Chlorinated Hydrocarbons," August 21, 1944, Love Canal Archives; S. B. Osborne (Hooker Electrochemical), file memo regarding process waste disposal, June 17, 1948, Love Canal Archives.

56. Wilcox to Bartlett, memo, August 16, 1946, p. 2.

57. Jerome Wilkenfeld (Hooker, assistant technical superintendent) to R. F. Schultz (Hooker, works manager), memo regarding exposed residue at the Love Canal, June 18, 1958, Love Canal Archives; M. L. Parker (Hooker, production manager) to J. S. Coey (Hooker, vice-president), memo regarding disposition of Hooker Property, December 4, 1962, Love Canal Archives; A. W. Chambers, Jr. (Hooker, associate counsel) to Niagara Falls Board of Education, correspondence, July 30, 1971, Love Canal Archives; A. R. Pasqualichio (Niagara County Department of Health) report of investigation regarding complaint, May 16, 1972, Love Canal Archives.

58. Wilkenfeld to Schultz, memo, June 18, 1958.

59. Parker to Coey, memo, December 4, 1962.

60. Niagara Falls Board of Education, minutes, regular meeting, November 7, 1957, Love Canal Archives, New York City.

61. "Hooker Cites Stand on Sale of Land Given for Schools," *Niagara Gazette*, November 8, 1957.

62. "School Site Purchase Falls Through Entirely," *Courier-Express*, Niagara Falls Bureau, November 21, 1957, Love Canal Archives.

63. "School Site Purchase Falls Through Entirely," *Courier-Express*, Niagara Falls Bureau, November 21, 1957, Love Canal Archives.

64. A. W. Chambers, Jr. (Hooker Electrochemical) to W. L. Salacuse (Niagara Falls Board of Education), correspondence regarding 99th Street property, November 21, 1957, Love Canal Archives.

65. Ansley Wilcox, 2nd (Hooker Electrochemical) to Dr. Charles Brent (president, Niagara Falls Board of Education), correspondence regarding 99th Street property, November 21, 1957, Love Canal Archives, New York City.

66. Niagara Falls Board of Education, minutes of regular meeting, January 21, 1954, Love Canal Archives, New York City.

67. Robert P. Whalen, M.D. (New York State Health Department, commissioner), "Order—The Love Canal Chemical Waste Landfill Site . . . " (Albany, NY: New York State Health Department, August 2, 1978).

68. *Syracuse Post-Standard*, December 29, 1953, p. 1.

69. Onondaga County Clerk's Office, Deed Book 1666, 236 (Syracuse, NY: December 21, 1953).

Index